RIPPLES

How Small Actions Can Create Big Change & Close America's Wealth Gap

Adam Robeck

Copyright © 2024 Adam Robeck

All rights reserved. No part of this publication may be reproduced, distributed, or transmitted in any form or by any means, including photocopying, recording, or other electronic or mechanical methods, without the prior written permission of the publisher, except in the case of brief quotations embodied in critical reviews and certain other non-commercial uses permitted by copyright law.
ISBN-13:9798302900616

A Path to Human Progress
9

Advocating for Policy Change
41

Corporations Exploiting Taxpayer Dollars
59

Predatory Lending and Debt Traps
67

Education Access & Reform
77

Promoting Local Businesses
99

Community Investment
108

Financial Literacy Programs
113

Supporting Fair Employment Practices
123

Engaging in Philanthropy
129

Voting and Civic Participation
135

Raising Awareness
141

Building Coalitions
147

HEALTHCARE
153

Mental Health Awareness & Support
165

Improving the Care, Treatment, & Funding for the Disabled & Elderly
173

BIG PHARM BIG PROBLEM
187

THERES NO PLACE LIKE HOME
239

Public Transportation
253

Corporate Greed in Essential Services
261

Hurricane-Prone Areas and the Insurance Scam
279

How the 1% Manipulate the Narrative
291

The Road Ahead
297

A Path To Human Progress

The Ripple Effect of Happiness and Society's Strength

Imagine waking up every day knowing that your needs are met—not just in the barest sense, but in a way that enables you to thrive. You have access to affordable healthcare, a job that provides both financial security and a sense of purpose, clean air to breathe, and an education that empowers you to pursue your dreams. You are connected to a community of people who support you—family, friends, neighbors, and even strangers who are eager to help when you need it. You feel safe, valued, and, above all, happy.

Now, imagine this scenario extending to the broader world—where happiness is not just an individual pursuit but a shared experience that echoes through entire nations, continents, and the globe. The quality of life that supports not only individual well-being but societal flourishing is not just an idealistic dream. It's a possibility within our grasp, and it starts with a profound understanding of how happiness and societal strength are intertwined.

At first glance, the connection between personal happiness and societal strength may not be obvious. After all, societies are vast, complex structures, while happiness is often seen as an individual matter—dependent on personal choices, attitudes, or even luck. But if we dig deeper, we begin to see how these two concepts are inextricably linked. The happiness of individuals contributes to the collective well-being of society, which in turn strengthens the societal structures that enable people to lead better lives. It is in this cycle, this virtuous loop, that human progress is realized.

A Powerful Vision

Think for a moment about the happiest places in the world. Countries like Finland, Denmark, and Norway consistently top global happiness rankings, but why? What do these nations have in common that leads to such consistently high levels of happiness among their citizens? While we can point to certain material factors—such as high standards of living, social welfare systems, and universal healthcare—their success lies not only in what these societies provide to individuals, but how they create an environment where happiness is culturally supported.

These nations have developed social structures that ensure that basic human needs—like health, education, and security—are accessible to all citizens. But more importantly, they place a high value on trust, social cohesion, and community well-being. In these societies, happiness doesn't stop at the individual level; it reverberates across families, neighborhoods, cities, and ultimately entire nations. Happiness, in this sense, isn't a fleeting emotion or personal achievement but a shared resource that strengthens communities.

When individuals are happy, they not only feel better; they contribute more to society. They are more productive, more
empathetic, and more likely to engage in behaviors that promote the greater good. They invest in their families, their communities, and their countries. They become the agents of change that drive social progress and innovation.

A Powerful Catalyst for Progress

But happiness isn't just a good thing for its own sake—it's the engine that drives societal progress. When individuals are happy and healthy, they are more likely to participate in civic life, whether that's volunteering, voting, or advocating for causes that benefit others. They are more inclined to collaborate and solve problems together, to act with a sense of shared responsibility, and to imagine a world that is better for all.

Think of a community clean-up day, or a group of people working together to create a local community garden. When people are happy, they are more likely to act for the collective good. They feel more connected to their neighbors, more committed to making the world a better place, and more confident in their ability to contribute to positive change.

This, in turn, strengthens the social fabric of society. When citizens are actively involved in creating a better environment, whether at the local or national level, they create resilient societies that can weather challenges like economic downturns, natural disasters, and social unrest. Societies with happy, engaged citizens are more likely to innovate, adapt, and create solutions that lead to progress.

However, the true potential of a society of happy citizens is fully realized when it translates into a movement—an ambition not just for personal or national improvement, but for global advancement. A society that fosters happiness, inclusion, and collaboration doesn't just uplift its own people; it plays a critical role in advancing the human race as a whole. It becomes a beacon of progress, leading the way in addressing issues like climate change, poverty, global health, and technological innovation. It shows the world that when we prioritize human well-being and societal strength, the collective possibilities are boundless.

From Local Communities to Global Transformation

This idea of ripple effects is central to understanding how societal strength drives global progress. Just as a pebble tossed into a pond sends ripples across the water, the strength of one community can create waves that extend outward, impacting other communities, nations, and ultimately the planet. The actions of one individual, one group, one nation—if done with the right values and shared vision—can spark global transformation.

Consider the global movements of recent years—movements focused on climate action, racial justice, and gender equality. These movements started with small, localized efforts, but grew exponentially because they tapped into a broader human desire for a better, fairer world. As more people joined these movements, a shared vision of a more inclusive and equitable world emerged. As the energy of the people multiplied, it led to policymaking, global cooperation, and technological advances that were once unimaginable.

Similarly, societies that emphasize the collective good tend to invest in projects that benefit everyone—renewable energy projects, education programs, and global health initiatives—that not only improve the quality of life for their own citizens but for the world at large. This is where societal strength and global advancement come together: by focusing on the happiness and well-being of their own citizens, countries become better equipped to address global challenges and make lasting contributions to the betterment of all humanity.

Building a Better Future Together

The purpose of this book is to explore how improving the quality of life for everyone—not just a privileged few—can lead to happier citizens, which in turn creates a stronger society. And this, ultimately, leads to the advancement of the human race. By emphasizing well-being—mental, emotional, physical, and social—we can empower individuals to contribute to the common good, create resilient communities, and build a better, more sustainable world for future generations.

In a world where challenges often feel insurmountable—be it the environmental crises we face, the social inequalities that persist, or the rapid pace of technological change—the idea that we can create a better future by fostering happiness and societal strength may feel ambitious. But it is not just possible—it is essential. The world's problems won't be solved by a few elite thinkers or powerful corporations alone. They will be solved by communities, nations, and ultimately the global collective, working together to harness the full potential of every individual.

This journey to a better world starts with a simple truth: happy people make stronger societies, and strong societies are the catalysts for the advancement of the human race.

Let's explore how the quality of life, when nurtured for all, leads to the flourishing of individuals, the empowerment of societies, and the advancement of the global good.

Happiness, societal strength, and human advancement are deeply interconnected. We all want to live in a world where personal well-being translates into collective action, where societies built on trust, opportunity, and inclusivity create the conditions for global progress. The following pages will continue to unpack this idea, taking a deeper look at how happiness leads to stronger societies, and how these societies, in turn, pave the way for the collective advancement of humanity. The journey to a better future is not just a personal one—it is a shared journey, and it starts with all of us.

Defining Quality of Life and Why It Matters

Quality of life—sounds straightforward enough, right? It's a term we hear tossed around in discussions about well-being, but when we really dive into it, we see that it's far more than just a surface-level idea. It's about how we live, how we feel, and how we engage with the world around us. It's both a reflection of individual circumstances and a larger societal ambition. From the basics like food and shelter to the more abstract aspects like emotional fulfillment and a sense of purpose, quality of life touches every corner of human existence.

In this section, we'll unravel the complex, multi-faceted nature of quality of life—what it includes, why it matters, and how improving it is not just a personal goal but a societal necessity. Because when people are thriving, society as a whole thrives.

1. The Many Layers of Quality of Life

Quality of life isn't just one thing—it's many things. Imagine it as a quilt, with each patch representing a different aspect of life. Some pieces are tangible, like your income and healthcare; others are more personal, like how connected you feel to others or how satisfied you are with your life. Together, these pieces form a holistic picture of how well we're living. So, let's take a look at the different layers that make up this rich, multi-dimensional concept.

a. Basic Needs and Material Well-Being: The Foundation of a Good Life

Let's start with the basics. No matter how optimistic or adventurous you are, you can't feel truly happy or fulfilled if you're struggling to meet your basic needs. A good quality of life starts with being able to feed yourself, sleep under a safe roof, and take care of your health. If these needs aren't met, everything else can start to feel like it's falling apart.

Food and Nutrition: You can't function well if you're hungry or malnourished. Good nutrition is the fuel that powers our bodies and minds, keeping us healthy, sharp, and energized. When food insecurity is present, it doesn't just affect physical health—it impacts mental well-being, too, often causing stress and anxiety.

Shelter and Housing: A place to call home isn't just about having a roof over your head. It's about security, privacy, and stability. A safe and comfortable home gives you a sense of peace and grounding. Without it, life can quickly spiral into a cycle of uncertainty and stress, damaging both physical health and emotional well-being.

Healthcare: Imagine going through life with untreated illness or injury. Without access to proper healthcare, what could have been a manageable condition could become a lifelong struggle. Healthcare is essential not just for physical health but also for mental peace—because the anxiety of living with unresolved health issues can seriously erode your happiness.

b. Economic Stability and Employment: The Power of Financial Peace

While money can't buy happiness, the freedom from financial worry certainly makes life easier and more enjoyable. Economic stability is about more than just meeting basic needs—it's about ensuring that you have the opportunity to thrive, grow, and build a future without the constant stress of financial insecurity.

Income: Having enough money to live comfortably is key. But beyond that, it's about not having to worry about how you'll pay for healthcare, housing, or food every month. Research shows that after you hit a certain threshold (around $75,000 annually in the U.S.), money doesn't have as much of an impact on happiness, but financial security still plays a huge role in overall life satisfaction.

Employment Opportunities: A fulfilling job can add purpose and meaning to your life. It's not just about the paycheck—it's about using your skills in a way that feels meaningful. People with jobs that align with their passions and goals are happier, more motivated, and more productive. On the flip side, unemployment or underemployment can lead to feelings of isolation, anxiety, and lack of self-worth.

Work-Life Balance: The best jobs don't just pay well—they allow you time to live your life. A healthy work-life balance means you can thrive both professionally and personally. Without it, stress and burnout can creep in, affecting your well-being and relationships.

c. Education and Intellectual Fulfillment: The Pursuit of Knowledge and Growth

Education is the ultimate life hack—it opens doors, enriches your mind, and gives you the tools to make informed decisions about your future. But it's not just about formal schooling—it's about continual growth and learning, no matter your age or stage in life.

Access to Quality Education: A well-educated population tends to be healthier, wealthier, and more engaged in society. Education equips individuals with the tools to succeed in life—whether that's landing a great job, understanding the world, or making informed decisions that benefit their health and happiness.

Lifelong Learning and Personal Fulfillment: Education doesn't stop when you leave school. It's about continuing to grow, explore new

ideas, and pursue passions. Whether it's picking up a new skill or delving into a hobby, the act of learning and growing gives life meaning and satisfaction.

d. Health and Well-Being: The Bedrock of a Good Life

Health—both physical and mental—is the ultimate foundation for living well. Good health allows us to engage fully with life, pursue our passions, and handle challenges with resilience. On the flip side, poor health can drain the joy out of life, making it hard to enjoy even the best circumstances.

Physical Health: Living a healthy lifestyle is essential to feeling good and doing good. It's about more than avoiding illness—it's about nurturing your body with good food, exercise, and regular check-ups. When we're physically healthy, we feel energized, motivated, and capable of tackling anything life throws our way.

Mental Health: Mental well-being is just as crucial. Without emotional balance and mental clarity, everything else in life becomes harder. People who experience mental health challenges like depression or anxiety can struggle to find joy in life, but the good news is that with support and care, emotional well-being can be restored.

Social Determinants of Health: A good quality of life isn't just about individual health; it's about the conditions in which you live. Factors like income inequality, neighborhood conditions, and environmental quality—like clean air, green spaces, and access to recreational activities—are just as important in determining health and well-being.

e. Emotional and Psychological Well-Being: The Heart of Happiness

When it comes to quality of life, it's not just about what you have, it's about how you feel. Emotional well-being—how content, purposeful, and connected you feel—plays a massive role in determining overall life satisfaction.

Social Relationships: Humans are social creatures, and our relationships shape our emotional health. Whether it's family, friends, or a supportive community, social connections provide emotional support, foster a sense of belonging, and make life richer.

Sense of Purpose: People who feel like their life has meaning—whether through their work, family, or volunteer efforts—tend to have a stronger sense of satisfaction and happiness. Purpose fuels motivation, resilience, and a deeper sense of fulfillment.

Freedom and Autonomy: The ability to make choices about your life and live according to your values is fundamental to psychological well-being. Societies that respect individual freedoms and allow people to pursue their own path tend to have happier, more satisfied citizens.

2. The Subjective Side of Quality of Life

While we often talk about the tangible, measurable factors that shape our lives—like income, health, and education—there's also a personal, emotional component to quality of life. This is where things get interesting. How you feel about your life—regardless of your circumstances—can make all the difference.

Life Satisfaction: This is the big picture—how content you are with your life overall. People who feel satisfied with their lives tend to report higher levels of happiness and are more likely to contribute positively to society.

Happiness: The emotional highs and lows of life—the moments of joy, excitement, and contentment—are the essence of what we think of when we talk about happiness. Countries with supportive social systems and freedoms tend to have happier populations.

Perception of Well-being: How you perceive your life—how you view your ability to achieve your goals, manage your challenges, and interact with others—matters just as much as the objective factors. When you feel in control and confident, your well-being improves.

3. Why Improving Quality of Life Matters

At the end of the day, improving quality of life is about more than just personal happiness—it's about building a better society. When individuals live in conditions that support their well-being, they are more productive, healthier, and more likely to contribute to positive change. Societies that prioritize quality of life experience greater social stability, economic growth, and innovation. It's a win-win.

Improving quality of life is a collective effort, but the rewards are immense. By creating environments where people have access to basic needs, opportunities for growth, and the freedom to pursue what brings them joy, we can unlock human potential and create a happier, healthier, more prosperous world for everyone.

The Link Between Quality of Life and Citizen Happiness

Happiness—the deeply satisfying feeling of joy, contentment, and fulfillment—is a universal goal, one that transcends borders, cultures, and personal circumstances. But what exactly makes us happy? While happiness is often seen as a personal or subjective experience, studies consistently show that the quality of life plays a monumental role in determining how happy individuals feel. And quality of life isn't just about having a good income or a big house; it's about having access to the things that truly nourish our well-being: basic needs, health, education, community, and the freedom to pursue what gives us joy.

There is a powerful link between quality of life and happiness. Let's explore how a life that meets both basic and emotional needs fosters long-term contentment. We'll look at the building blocks of happiness—from securing essential needs like food, shelter, and healthcare to nurturing social relationships and personal fulfillment—and how these factors work together to create a foundation for a joyful, meaningful life.

1. Basic Needs and Material Well-Being: Laying the Groundwork for Happiness
At the core of happiness lies the fulfillment of our most basic needs—things like food, shelter, healthcare, and safety. These are the fundamentals that

not only keep us alive, but also create the stability and peace of mind necessary for emotional well-being. When these needs are not met, the resulting stress and uncertainty can drain the joy from our lives.

a. Food Security and Nutritional Health: Fueling Happiness

Imagine trying to be happy when you don't know where your next meal will come from. Food insecurity—when access to sufficient, nutritious food is uncertain—is one of the biggest detractors from happiness. Research has shown that hunger, malnutrition, and the constant anxiety of not having enough food can lead to increased stress, anxiety, and depression. People struggling with food insecurity often face physical and mental health challenges, which compound the feeling of discontent.

On the other hand, food security—the reliable access to nutritious food—has a direct, positive impact on happiness. Studies consistently show that when people have consistent access to healthy food, their well-being improves. In fact, nutrition not only affects our physical health but also boosts our mental clarity and emotional resilience, leading to greater happiness and life satisfaction. Simply put, good food is good for the soul!

b. Housing Stability and Shelter: A Safe Haven for Well-Being

Think about the sense of calm you feel when you're nestled in your home after a long day, knowing that you're safe and secure. Stable housing is more than just a roof over our heads—it's a sanctuary that provides emotional comfort, security, and privacy. Homelessness or housing instability, on the other hand, is linked to severe stress, anxiety, and social isolation—factors that drain happiness and health. Those without stable housing often face discrimination and a lack of social support, which further diminishes their emotional well-being.

On the flip side, having a secure, comfortable home is one of the strongest predictors of happiness. It gives us emotional stability, social integration, and a sense of ownership over our lives. It's not just about having a place to sleep; it's about having a foundation where we feel safe, valued, and connected. Research shows that nations with higher standards of housing quality tend to have higher levels of mental health and social well-being, illustrating just how much a safe home environment contributes to overall happiness.

c. Healthcare Access and Health Security: Wellness as a Pathway to Joy

When we're healthy—physically and mentally—we're in a better position to enjoy life, pursue passions, and thrive. But when health issues go untreated, they can create a constant cloud of worry, lowering our happiness. Access to quality healthcare—from preventive care to treatment for both physical and mental health—is a cornerstone of a fulfilled life. Without it, people often face suffering, isolation, and feelings of hopelessness, all of which negatively affect happiness.

Countries with universal healthcare systems, like those in Scandinavia and parts of Europe, tend to see their citizens report higher levels of happiness. The reason? When people have access to healthcare, they can manage health issues before they become overwhelming, leading to a greater sense of control and security in their lives. Knowing you have access to treatment not only reduces physical suffering but also contributes to a peace of mind, which enhances emotional well-being.

2. Economic Stability: Income, Employment, and the Pursuit of Happiness

It's no secret that money can't buy happiness—but it sure helps. Economic stability—the ability to meet your basic needs without constant worry—lays the foundation for a fulfilling life. Financial security means you're less burdened by stress and can enjoy life more fully. It also provides the freedom to pursue activities that bring joy and purpose.

a. Income and Financial Security: The Link Between Wealth and Well-Being

While happiness doesn't grow exponentially with wealth, income does have a direct correlation with happiness—especially when it ensures financial security. People who earn enough to comfortably meet their basic needs (food, shelter, healthcare) tend to be much happier than those who struggle to make ends meet. However, research shows that the relationship between income and happiness isn't linear. After a certain point—once basic needs and a level of comfort are secured—the additional boost to happiness from increasing income is less significant.

Daniel Kahneman and Angus Deaton's research found that in the United States, happiness increases with income up to about $75,000 per year, after which the returns on happiness begin to level off. This phenomenon highlights that while financial security is key to happiness, beyond a certain point, it's the freedom from financial stress—the feeling of being able to meet your needs comfortably—that matters most.

b. Employment and Job Satisfaction: The Role of Meaningful Work in Well-Being

Beyond earning a paycheck, work plays a major role in happiness. A stable, fulfilling job not only provides financial security but also gives people a sense of purpose, belonging, and identity. People who feel valued in their work, who enjoy what they do, and who have opportunities to grow tend to be happier and more engaged in their communities.

However, the opposite is true for those who face job insecurity, underemployment, or workplace stress. Unemployment or a job that feels meaningless can result in depression, anxiety, and a loss of self-worth, all of which lower happiness levels. A healthy work-life balance, job stability, and work that feels rewarding and purpose-driven are essential components of well-being. When people feel their work matters, they feel empowered and fulfilled—contributing to higher levels of happiness.

3. Health and Well-Being: The Dual Impact of Physical and Mental Health on Happiness

A person's health, both physical and mental, is foundational to happiness. When we're in good health, we have the energy to enjoy life, pursue goals, and engage in fulfilling activities. However, poor health—whether physical or mental—can be a major barrier to happiness, casting a shadow over every other area of life.

a. Physical Health and Vitality: Living with Energy and Joy

Good health isn't just about the absence of illness; it's about feeling good in our bodies. When we have the energy to move freely, exercise, and participate in activities we enjoy, we experience a greater sense of well-being. Chronic illness, pain, or disability can diminish our ability to experience life fully, but when we're healthy, we have the capacity to live vibrantly and enjoy the beauty of the world around us.

b. Mental Health and Emotional Well-Being: Strengthening the Mind for Lasting Happiness

Mental health plays just as crucial a role in happiness as physical health. People with good mental health—characterized by emotional stability, resilience, and a positive outlook—tend to be happier and more productive in all areas of life. Mental health challenges like anxiety, depression, and chronic stress can drain energy and lower life satisfaction. Social support systems, access to mental health care, and reducing stigma around mental illness are critical in fostering emotional well-being. Countries that prioritize mental health services and social support often have happier, more resilient citizens.

4. Education and Personal Fulfillment: The Joy of Knowledge and Lifelong Learning

The link between education and happiness is undeniable. Education provides the tools to improve one's economic situation, broaden opportunities, and develop a deeper sense of purpose and fulfillment. Whether it's formal schooling, lifelong learning, or simply pursuing a passion, knowledge enriches the human experience and contributes to lasting happiness.

a. Access to Education and Empowerment: The Key to Unlocking Potential

Education opens doors, but it also empowers individuals to shape their lives. People with higher levels of education tend to report greater job satisfaction, more financial stability, and higher levels of happiness. Beyond economic benefits, education fosters intellectual curiosity, personal growth, and a sense of accomplishment—all of which contribute to self-esteem and life satisfaction.

b. Opportunities for Personal Growth: The Path to Fulfillment

Learning doesn't stop after school. Lifelong learning—whether it's picking up a new hobby, taking an online course, or reading a book—keeps the mind sharp and the spirit engaged. The more we grow, the more we feel proud and fulfilled, which boosts our overall happiness.

5. Social Connections and Relationships: Building a Supportive Network for Joy

Human beings are social creatures, and the quality of our relationships plays a huge role in determining how happy we feel. Strong, supportive relationships with family, friends, and community members provide a sense of belonging and security, which are crucial for navigating life's challenges and celebrating its joys.

a. Social Support and Emotional Security: The Power of Connection

Social connections provide emotional support, reduce stress, and offer a sense of purpose. Having someone to lean on during tough times—whether it's a friend, family member, or community group—can make all the difference. The strength of these relationships is a powerful indicator of happiness.

b. Social Capital and Collective Well-Being: Building Trust and Community

When communities are built on trust, cooperation, and shared values, happiness flourishes. Social capital—the networks of relationships and social ties—forms the foundation for collective well-being. Countries with high levels of social trust and community engagement tend to have happier populations. This sense of connectedness creates a culture where everyone has the chance to thrive.

The connection between quality of life and happiness is undeniable. When individuals have access to basic needs, healthcare, economic stability, education, and social support, happiness thrives. By prioritizing policies and practices that improve these areas, societies can create a virtuous cycle where the well-being of individuals feeds into the well-being of the whole community. Ultimately, when people are happy, society flourishes—creating a harmonious, prosperous world where everyone can reach their full potential.

How Happy Citizens Create a Stronger Society

Imagine living in a society where people are not only satisfied with their lives, but genuinely happy—where people's basic needs are met, where they feel safe, valued, and connected to others, and where they are empowered to pursue their passions and purpose. This vision of happiness may seem utopian, but it's a vision that we have the power to move toward by understanding and nurturing the profound link between individual happiness and the strength of society.

It's easy to assume that societies function based purely on external structures—governments, economies, laws, and institutions—but the real engine that drives long-term progress and positive change is the happiness of its citizens. When individuals are happy, they become more productive, more creative, more generous, and more connected to their communities. In turn, these ripple effects create a virtuous cycle that strengthens the fabric of society itself.

Happiness is contagious, it fosters greater collaboration and trust, and it drives civic engagement and innovation. Let's look at how happy people—working together—create a stronger, more resilient, and more compassionate society.

1. Happiness is Contagious: The Ripple Effect of Well-Being

One of the most remarkable findings from psychology and social science is that happiness is contagious. When individuals are happy, their positive emotions often "spill over" to those around them, creating a ripple effect of joy, optimism, and energy that spreads throughout communities. This is the basis of the "social contagion" theory, which shows that happiness and well-being are not confined to the individual but can influence entire networks of people.

When you're surrounded by positive, happy people—whether they're family members, coworkers, neighbors, or even strangers in a public space—you're more likely to feel positive and happy yourself. A study published in the journal BMJ found that happiness can spread like an emotional virus: a person's happiness can increase the chances of their friends, family, and even distant acquaintances being happy by up to 25%. The connection is real, and it works in both directions: a society filled with happy people is, by nature, a more vibrant and cohesive place to live.

This contagion effect has profound implications. Imagine if a critical mass of citizens within a society were empowered with happiness—not just through external circumstances, but as a result of fostering mental health, building supportive relationships, and creating a culture of positivity. Such a society would exude energy and optimism, making it easier for others to see the possibilities for improvement, innovation, and connection.

This dynamic doesn't just stop at the individual level. It affects collective action. When happiness spreads, it motivates people to participate more actively in social, economic, and political life. They become more generous, more willing to help others, and more likely to support causes that benefit the broader community. In a society where happiness is contagious, everyone's well-being improves as a result of the positive actions taken by others.

2. Building Trust: Happy Citizens Foster Stronger Social Connections

At the heart of any successful society lies trust—the foundation upon which individuals and communities rely to work together toward common goals. Trust doesn't just mean believing that people will follow the law or respect social norms; it means that people have faith in each other's intentions, capabilities, and goodwill. Trust is built on relationships, and relationships thrive in a society where people are happy, feel secure, and are emotionally invested in the welfare of others.

Happy citizens are more likely to trust one another. Research shows that when people feel secure in their own lives—whether financially, emotionally, or physically—they are more likely to trust others. They are less anxious about competition, scarcity, or betrayal and more willing to extend themselves to others. In societies where people are happy, social capital flourishes—the networks of relationships, mutual respect, and community bonds that bind people together.

For example, consider how happy, healthy relationships contribute to community resilience. Communities where trust is high are more likely to collaborate during crises—whether that's responding to natural disasters, economic downturns, or health emergencies. During the COVID-19 pandemic, many communities that were built on high levels of trust were more effective at responding to the challenges they faced. People were more likely to follow public health guidelines, support one another, and engage in acts of kindness and solidarity, knowing that they were all in it together.

When people are happy, they are also more likely to build and maintain strong social networks—family bonds, friendships, and community ties. These social connections are essential for navigating life's challenges, but they also foster a sense of belonging and purpose. In communities where social connections are strong, people feel supported, understood, and motivated to act for the greater good.

3. Civic Engagement: Happy People Are More Likely to Participate in Society

One of the most important ways in which happy citizens strengthen society is through civic engagement. When people are content with their lives, they are more likely to engage in activities that benefit the broader community. They volunteer, vote, participate in local organizations, and advocate for social change. Civic engagement is not just about individual happiness—it's about improving the collective well-being of society.

Happy citizens are more likely to be involved in their communities and engage with issues that impact others. Studies have shown that people who report higher levels of life satisfaction are more likely to vote, participate in community service, and contribute to charitable causes. They feel a sense of duty, a moral imperative to give back, and a belief that their actions can make a difference. In short, happiness breeds social responsibility.

Consider how volunteerism contributes to stronger societies. In the United States, for instance, nearly one-quarter of adults engage in some form of volunteer work. Volunteers often report higher levels of happiness themselves, but they also create tangible benefits for their communities. Whether it's providing food for the homeless, tutoring children, or helping to clean up a local park, the collective effort of individuals who give their time and energy improves social cohesion and quality of life for everyone.

In addition to volunteering, happy citizens are more likely to engage in political activism and advocate for social change. Research by political scientists has shown that happiness and life satisfaction correlate strongly with increased participation in democracy. Happy people are more likely to vote, to support political candidates who align with their values, and to become involved in activism to improve societal conditions. In turn, these individuals help to shape policies that benefit the public good, such as those that address climate change, inequality, healthcare, and education.

4. Innovation and Creativity: Happy Citizens Drive Progress

One of the most exciting benefits of a happy, fulfilled populace is the creativity and innovation it fosters. People who are content with their lives tend to be more curious, open-minded, and willing to take risks—three essential ingredients for innovation. Happy citizens are more likely to pursue new ideas, explore diverse interests, and push boundaries, all of which propel society forward.

Happiness provides the mental and emotional space for people to think creatively. It reduces stress and anxiety, allowing people to focus on problem-solving and innovative thinking. In environments where happiness is cultivated—whether in schools, workplaces, or communities—people are encouraged to be creative and are less afraid of failure. This willingness to take risks leads to breakthroughs that can reshape industries, improve technologies, and solve global problems.

For example, consider the Silicon Valley innovation hub in California, where many of the world's most successful tech companies have been founded. The culture of the Valley is known for its optimism, risk-taking, and collaboration—characteristics that are deeply tied to the happiness and satisfaction of the people who live and work there. Individuals in such environments feel empowered to pursue their dreams, create new technologies, and solve complex problems because they are not bogged down by negative emotions like fear, anxiety, or despair.

In broader society, the creativity fostered by happiness has the potential to address some of the world's most pressing issues. Climate change, poverty, public health crises—all of these challenges require innovative solutions. In a world where citizens are happy, where mental health is supported, and where people feel a sense of purpose, the collective creativity of society can come together to tackle these problems with energy and optimism.

5. Positive Societal Outcomes: Happiness as a Pillar of Social Well-Being

At a broader level, the overall happiness of a society is associated with a host of positive societal outcomes. These outcomes are not only beneficial for the individuals involved, but they ripple outward, creating a society that is more stable, prosperous, and harmonious.

Countries with higher levels of happiness tend to have lower crime rates, better health outcomes, and stronger economies. This is partly because happy people are less likely to engage in destructive behaviors or contribute to societal problems like crime, violence, or addiction. Happy people also tend to make healthier life choices—such as eating well, exercising, and seeking medical care—leading to a healthier and more productive society overall.

In terms of economic outcomes, happy societies tend to experience higher rates of productivity, job satisfaction, and innovation. People who are content with their lives are more likely to pursue careers they are passionate about, leading to greater success in the workplace. Happy workers are also more likely to collaborate, contribute ideas, and help their colleagues, fostering an environment of cooperation and mutual success.

Moreover, happiness is linked to greater social equality. Societies that prioritize the well-being of their citizens are more likely to have policies in place that promote fairness, equity, and opportunity for all. When people are happy, they are more likely to be concerned with the well-being of others, leading to a more inclusive, compassionate society.

The connection between happy citizens and a stronger society is profound. When people are happy, they engage more fully in their communities, build trust with others, foster creativity and innovation, and work together to solve societal problems. Happiness is not a solitary pursuit—it is a collective one. By creating environments that nurture the happiness and well-being of individuals, we create a society that is more cohesive, more innovative, and more resilient.

The beauty of this connection is that it is not just theoretical. It is something we can cultivate, starting with small acts of kindness, building trust within our communities, supporting one another, and advocating for policies that ensure everyone has the opportunity to live a fulfilling and happy life. When we prioritize happiness, we're not just enhancing individual lives; we're paving the way for a stronger, more harmonious, and more prosperous society—one that can achieve great things together.

How Societal Strength Leads to the Advancement of the Human Race

When we think about human advancement, it's easy to focus on technological breakthroughs, scientific discoveries, or global achievements like space exploration or the eradication of diseases. These monumental feats seem to define our progress. However, there's an underlying foundation that makes these achievements possible: the strength of society itself.

At its core, the advancement of the human race is not solely about the ingenuity of isolated individuals, nor is it only about scientific or technological prowess. True progress is driven by the collective efforts of a society that is united, collaborative, resilient, and empowered. A society in which the majority of its citizens are happy, healthy, and engaged in meaningful endeavors has the potential to accomplish remarkable things—not just for the benefit of a few, but for all of humanity.

A thriving society serves as a springboard for human flourishing—from tackling global challenges like climate change and poverty to fostering a culture of inclusion, peace, and innovation. In this section, we'll explore how a strong society, one in which its citizens are empowered, supported, and encouraged to contribute, creates the conditions that allow humanity to reach

its fullest potential.

1. Societal Strength Fuels Innovation and Technological Progress

When a society is strong—when its citizens have the resources, opportunities, and security to pursue their passions—it fosters creativity, innovation, and problem-solving. Throughout history, major technological and scientific advances have often been the result of collaboration and the pooling of collective knowledge. From the invention of the printing press to the development of the internet, human progress has been fueled by societies that encouraged intellectual freedom, curiosity, and collaborative efforts.

In a society where people are happy and well-supported, individuals are freer to think, experiment, and innovate. People are not burdened by the constant pressures of poverty, disease, or insecurity. Instead, they can focus on creating new solutions, whether that's developing renewable energy technologies to fight climate change, advancing artificial intelligence to improve healthcare, or exploring space to push the boundaries of human knowledge.

Happy societies create the space for creative freedom. The lower levels of stress and anxiety that accompany a society with strong social safety nets, equitable access to resources, and healthy lifestyles enable people to think more clearly and boldly. For example, cities that offer access to affordable healthcare, education, and housing often become the epicenters of innovation, attracting brilliant minds who seek to collaborate and make a difference.

Look at Silicon Valley, home to some of the world's most transformative companies. Why is it such a hotbed of innovation? It's not only about the cutting-edge technology and venture capital funding—it's about the culture that exists there, a culture rooted in inclusivity, optimism, and opportunity. People in Silicon Valley have the freedom to explore and experiment, knowing that they're supported by a robust infrastructure, access to information, and the belief that their contributions will matter. This environment encourages risk-taking, and risk-taking leads to breakthrough discoveries.

When societies invest in the well-being of their citizens—through education, mental health care, and economic support systems—they unlock the full potential of their people. This leads to rapid technological progress, the emergence of new ideas, and creative solutions to pressing global problems.

2. Strengthening Society Builds Resilience to Global Challenges

The advancement of the human race doesn't happen in a vacuum. It requires global cooperation and the ability of societies to work together in the face of crises and challenges. Whether it's the threat of climate change, the rise of global health pandemics, or the persistence of inequality, the world faces crises that require global action—and that action can only happen when society is strong and its citizens are willing to collaborate for the greater good.

When a society is healthy, happy, and cohesive, it is better equipped to face adversity. Strong societies are more resilient. They can withstand natural disasters, economic downturns, and social upheavals. This resilience is the result of strong social bonds, trust, and shared purpose—all of which are nurtured in societies that prioritize the well-being of their citizens.

Consider the global COVID-19 pandemic. While the virus affected nearly every country, some nations were able to respond more effectively than others due to the strength of their societies. New Zealand, for example, was able to implement strict lockdown measures early and successfully limit the spread of the virus because it had a high level of trust in the government, a unified response from citizens, and a well-organized public health infrastructure. In contrast, countries with weak social cohesion or political instability faced more difficulties in controlling the virus.

Similarly, addressing climate change—perhaps the greatest existential threat to humanity—requires coordinated efforts across borders. In societies where people feel a sense of collective

responsibility and where social and economic equity are priorities, citizens are more likely to support policies that address environmental degradation, advocate for sustainable practices, and invest in green technologies. Strong societies recognize the importance of long-term thinking and are more likely to support initiatives that benefit the future, not just the present.

The ability of societies to come together in the face of global challenges is not only a matter of political will—it is a reflection of societal strength. Societies that encourage shared values, community involvement, and cooperation are better able to confront crises and move toward collective solutions. Human progress happens when we recognize that we are all in this together, that the advancement of one is the advancement of all.

3. Inclusive Societies Foster Global Cooperation and Peace

At its core, advancing the human race is about creating a world where all people can thrive, not just those in privileged positions. Strong societies are those that ensure equality, justice, and inclusion for all their members. These societies actively work toward dismantling systemic barriers, empowering marginalized groups, and ensuring that every individual has the opportunity to contribute to the greater good.

The principle of inclusivity is essential to the long-term success of humanity. A society that fosters inclusivity builds strong, resilient relationships within its borders, creating a culture of peace and mutual respect. When citizens feel seen, heard, and valued, they are more likely to engage in constructive behavior and support efforts that benefit society as a whole.

For example, the advancement of women's rights has been one of the most transformative social movements in recent history. In societies where women are empowered to participate fully in the workforce, politics, and social life, entire nations experience greater levels of prosperity and well-being. Women's education, economic participation, and political leadership have led to stronger, more resilient societies and more sustainable development outcomes.

Global cooperation—the ability of nations to work together to address issues like climate change, health crises, and poverty—depends on fostering relationships built on mutual respect and understanding. Strong societies, by virtue of their internal commitment to equity, are more likely to reach out to other nations in friendship and collaboration. When people see the benefits of cooperative effort at home, they are more willing to extend that collaboration to global partnerships.

This is why international agreements like the Paris Climate Agreement and the Sustainable Development Goals of the United Nations are so crucial. They represent not just the political will of governments, but the collective action of strong societies working together to ensure the survival and prosperity of future generations.

4. Economic Prosperity and Global Development: The Impact of a Strong Society

Economic prosperity is often seen as a byproduct of societal strength. Strong societies provide the education, healthcare, and infrastructure needed to produce highly skilled, innovative, and productive workers. When people are healthy, educated, and empowered to contribute, they can generate new ideas, create businesses, and drive economic growth.

A strong society is one that actively works to close the income gap, ensure access to opportunity, and reduce poverty. This not only benefits the people in that society but also has global implications. The more prosperous a nation becomes, the more it is able to invest in global development, aid efforts, and sustainable practices that benefit the entire world.

For example, wealthier nations that prioritize social programs can allocate resources to tackle global poverty, hunger, and disease. When a country's economy is stable and its people are happy, it can invest in foreign aid, education, and healthcare programs in less developed parts of the world. Additionally, the global supply chains that drive trade are strengthened when societies embrace fair trade, ethically sourced goods, and sustainable economic practices.

Economic prosperity in strong societies allows for investment in infrastructure, such as clean energy technologies, transportation systems, and education. These systems create more opportunities for human development, creating an upward cycle of prosperity that benefits not just one nation, but the entire global community.

5. The Long-Term Vision: A Strong Society Lays the Foundation for a Better Future

Ultimately, the strength of society lays the groundwork for a better future. When citizens are happy, connected, and empowered, they develop the collective vision and will to create positive change. They're not focused solely on their own survival, but on advancing society in ways that improve the lives of everyone—now and for future generations.

A strong society encourages long-term thinking, where citizens recognize that progress must benefit the planet, future generations, and the global community. This vision of shared responsibility is key to solving the most urgent problems of the 21st century, from climate change to geopolitical instability. When societies work toward the greater good, the human race as a whole advances—not just in terms of technology, but in terms of human dignity, justice, and sustainability.

The strength of society is not just a matter of economic stability or political power—it is the foundation upon which the future of humanity rests. When societies prioritize the happiness and well-being of their citizens, when they foster trust, collaboration, and creativity, they create the conditions for global cooperation and long-term prosperity. A strong society is not only resilient in the face of challenges, but it is also equipped to contribute to the advancement of the human race. By building strong, inclusive, and forward-thinking societies, we can meet the challenges of the future, achieve remarkable feats, and create a world where humanity flourishes as one.

Why the Wealth Gap Should Matter to You

Imagine it's a typical Sunday morning. You're sipping your coffee, scrolling through your phone, and catching up on the news. As you flip between stories, you're hit with headlines about billionaires building private space stations, CEOs taking home mind-boggling salaries, and the latest statistics showing how much of the nation's wealth is concentrated in the hands of a tiny few. You think to yourself, Yeah, that's a problem, but what can I really do about it?

It's easy to feel small when confronted with such massive disparities. The wealth gap in the U.S. is staggering, and sometimes it seems like no matter what happens, the rich just keep getting richer, while so many others are left struggling to stay afloat. It's easy to dismiss it as an intractable issue—

something only policymakers or Wall Street insiders can address. But here's the good news: You can make a difference.

Before you roll your eyes and dismiss me as another idealist, hear me out. The truth is, the wealth gap isn't some abstract, distant problem. It's right here, in the neighborhoods we live in, the communities we care about, and even in the everyday decisions we make. In fact, tackling it doesn't always require grand gestures—it starts with small, deliberate actions we can all take.

Sure, fixing the wealth gap may seem like a Herculean task, but when enough individuals and communities band together, big change happens. This book is all about exploring those steps—practical, actionable ways we can work together to bridge the divide between the haves and the have-nots.

The Great Divide: Why It Matters More Than Ever

Let's get real for a moment. The wealth gap isn't just about the numbers—it's about real people, real lives. It's about families struggling to make ends meet while the ultra-wealthy add another zero to their bank accounts. It's about the single mother working three jobs to feed her kids, while the CEO of her company takes home a bonus that's more than her annual salary. And it's about the communities where access to quality education, healthcare, and even clean water is a luxury few can afford.

The gap has been widening for decades. In 1979, the top 1% of Americans held about 9% of the country's wealth. By 2019, that number had jumped to nearly 40%. And then we haven't even processed the long term effects the pandemic had on the economy. The rich got richer especially the large pharmaceutical companies, while the poor lost jobs, homes and places of business. At the same time, wages for the average American have stagnated, while housing, healthcare, and education costs have skyrocketed. This isn't just an economic issue—it's a social justice issue. Over the years we have had banks, airlines, and car manufacturers "bailed out" by our government. Their executives still pocket millions of dollars annually while the average American salary is around $50,000. The Fed keeps raising interest rates and inflation is skyrocketing at alarming rates.

Despite how overwhelming this all may seem, we're not powerless. Change doesn't need to start with a sweeping, nationwide reform (though, yes, that would certainly help). Change starts with you. And no, this isn't some feel-good rhetoric. There are real, concrete ways that individuals and communities can take action to reduce inequality and build a more equitable future.

Small Actions, Big Impact

You don't have to be a billionaire philanthropist to make a difference. You don't need to run for office or launch a nationwide protest (though those things are important, too). What matters is what you do every day—the choices you make and the ways in which you support your community.

Let's start with something as simple as where you spend your money. By supporting local businesses and entrepreneurs, especially those in under-resourced neighborhoods, you're directly helping to stimulate the economy where it matters most. When you purchase from small businesses, you're not just buying a product—you're investing in the people behind it, their families, and the broader community. It's a small but powerful way to promote economic mobility.

But it doesn't end there. What if we could help break the cycle of poverty by ensuring that everyone had access to the tools to succeed? That's where education and financial literacy come in. It's not just about getting a degree or going to college—it's about ensuring that all individuals, no matter their background, have the skills and resources they need to succeed. That includes vocational training, financial education, and mentorship programs. When we empower people with knowledge, we're giving them the keys to unlock a better future.

Let's talk about voting. Yes, you've heard it before—but it's still one of the most powerful ways to create change. Who you vote for and what policies you support can directly impact economic inequality. Voting for leaders who prioritize raising the minimum wage, expanding access to healthcare, and ensuring fair wages can change the direction of a country. But voting isn't just about national elections—it's about supporting local candidates who understand the needs of your community.

It's not just about putting the right people in office—it's about holding them accountable. When citizens engage in local community organizing and advocacy, they force governments and corporations to pay attention. Change comes from the bottom up, not just from the top down. It's about joining forces with grassroots organizations and labor unions to demand better working conditions, fairer wages, and more equitable opportunities for all.

Turning Awareness Into Action

I know, I know—this all sounds a little overwhelming. You might be thinking, This is great in theory, but I'm just one person. What difference can I really make?

More than you think.

When people raise their voices, when communities work together, the ripple effect can be huge. The truth is, awareness is the first step toward action. Once you recognize the problem, you can begin to make more informed choices. You can share your knowledge with others and use your voice to advocate for change. Social media is a powerful tool for raising awareness, so why not use it to spread the word about the impacts of the wealth gap? One post, one conversation, one share—it all adds up.

Remember, this isn't just about charity—it's about fairness. It's about creating a society where everyone has a fair shot at success, no matter their background. When we support equitable hiring practices, advocate for tax reforms, and push for policies that prioritize the public good, we create a more just and balanced system. This is about addressing the symptoms of inequality—it's about changing the structures that perpetuate it.

Let's Get Started

The road to closing the wealth gap won't be easy, and it won't happen overnight. But that doesn't mean it's hopeless. In fact, it's the small, everyday decisions that can lead to big change. Whether it's supporting local businesses, advocating for better wages, participating in financial literacy programs, or voting for leaders who prioritize equity, each action contributes to the larger movement.

So, if you've ever found yourself feeling frustrated or helpless about the state of the world, know this: you're not alone, and you're not powerless. In fact, you're in the perfect position to help spark change. The wealth gap may be vast, but together, we can narrow it.

Ready to roll up your sleeves and get started?

Advocating For Policy Change

If you're reading this book, you're probably aware that the wealth gap in the U.S. is a little out of control. I mean, how can you ignore it when Jeff Bezos goes to space like it's just a quick weekend getaway, while half the country struggles to pay rent? The disparity between the haves and the have-nots has never been starker, and if you're anything like me, you've probably spent more time than you care to admit screaming at your TV or shaking your fist at the heavens wondering: What can we do about it?

The answer, my friend, is: policy change. That's right—good ol' government action. It might not have the same immediate gratification as canceling your gym membership after three weeks of good intentions, but if we want to address the wealth gap, we've got to start with the people who have the power to actually make systemic changes. No, I'm not talking about your uncle who posts about "taxing the rich" on Facebook every time a billionaire buys a yacht (though, kudos for his passion). I'm talking about advocating for policies that can change the way the economy functions—for everyone.

In this chapter, we're going to break down a few key areas where policy change can make a real difference in narrowing the wealth gap. From pushing for better wages to making sure the rich—both people and corporations—pay their fair share, these are the kinds of shifts we need if we want to create a fairer, more balanced society. And yes, you can actually be part of making that happen. Grab your metaphorical megaphone, because we're going to start advocating for change like it's 1999 and "The West Wing" is still on air.

First Things First: Why Policy?

Let's take a moment to pause and ask: Why do we even need policy change in the first place? It's easy to get caught up in the noise and confusion of everyday life, but when it comes to the wealth gap, we need to step back and think critically about the forces shaping our economy—and how we got here.

You've probably heard it before, often from someone who is very calm and very collected, like your uncle at Thanksgiving or the guy on cable news with the perfectly groomed beard. They say something along the lines of: "If people would just work harder, they'd be able to make more money." It's a refrain we've all heard at some point, maybe with the smug assurance of someone who's never had to decide between paying for rent or paying for prescription medication. It's often accompanied by an image of a determined, tired person working 80 hours a week, yet still unable to afford the basics—like food, shelter, or even the dignity to take a sick day.

And while it may seem like common sense—this idea that working harder will automatically lead to more money—there's one small flaw with that logic: it's not just about how hard people work. It's about how the system is set up.

Think about it. If hard work were the ultimate predictor of success, then why are millions of people working full-time jobs, sometimes multiple jobs, and still struggling to make ends meet? Why are some people getting richer at the speed of light while others can barely catch their breath? The truth is, the wealth gap isn't some natural law of the universe that's just part of the "human condition." No, it's a product of decisions—decisions made over decades, often with the explicit goal of creating a system that favors the wealthy and leaves everyone else in the dust.

If we're being honest, the wealth gap didn't just happen. It was built. The policies—or lack thereof—that have shaped our economy over time have allowed wealth to accumulate in the hands of a tiny group of people. And let's be clear: the system isn't broken—it's working exactly as it was designed to work. For those at the top.

The idea that "everyone can succeed if they just work hard enough" has a certain ring to it, especially in a country built on the myth of the "American Dream." But this idea disregards the reality of the systemic barriers that exist in our society, the ones that keep wealth concentrated at the top and make it harder for everyone else to get ahead. Policies that benefit the wealthy, tax breaks for corporations that pay workers next to nothing, and loopholes in the system have allowed the rich to get richer while leaving the rest of us scrambling for scraps.

In fact, the wealth that is concentrated at the top trickles down at a rate somewhere between "slower than molasses" and "who's got time for that?" Meanwhile, the vast majority of us are stuck running on the hamster wheel, trying to keep up. We hustle, we work, we sacrifice, and yet we are still unable to climb up the ladder. For many people, the idea of achieving financial stability feels like a dream that gets farther away with every passing year. It's like playing a game where the rules are stacked against you—and someone keeps changing the rules just to make sure you don't win.

Now, imagine if we flipped that script—what if we made the system work for everyone? What if there were policies in place that helped level the playing field, that helped redistribute opportunities so that everyone had a fair shot, regardless of where they started?

That's where policy change comes in. Policy is the lever we can pull to fix the system that lets billionaires hoard wealth while the waitress at the local diner has to choose between feeding her family and paying for her child's prescription. Policy is the tool we use to redistribute opportunities so that people aren't just stuck in an endless cycle of hard work with no reward.

Here's the cold, hard truth. When we talk about the wealth gap, we're not talking about some abstract or inevitable problem. We're talking about a man-made problem, one that was created through laws, tax codes, and business practices that prioritize the accumulation of wealth for the few while the rest of us fight to stay afloat. Whether it's an underfunded education system, stagnant wages, or a tax code that rewards the richest individuals and corporations, the policies we have in place right now are fueling inequality. The people at the top don't need to work any harder to get ahead—they've already rigged the system. The rest of us? We're working ourselves into the ground just to stay in place.

And that's why we need policy change. Policy is the only way we can rewire the system to work for everyone, not just the lucky few who were born into wealth or inherited a family business. The truth is, no matter how much you work, you can only get so far in a system that is stacked against you from the start. If the game is rigged, no amount of hustle is going to fix it. But with the right policies in place—policies that promote fair wages, empower workers, close tax loopholes, and expand access to education—we can shift the balance. We can make the system fairer, so that everyone has a shot at success.

The idea here is simple. The wealth gap isn't a personal failure; it's a collective problem that requires a collective solution. It's not about blaming individuals for their lack of wealth or accusing them of laziness. It's about recognizing that the system is broken—and advocating for policies that fix it. These are policies that ensure that wages keep pace with the cost of living, that working people have access to health care and paid leave, and that corporations pay their fair share in taxes. It's about creating a system that rewards people for their hard work and talent, not just their ability to game the system.

What's even more critical is that policy change is something we can influence. Unlike the idea of "pulling yourself up by your bootstraps"—which conveniently ignores the fact that not everyone has boots—policy change is something we can all advocate for. We have the power to elect leaders who care about reducing inequality. We can push for tax reforms that close loopholes and ensure that billionaires pay their fair share. We can demand policies that lift wages and protect workers' rights.

So, next time someone tells you that the wealth gap is just a matter of personal responsibility or that everyone has the same chance to succeed if they just "work harder," you can tell them: "Well, if the system wasn't designed to favor the wealthy, maybe more of us could actually succeed." And then, you can talk about how policy change is the key to creating a more equitable world for all.

Increasing the Minimum Wage

Let's get this out of the way right off the bat. $7.25 an hour is a joke. And not a funny one—the kind where you awkwardly laugh because you're not sure if the person is serious. No, this is the kind of joke that makes you want to scream into a pillow.

In case you haven't checked in recently, the current federal minimum wage in the United States is $7.25 per hour. That's right—$7.25. Now, I get it, some people might say, "Oh, but that's not supposed to be a living wage. It's for teenagers and people just starting out in the workforce." To that, I say: Really? Is that the best you've got?

First of all, let's clear something up. The average age of a minimum wage worker in the U.S. is 35 years old. Yes, you read that right. It's not just teenagers flipping burgers or college students working part-time to pay for their weekend Starbucks habit. People in their 30s—people with kids, bills, rent, and all the grown-up responsibilities—are working these jobs, and they're doing it full-time. Some are even juggling multiple minimum wage jobs just to make ends meet. So the whole "minimum wage jobs are for kids" argument? It's not only outdated, it's out of touch with reality.

Here's where it gets even more ridiculous. The cost of living has gone up drastically since the last time the federal minimum wage was raised in 2009. Since then, we've seen the price of rent, healthcare, groceries, and just about everything else go up—while wages have remained stagnant. The value of the dollar has eroded, and $7.25 today is worth far less than it was 15 years ago. So, let's break it down: how far does $7.25 actually get you in today's world?

Let's say you work 40 hours a week (because, surprise, a full-time job doesn't mean you get weekends off in the real world). At $7.25 an hour, that's about $290 a week before taxes. After taxes? Maybe around $250. Congratulations, you now have enough money to pay for two weeks worth of groceries for a family of three—or if you're in a high-cost area like New York or San Francisco, you might be able to afford two takeout dinners. But don't plan on going out to the movies or taking a vacation any time soon.

If the federal minimum wage had been increased to keep up with inflation since 1968, it would be about $12 an hour today. Not a life of luxury, but at least enough to cover the basics—rent, utilities, a few groceries, maybe even a weekend getaway (if you're careful). Taking this idea slightly further, if the minimum wage had kept pace with productivity gains—meaning the increase in the output of the economy, the amount of value being created by workers—it would be closer to $23 an hour. So, while we've seen a huge increase in productivity, workers' wages have barely budged.

What does that mean? It means that workers are producing more than ever before, but they're not seeing the benefits of that increased productivity. The benefits, instead, are going to the top. Corporate profits have skyrocketed. CEOs are pulling in 320 times more than the average worker. And the disparity keeps getting worse: as workers are stuck earning the same low wages, the ultra-wealthy continue to accumulate more wealth at a pace that's downright obscene.

You don't need to be an economist to see the problem here. In a world where the cost of living is rising faster than you can say "inflation," $7.25 an hour isn't just unfair—it's completely out of touch with reality.

So, what can we do about it? Advocate for an increase in the federal minimum wage. I know it's not going to happen overnight—no change ever does—but it has to start somewhere. We need to shift the conversation from "Oh, this is just what people should expect" to "Wait a minute, this is an issue we can solve." And the solution is simple: we need to raise the minimum wage to a level that recognizes the value of the work people are doing.

The truth is, there's absolutely no reason why someone working full-time —working their butt off—shouldn't be able to afford a basic, decent standard of living. Raising the minimum wage isn't just about helping the people who need it most—it's about ensuring that work is dignified. People should not have to work multiple jobs, neglect their health, or forego spending time with their families just to get by. The wages people are paid should reflect the work they do, not just the bare minimum that companies are willing to offer.

And for those who argue that raising the minimum wage would "hurt small businesses" or "cause inflation," well, here's the thing: it's the wealthiest individuals and corporations who are benefiting the most from this wage stagnation. If companies like Amazon and Walmart can afford to pay their CEOs millions of dollars, they can afford to pay their workers more. The argument that increasing the minimum wage will lead to job loss or economic ruin doesn't hold water when we see record profits in the hands of those who least need it.

But we need to remember that raising the minimum wage isn't just about economic fairness—it's a matter of basic human dignity. It's about recognizing that the people who clean our offices, stock our shelves, serve our food, and drive our buses deserve more than just a pat on the back. They deserve a living wage. Their work matters. Their contributions to society are significant. And their pay should reflect that.

So, what's the next step? How do we advocate for this change? First, talk about it. Start conversations with people you know. Share the facts. Talk about how unfair it is that workers can't even afford to live on the money they make. Second, vote. Find out where your local and national representatives stand on the issue, and vote for those who support raising the minimum wage. Third, support businesses and organizations that advocate for workers' rights. There are tons of grassroots campaigns and worker advocacy groups fighting for a fair wage across the country. Get involved—whether that means signing petitions, attending rallies, or simply lending your support to those who are on the frontlines.

And finally—don't stop pushing. Demand change. This is an issue that affects everyone—not just the workers at the bottom of the wage scale. When workers are paid fairly, they're able to contribute more to the economy, spend more, and improve their communities. It's a win-win for everyone.

The bottom line, $7.25 an hour is not enough to live on. It's time to raise the minimum wage, and it's time for all of us to advocate for policies that ensure that work is not just about surviving—but about thriving. Because when workers do well, we all do well.

Labor Rights

Let's talk about labor rights for a moment, because workers are not robots. And yet, sometimes it feels like employers expect them to be. If you've ever worked a low-wage job—whether in fast food, retail, or any other service industry—you've probably heard some version of this argument: "The economy would collapse if all the fast food workers went on strike." And sure, there's a kernel of truth to that. Many of the jobs that keep the gears of the economy turning—like stocking grocery shelves, flipping burgers, or driving buses—are often the lowest-paying and the most under-appreciated. But just because a job is considered "unskilled" or "entry-level" doesn't mean it's unimportant.

In fact, let's set the record straight right now. The people working in grocery stores, in warehouses, in fast food chains, or as delivery drivers are not robots. They are real people. People with families, bills, dreams, and lives outside of work. They deserve to be treated with respect, to earn a fair wage, and to work in conditions that don't make them feel like cogs in a machine. Unfortunately, that's not always the reality.

In many industries, workers are not only underpaid, but their labor is taken for granted. Employers, especially in large corporations, often exploit their workers by paying them as little as possible and skimping on benefits, while making record profits. So here's the million-dollar question: Why should workers who are literally keeping everything running be paid so poorly?

Take a moment and think about the last time you ordered food from a fast food restaurant or picked up groceries. The people who prepared your food, bagged your items, or handed you your coffee didn't do that job because they "love" it (though some might genuinely enjoy their work). They did it because they need to make a living. Unfortunately, for many people working in these essential industries, that living is barely enough to cover the basics. In fact, millions of workers in these sectors rely on public assistance—like food stamps, Medicaid, and housing subsidies—just to make ends meet, all while their employers rake in billions in profits.

Let's talk about a company like Amazon. The online retail giant has more than 1.5 million employees worldwide. Amazon made over $500 billion in revenue in 2022. That's more than the GDP of many countries. And yet, Amazon workers—especially those in warehouses—often deal with harsh conditions: grueling hours, physical exhaustion, and even unreasonable performance quotas that can lead to injuries. In the U.S., Amazon has been accused of discouraging workers from unionizing, creating an environment where people are afraid to speak up about their conditions for fear of losing their jobs. And while Jeff Bezos—Amazon's founder and former CEO—was taking the company to new heights, his workers were getting low wages, limited benefits, and no real say in how they were treated.

This isn't an isolated incident. The wealth gap isn't just about what people earn, it's also about what they're denied. Workers who are treated poorly and paid poorly often have little power to improve their situation. This dynamic creates a cycle of exploitation that's hard to break. It's a classic case of labor being undervalued while employers line their pockets. The good news is we can change this. And no, it's not a pipe dream. It's already happening.

We've seen the power of collective action in real-time. Just look at the efforts of workers organizing in places like Amazon warehouses, Starbucks stores, and even McDonald's restaurants. For years, workers in these industries were often told to just "deal with it" or "be thankful for the job." But increasingly, people are saying, "No, we deserve better."

In Amazon warehouses, workers started organizing to demand better working conditions, higher wages, and a seat at the table. Amazon responded by attempting to squash these efforts at every turn, from firing employees involved in organizing campaigns to spending millions on anti-union efforts. But despite the challenges, Amazon workers have won significant victories in various regions—fighting for better pay, safer conditions, and more job security.

Similarly, in Starbucks, baristas and other employees started unionizing in 2021, with an outpouring of support from workers at locations across the country. Starbucks, like many big corporations, tried to prevent unionization by offering employees perks and bonuses as a distraction, or outright firing those who spoke out. But workers kept pushing, and since then, hundreds of Starbucks stores have successfully voted to unionize, sending a powerful message to the company and to the broader economy: Workers have a voice, and they're not afraid to use it.

These victories, though hard-won, show us that collective bargaining works. When workers come together, they can negotiate for better wages, improved benefits, paid sick leave, safer working conditions, and even more reasonable working hours. When workers are empowered, they can get a better deal—and they don't have to do it alone. By banding together, they gain bargaining power that no individual could have on their own.

So, how can we help? Advocate for stronger labor protections—policies that make it easier for workers to organize, unionize, and collectively bargain without the fear of retaliation. In the U.S., there are still states that make it incredibly difficult for workers to form unions, and there are too many companies that find loopholes to avoid paying fair wages and offering decent benefits. If we want to create a more just economy, we need to fight for policies that level the playing field between workers and corporations.

We also need to support the right of workers to unionize without fear of retaliation or job loss. We've seen far too many examples of companies threatening workers who want to join a union, firing union supporters, or even using illegal tactics to suppress union efforts. That's not how democracy is supposed to work. A free and fair labor market relies on workers having the freedom to organize and fight for their rights.

One of the best things we can do to support workers is vote for leaders who are committed to protecting labor rights. This includes supporting candidates who back policies that make it easier to form unions, improve wage laws, and strengthen protections for workers who stand up to their employers. Whether it's through local, state, or federal elections, political power is an important tool for changing labor laws and ensuring workers are treated fairly.

In addition to voting, stand in solidarity with workers. Attend rallies and demonstrations that support labor rights, participate in campaigns to raise awareness about worker exploitation, and—when possible—buy from businesses that treat their workers well. Choose to spend your dollars at places that offer fair wages and benefits, and support companies that make a point of treating their employees with dignity and respect. You'd be amazed at how powerful consumer choices can be in driving change.

At the end of the day, labor rights aren't just about better working conditions for workers. They're about creating a stronger, more equitable economy. When workers are paid fairly, treated with dignity, and given the rights they deserve, the whole economy benefits. They spend more money, invest in their communities, and contribute to a more thriving economy. The truth is: an economy that lifts up its workers lifts up all of us.

So the next time you hear someone say, "Those fast food workers don't deserve more," or "People don't need unions to get ahead," remind them: Labor is the backbone of our economy, and when workers succeed, we all succeed.

Expanding Social Safety Nets

The truth is that social safety nets are not bad. In fact, they are absolutely essential for keeping our society from falling apart at the seams. And yet, every so often, you'll hear someone argue that people who rely on government assistance are "lazy" or "undeserving." And you know what? That's not just a misguided opinion—it's flat-out wrong.

Life is unpredictable. The reality is, no one can control every twist and turn that life throws at them. You might get sick. You might lose your job due to no fault of your own. A global pandemic might hit (remember that?) and turn everything upside down. Or you might be working hard every day, only to find that your wages aren't enough to cover the rising costs of rent, healthcare, or education.

The thing is no one can succeed entirely on their own. While the myth of the "self-made" person persists, the truth is that we all rely on a system of support—whether it's in the form of family, friends, or, yes, social safety nets—to get by when things go wrong. These programs were created to ensure that when life gets tough, people aren't left to fend for themselves in a broken system. Social security, Medicare, unemployment benefits, food assistance, and other safety nets are there to catch us when we stumble, to help us get back on our feet, and to prevent us from falling through the cracks.

Let's take a quick look at some of these programs and what they do. Social Security is a retirement safety net for millions of Americans—especially the elderly, who often have little to no other source of income. Medicare provides healthcare to those 65 and older, a group that's particularly vulnerable when it comes to medical costs. Unemployment benefits provide temporary financial relief for people who lose their jobs, helping them stay afloat as they search for new employment. And let's not forget food assistance programs like SNAP, which help ensure that millions of families don't go hungry, even when life throws them a curveball.

These programs are not perfect, and they are not enough. In fact, they often fall short, leaving people in need struggling to make ends meet. The cost of healthcare has soared to such an extent that even people with insurance are burdened by exorbitant out-of-pocket expenses. Housing prices in many parts of the country have skyrocketed, making it nearly impossible for low-income individuals and families to afford a place to live. And as for education, student debt has become a crushing weight on millions of young people, many of whom are left with degrees that don't guarantee a stable job or financial security.

So, what do we do about it? First, let's get one thing straight. There is no shame in needing help. None. We are all part of a larger society, and when the system works as it should, we take care of one another. When someone falls on hard times, it's not a personal failure—it's a sign that the system needs to step in and provide support. The idea that someone who receives assistance is lazy or "not trying hard enough" is not only insulting but deeply harmful. We are all vulnerable to life's uncertainties, and social safety nets are how we protect each other in those moments.

So, how do we ensure that these programs continue to serve the people who need them most? Well, the answer is simple: We advocate for their expansion. We need to make these programs stronger, more accessible, and more effective.

Let's start with universal healthcare—or at the very least, a public option. Right now, millions of Americans go without healthcare because they can't afford it. Even people with insurance face sky-high premiums, deductibles, and out-of-pocket costs that often force them to choose between seeing a doctor and paying for food or rent. This is unacceptable. Healthcare should not be a luxury. It should be a right. If we can't achieve universal healthcare right away, then we need to push for a public option—a government-run plan that would allow anyone to buy into the system, regardless of income. By expanding access to healthcare, we can ensure that fewer people have to choose between their health and their survival.

Next, we need to strengthen unemployment benefits and ensure that they are more than just a lifeline—they should be a springboard. Right now, many unemployment benefits are woefully inadequate, especially in states where benefits are limited to just a few weeks or months. Meanwhile, the job market is evolving rapidly, and many workers need more time to retrain or find a new job that matches their skills. Instead of punishing people for being out of work, we should offer a robust safety net that gives them the resources they need to transition to new employment without falling into poverty.

Then there's the issue of housing. The cost of living in cities across the country has skyrocketed, and affordable housing is becoming increasingly rare. We need more affordable housing programs, whether through increased public housing, rent control policies, or subsidies that help low-income families pay for housing. Housing isn't just about having a roof over your head—it's the foundation for everything else. Without stable housing, it's nearly impossible to maintain a job, stay healthy, or give children the kind of stable environment they need to succeed. Affordable housing is not just a luxury—it's a necessity.

And let's not forget about food security. With food prices climbing, millions of families are finding it harder and harder to put enough food on the table. We need to expand food assistance programs like SNAP, increase the eligibility for these programs, and ensure that more families have access to nutritious meals. The fact that there are people in this country who are working full-time jobs but still don't earn enough to feed themselves or their families is a tragedy. No one should go hungry, especially in a nation as wealthy as ours.

So, what can you do about it? Advocate for the expansion of social safety nets in your community, in your state, and at the national level. Support candidates who prioritize policies that provide a livable income for those who are unemployed, underemployed, or facing hardships. Push for universal healthcare, affordable housing, and better food assistance programs. Join the movement to strengthen our social safety nets—because when we take care of each other, we all benefit.

It's also important to recognize that the social contract doesn't mean that those who can work should always be the ones providing. In an ideal world, everyone would have a job that pays them fairly and gives them the opportunity to thrive. But the reality is, sometimes people can't work, sometimes they need help, and sometimes the system itself fails. When we make it easier for people to get the help they need during those tough times, we're not just providing a safety net—we're strengthening the very fabric of our society.

Because life isn't a one-man show. It's a shared experience. And when we make sure everyone can stand on their own two feet, we all rise together.

Taxing the Rich: Seriously, It's About Time

Alright, let's talk about the elephant in the room—the 1% of the population that's hoarding more wealth than a dragon guarding its treasure hoard. You know the ones—the ones with enough money to buy yachts, private jets, and an entire fleet of luxury cars. They can order avocado toast in every city on the planet without worrying about the price tag, while the rest of us are counting every dollar to make sure we can afford rent, groceries, and maybe a Netflix subscription.

But here's the thing that's truly maddening, the wealthiest 1% are not paying their fair share in taxes. And when I say the "wealthiest 1%," I'm not just talking about those few ultra-rich individuals who can fill their garages with luxury cars—I'm talking about the entire class of corporate moguls and billionaires who, thanks to a myriad of loopholes, shelters, and tax tricks, pay a far lower percentage of their income in taxes than regular folks like you and me. That's right. Some billionaires pay a lower effective tax rate than a teacher, nurse, or mechanic. How? Let's break it down...

First of all, let's be clear about one thing, the rich don't make their money the same way the rest of us do. For most of us, our income comes from earned wages—that's our paycheck, our hourly wages, or our salary. And that income is taxed through things like payroll taxes (which fund Social Security and Medicare) and income taxes, which are taken right out of our paycheck before we even see it. The more we earn, the higher the percentage we pay, and that's the way it's supposed to work—progressive taxation is meant to ensure that those who can afford to pay more do so.

But billionaires? They're not relying on earned income. Instead, they make their money through capital gains—that is, income derived from their investments, stocks, or assets like real estate. And the thing is, capital gains are taxed at a much lower rate than earned income. In fact, the top rate on capital gains is 20% (if you're lucky), while the top rate on earned income can be as high as 37%. But that's not where it ends. There are also loopholes, offshore tax shelters, and other legal tricks that let the ultra-wealthy shield their money from the taxman altogether.

One of the most notorious tricks is the carried interest loophole, which lets hedge fund managers and private equity partners treat their income from managing investments as capital gains, even though they are getting paid for their work. So, instead of paying regular income tax rates, they pay a lower rate meant for long-term investments. That's just one of many clever ways the rich minimize their tax liabilities—sometimes paying less than the average middle-class worker who's simply trying to make ends meet.

Another classic example is the use of offshore tax havens. These are countries or territories (like the Cayman Islands or Luxembourg) where billionaires and multinational corporations can park their money to avoid paying taxes in their home country. In fact, Apple, Amazon, and other major corporations have been known to stash billions in profits offshore, where they pay little to no tax. That's right—while small businesses and individuals can't escape paying their fair share, big corporations are jumping on planes to avoid paying taxes on billions of dollars.

While the ultra-rich are getting off scot-free, the rest of us are stuck with a tax system that doesn't play fair. In addition to income taxes, many people in the working class pay regressive taxes—taxes that hit people harder the less money they make. Sales taxes and payroll taxes are the prime offenders.

Sales taxes are a great example of a tax that disproportionately impacts lower-income individuals. Whether it's buying groceries, clothes, or even the essentials, the working class pays sales taxes on almost everything they purchase. And the higher the price of an item, the more sales tax you pay. For someone earning minimum wage, that's a much higher percentage of their income than it is for someone earning millions.

But perhaps the most infuriating example is the payroll tax, which funds Social Security and Medicare. The problem here is that the payroll tax is regressive—meaning that once you make over a certain threshold (currently around $160,000), you stop paying it. So, someone making $160,000 a year and someone making $1 billion are both paying the same amount in payroll taxes. That means billionaires are paying far less into the system that supports seniors, disabled people, and the unemployed than the average worker, even though they benefit disproportionately from the government's infrastructure and economy.

While the average worker is paying taxes on income earned from actual labor, the rich have figured out how to game the system. They don't need to rely on earned income, they have money making more money for them. They're investing in stocks, properties, and offshore accounts—and their wealth is growing in ways that aren't taxed as heavily.

To make matters worse, corporations are getting in on the action, too. In 2017, the U.S. passed a corporate tax cut that reduced the corporate tax rate from 35% to 21%. While the argument was that this would encourage companies to reinvest in their workers and the economy, the results were not at all the case. In fact, many large corporations used their tax breaks to buy back their stock, which boosts the value of their shares and benefits their executives, all while doing little to improve the wages or working conditions of their employees. Amazon paid zero dollars in federal income taxes in 2018 and 2019, despite making tens of billions in profits. Netflix did the same in 2019. And Apple? Well, they've been parking billions in offshore accounts to avoid paying their fair share for years.

So, now that we've laid out the problem, what can we do about it? Tax reform. And not just some small tweaks here and there—we need real, structural changes that hold the wealthy accountable.

First, we need to ensure that capital gains are taxed at the same rate as earned income. This could be a game-changer in the fight for tax fairness. Why should someone who makes millions from investments pay a lower rate than someone who's working 60 hours a week to make ends meet? That's just common sense.

Second, we need to close the loopholes that allow the ultra-wealthy and corporations to avoid paying their fair share. This means getting rid of things like the carried interest loophole and cracking down on offshore tax havens. There's no reason that billionaires should be able to park their money in a foreign country and avoid paying taxes to the government that made their success possible.

Third, we need to reintroduce higher taxes on the wealthiest individuals and corporations. This doesn't mean punishing success—it means ensuring that those who benefit the most from the system also contribute to keeping it running. The top tax rate for individuals hasn't been this low in over 100 years. Back in the 1950s, when the economy was booming, the highest marginal tax rate was over 90%. In fact, under President Eisenhower, the highest earners were taxed at 92%. Now, the top rate is just 37%. So let's bring back progressive tax policies that ensure the rich pay their fair share.

Finally, let's support policies that tax wealth itself, not just income. A wealth tax—where individuals pay taxes on the value of their assets, such as stocks, bonds, and real estate—could be one way to address the vast accumulation of wealth at the top. There's already a precedent for this. Countries like Switzerland and Norway have wealth taxes that help redistribute some of the wealth that's become so concentrated at the top. It's time to have that conversation in the U.S.

Let's be clear about one thing, tax reform isn't about punishing success. It's about ensuring fairness. It's about making sure that the system works for everyone—not just the ultra-wealthy who are already beating the system. When the rich pay their fair share, it helps fund public goods and services that benefit all of us: schools, healthcare, roads, and public infrastructure. It strengthens our economy and ensures that we all have access to the resources we need to thrive.

So, what can you do? Start by advocating for tax reform. Support candidates and policies that prioritize progressive tax structures, closing tax loopholes, and ensuring that the wealthy contribute to the common good. It's time to level the playing field and make sure the ultra-rich are paying their fair share. The system is rigged in their favor, but with enough political pressure, we can tip the scales back toward fairness. Because the truth is, when the wealthiest 1% pay their fair share, we all benefit. It's about time.

Corporations Exploiting Taxpayer Dollars

Let's talk about a popular concept in economics called "corporate welfare"—and no, it's not the kind of welfare where your neighbor gets food stamps. It's the other kind, where massive corporations receive government subsidies, tax breaks, bailouts, and lucrative contracts at the expense of, well, you guessed it—taxpayers. So while ordinary Americans are scraping to make rent, corporations are partying with taxpayer dollars. But instead of reinvesting those funds in their workers or communities, many of these corporations take the money and run, leaving little behind except more wealth for the already-wealthy. This practice raises serious ethical concerns, and it's a key factor in perpetuating the wealth gap.

Corporate Welfare 101: Who's Getting the Handouts?
In the U.S., corporate welfare comes in many forms: tax breaks, direct subsidies, bailouts, and contracts that don't require the same level of scrutiny as the average citizen's application for, say, a small business loan. In short, corporations often get a free ride from the government, while the rest of us are expected to pay our fair share of taxes and follow the rules. It's a bit like the popular kid in school who gets extra credit for doing nothing, while the hardworking students are left asking, "Wait, where's my reward?"

For example, Amazon is a prime (pun intended) offender when it comes to corporate welfare. In 2018, Amazon paid zero dollars in federal taxes despite earning $11.2 billion in profits. Instead, Amazon received a $129 million tax rebate. How? By using tax loopholes, incentives, and various subsidies meant for small businesses and innovation. This is the same company that's been celebrating record profits while its warehouse workers have to rely on food stamps to make ends meet. Amazon is far from alone in this, either. Walmart,

ExxonMobil, and Chevron—giants of their respective industries—have also been recipients of tax breaks that let them profit more from their businesses than the average taxpayer. And don't get me started on the bailouts.

Bailouts: The Billionaire's Safety Net

Remember the 2008 financial crisis? It was like the ultimate "oops" moment for Wall Street, and the government responded by bailing out banks and corporations to the tune of $700 billion. Yet, how many average Americans got a similar bailout when their homes were foreclosed, their jobs were lost, or their retirement funds were wiped out? The answer is a resounding zero. But the executives at companies like AIG and Bank of America? They were rewarded with multimillion-dollar bonuses, and their companies emerged from the financial wreckage with a shiny new lease on life—largely funded by taxpayer dollars.

These bailouts didn't come with any strings attached, either. No mandatory wage increases for workers, no job creation in the communities that got hit hardest by the recession—just corporate executives continuing to make bank while the rest of us picked up the tab. So, taxpayers saved the day… for billionaires.

Corporate Contracts: More Money for Less Work

Now, let's talk about government contracts. Every year, billions of dollars in taxpayer money go to private corporations for things like defense contracts, infrastructure projects, and even healthcare services. The most well-known examples come from companies like Lockheed Martin, Boeing, and Halliburton, which have raked in enormous government contracts—some of which, let's be real, probably should've been scrutinized a little more closely. Despite receiving these massive sums of public money, there's often little accountability when it comes to actually benefiting the public.

For instance, Lockheed Martin, a defense contractor, has received billions of dollars for weapons systems, military jets, and other defense-related technologies. Yet, a 2019 report found that Lockheed had been overcharging the U.S. government for these systems, costing taxpayers tens of billions of dollars. Meanwhile, many of the workers on the production line were making far less than the company's executives, who were pocketing tens of millions in salary and bonuses. In other words, taxpayers were subsidizing the profits of wealthy shareholders, while workers saw few benefits from the booming business.

It's like paying a contractor to build a new deck on your house, but when the work's done, you find out they've used subpar materials, overcharged you for the supplies, and paid their workers minimum wage—while the owner of the company gets a shiny new Ferrari.

Boeing's Broken Wings: Cutting Corners, Risking Lives, and Reaping Profits

And then there's Boeing, which is a textbook example of corporate greed in action—this time with a life-and-death twist.

Boeing, one of the largest defense and aerospace contractors in the world, has a long history of government contracts—especially with the U.S. military. But in recent years, the company's practices have been called into question after the crashes of two 737 MAX aircraft, which killed 346 people. The scandal revealed that Boeing executives, in their rush to stay competitive and increase profits, cut corners on safety and rushed production of the aircraft, putting the lives of passengers and crew members at risk.

This wasn't just a case of a bad design—it was about intentionally ignoring warnings, downplaying safety concerns, and failing to disclose critical issues about the plane's flight control system. The company withheld information from regulators and downplayed the severity of the issue, all to speed up production and reduce costs. After the crashes, Boeing faced widespread outrage, and investigations revealed that they had ignored safety protocols and pressured regulators to approve their planes quickly.

But what about the billion-dollar contracts Boeing has received from taxpayers? You guessed it. They were still getting paid. In the wake of the crashes, the U.S. government gave Boeing a $13 billion bailout to "help" the company recover. Meanwhile, executives, who were directly responsible for the safety failures, were still collecting hefty salaries and performance bonuses. CEO Dennis Muilenburg, despite the disastrous safety failures, still received $23 million in compensation in the year after the crashes. Shareholders continued to see their dividends while the public, many of whom were affected by the company's negligence, had to foot the bill for the bailout.

It's like the ultimate con. Taxpayers get stuck paying for a company's gross negligence (in both public safety and financial stability), while executives rake in millions, and the workers who actually build the planes are still getting paid peanuts compared to the windfall the executives and shareholders walk away with.

A Win for the 1%, A Loss for the Rest of Us

Boeing's corporate interests and government contracts align with the broader issue of the wealth gap in America. As companies like Boeing, Lockheed Martin, and others receive massive taxpayer dollars, safety and quality often take a backseat to profit margins and executive paychecks. Meanwhile, the average taxpayer—the very people funding these contracts—is left in the dark, trusting that their money is being used to improve public safety and infrastructure, only to find out later that it's being funneled into executive bonuses and corporate profits.

The public's safety is treated as expendable if it means cutting costs, while the rich continue to get richer. If we're honest about it, corporate contracts have become less about serving the public good and more about corporations and their executives continuing to get rich off the backs of taxpayers—many of whom have no say in how their money is spent.

The scandal at Boeing is just one example of how corporations manipulate government contracts for their own gain. It's a system where profits come before people, and the public is left to clean up the mess—financially and morally.

Accountability? Not for the 1%

So, what happens when a corporation like Boeing cuts corners, risks lives, and takes taxpayers for a ride? The wealthy executives get bailed out, the stock prices go up, and the workers? They get the same pay or, more often than not, the layoffs.

This is the kind of corporate culture that is spreading through America's economy. When taxpayer dollars fund massive contracts for companies like Boeing, there needs to be far greater accountability. Government oversight is critical to ensure that these corporations are held responsible for their actions—and that they aren't just padding their bottom line at the expense of public safety and the common good.

We need a system of accountability where corporate greed doesn't trump the public's well-being—where CEOs aren't allowed to make millions while cutting corners and putting lives at risk. If we can hold these companies accountable, then maybe—just maybe—corporate contracts will finally start working for the public good rather than just the 1%.

The Ethical Problem: Corporations Are Sucking Up the Public Good

So what's the ethical problem here? It's not just that corporations are getting handouts from the government—it's that they aren't doing enough to reinvest in the people or communities who make their wealth possible. Many of these companies pocket the subsidies and tax breaks, funnel the money to executives and shareholders, and don't create the jobs, infrastructure, or opportunities that could actually benefit society at large. Instead of using taxpayer dollars to lift up workers and local economies, they turn around and use that money to pad their bottom line or fund stock buybacks that make wealthy investors even wealthier.

It's essentially a wealth transfer from taxpayers to corporations—except, instead of creating public benefits (like better healthcare, education, or infrastructure), it simply increases inequality. Corporate welfare doesn't create a trickle-down effect; it just keeps the cash flowing in one direction: upward.

Take, for example, the fact that Amazon paid no federal taxes in 2018. Meanwhile, 34% of Amazon's warehouse workers rely on food stamps to feed their families. So, Amazon is taking in subsidies, paying no taxes, and making billions of dollars, while its workers are scraping by on government assistance. The irony here is that the taxpayer-funded safety net for workers is being funded by the very taxes Amazon isn't paying. It's like playing Monopoly with your friend who keeps taking extra $500 bills from the bank but refuses to land on "Income Tax" when it's their turn.

How Corporate Welfare Perpetuates the Wealth Gap

Corporate welfare is one of the primary mechanisms that drive the wealth gap in the United States. Think about it, If the government is giving huge corporations billions in tax breaks and subsidies, then that's money that could have gone to funding things like public education, healthcare, or social services that benefit the middle and lower classes. Instead, that money is funneled to the wealthy elites who already control most of the nation's resources.

As corporations get richer, they invest less in the communities that made them wealthy in the first place. So, while executives and shareholders are seeing record profits, the people working for them—those who make the products, sell the services, and fuel the economy—are stuck in lower-wage jobs with little opportunity for upward mobility. The result? The 1% gets richer, while the 99% gets left behind. The wealth gap isn't just widening; it's becoming a chasm.

A Call for Change: Who Should Be Held Accountable?

What's the solution to this mess? It's not as simple as saying "no more corporate subsidies." After all, some subsidies are designed to incentivize innovation or address market failures. But the ethical issue arises when those subsidies don't benefit society at large, but rather line the pockets of the already-wealthy few.

The government needs to reevaluate how it uses taxpayer dollars to support corporations, ensuring that any public funding directly benefits the workers, the communities, and the economy as a whole. That means holding companies accountable for the public funds they receive, and ensuring that those funds are reinvested into their workforce, local economies, and social infrastructure.

And, let's be honest, it wouldn't hurt to make sure that corporations like Amazon and Walmart actually pay their fair share of taxes—not only so the rest of us don't have to pick up the slack, but also so that taxpayers' dollars are used to reduce the wealth gap, not widen it.

Corporate welfare, while it may seem like a good idea to stimulate business—is often just a way for corporations to milk the system without giving anything back. It's an ethically questionable practice that perpetuates the wealth gap, stifles economic mobility, and keeps the rich getting richer while the rest of us are left holding the bill. If we want a fairer, more equitable society, we need to reconsider how taxpayer money is spent and ensure that it's invested in ways that benefit everyone, not just the 1%.

Predatory Lending And Debt Traps

Imagine you're struggling to make ends meet, scraping by with a paycheck-to-paycheck lifestyle. You've got rent to pay, bills stacking up, and then—suddenly—an emergency hits. Maybe your car breaks down, or a medical expense pops up out of nowhere. You need money, fast. In this moment of desperation, a "helpful" offer appears, promising a quick fix: a payday loan, a credit card with a high limit, or a subprime mortgage. Sounds like a lifeline, right? Well, not exactly. What these "helpful" financial products often lead to is a debt trap, and the only thing that's fast is how quickly you'll sink deeper into financial turmoil.

Let's talk about predatory lending—a practice that's been going on for decades, where vulnerable people are enticed into borrowing money under terms that are so unfair, they can never get out. And the real kicker? The government has largely failed to regulate these industries effectively, leaving people to drown in high-interest loans, sky-high fees, and debt that seems impossible to escape. The impact? These financial products are driving the wealth gap wider, creating a cycle of poverty that's hard to break and contributing to the growing inequality in the United States.

Predatory Lending 101: What is It?

Predatory lending involves targeting vulnerable individuals with high-interest loans and financial products that they have little chance of repaying without incurring substantial additional debt. The most common forms of predatory lending include:

Payday loans: Short-term, high-interest loans designed to be repaid by your next paycheck. These loans often come with exorbitant fees and interest rates that can reach up to 400% annually (and sometimes even higher).

Subprime mortgages: These are loans given to borrowers with poor credit scores, often accompanied by high interest rates and unfavorable terms. Subprime mortgages were a major contributor to the 2008 financial crisis, as millions of people were lured into taking out loans they could never afford.

Credit cards with exorbitant interest rates: Many people with poor credit end up with credit cards that charge sky-high interest rates, leading to a never-ending cycle of debt as they try to pay off balances while accumulating more interest charges.

The business model for predatory lenders is simple, trap people in debt. These companies make their money by offering loans that seem too good to pass up, but with terms that ensure the borrower can never repay them fully. Borrowers get stuck in an endless cycle of borrowing to pay off previous loans, taking on more and more debt until they're buried under a pile of interest, fees, and late charges.

Why It's a Problem for Vulnerable Populations

Predatory lending disproportionately affects low-income communities, minorities, and those without access to traditional banking services. These populations are often living paycheck to paycheck, so when an unexpected financial emergency arises, they have limited options. In these moments of financial desperation, predatory lenders swoop in with promises of fast cash and easy terms.

For instance, payday loans might look tempting. "Borrow $300 today, pay back $330 in two weeks." Sounds fair enough—except when you consider that many payday lenders charge an APR (annual percentage rate) of 400% or more. This means that if you fail to pay it back on time, interest keeps piling up, and suddenly, that $300 loan can balloon to $600 or even more. And what happens when you can't repay it? You borrow again—except now you're borrowing just to pay off your old debt. Welcome to the debt trap.

This is especially dangerous because people in these vulnerable populations often don't have the financial literacy to understand the long-term impact of these loans. It's like being given a lifeline that's actually a noose slowly tightening around your neck. The worst part is that these loans don't just put people in debt—they keep them there, sometimes for years.

Real-Life Examples of the Debt Trap:
The Payday Loan Nightmare

Consider the story of Jasmine, a single mother who needed a quick $500 to cover a medical emergency. She took out a payday loan at 400% APR, thinking she'd be able to pay it back when she got her next paycheck. But when payday came, she was short—and now she owed $600. So, she took out another payday loan, and the cycle began. In just a few months, she found herself drowning in a sea of high-interest loans, with no way to get out. Eventually, Jasmine lost her car to repossession and her credit score tanked, which made it harder to get a regular loan or even rent an apartment. The payday loan industry didn't just leave her financially worse off—it created a chain reaction that worsened every aspect of her life.

The Subprime Mortgage Crisis

The subprime mortgage crisis of 2008 is another infamous example. In the years leading up to the crash, millions of Americans were lured into buying homes with subprime mortgages, which are designed for people with poor credit. These loans often featured low "teaser" interest rates that adjusted to much higher rates after a few years. So, people who were already living paycheck to paycheck found themselves with homes they couldn't afford as their mortgage payments increased. When the housing market crashed, millions of people lost their homes to foreclosure, and the wealth gap widened dramatically. Predatory lenders who had issued these risky mortgages got off scot-free, while homeowners were left with ruined credit, lost property, and a shredded sense of security.

How Predatory Lending Perpetuates the Wealth Gap

Now, let's zoom out and look at the broader picture. Predatory lending is a direct contributor to the wealth gap in the U.S., and here's why:

Higher Debt Burdens for Low-Income Communities

Low-income households are disproportionately affected by predatory lending because they have fewer options for borrowing money. When these households are stuck with payday loans, high-interest credit cards, or subprime mortgages, it leaves them with little disposable income to invest in savings, education, or assets like a home or a retirement fund. Instead of building wealth, they're spending their money on interest and fees, further deepening their financial vulnerability.

Struggling to Build Credit

People stuck in debt traps often have to rely on high-interest credit cards, payday loans, or subprime loans to make ends meet. This not only keeps them in perpetual debt but also makes it incredibly hard for them to build or repair their credit. Good credit is essential for accessing better financial products, such as low-interest loans for homes or cars. But when you're stuck in a cycle of debt, your credit score gets crushed, making it harder to escape the cycle and enter the middle class.

Economic Mobility: The Myth of "Pulling Yourself Up by the Bootstraps"

Predatory lending undermines the myth that anyone can "pull themselves up by their bootstraps." For many people, taking out payday loans or using subprime mortgages isn't about luxury or excess spending; it's about survival. But instead of receiving help to overcome financial hardship, they get sucked into a system that keeps them trapped. They're denied the ability to save, invest, or improve their financial situation, all while others with access to cheaper, more reasonable credit (i.e., the wealthy) can continue to accumulate assets and wealth.

Concentration of Wealth

When money is siphoned off into payday loans, credit card debt, and high-interest subprime mortgages, the wealth that could be invested in local businesses, education, or health is instead funneled into the pockets of predatory lenders, who are often large corporations or hedge funds. These wealthy entities continue to accumulate wealth while the poor struggle to make ends meet, exacerbating the wealth gap.

Why Does This Happen? The Government's Failure to Regulate

While it's clear that predatory lending practices harm vulnerable populations and contribute to the wealth gap, the government has failed to provide sufficient oversight and regulation in this area. In fact, many states have weak or no laws restricting payday loans, leaving citizens exposed to exorbitant interest rates and predatory practices.

In the aftermath of the 2008 financial crisis, the Dodd-Frank Act was passed to curb risky lending practices. But despite this, the Consumer Financial Protection Bureau (CFPB) has been under constant attack by lobbyists and lawmakers, making it harder to enforce regulations. Even when regulations do exist, predatory lenders find ways to circumvent them through loopholes or by moving their operations to states with fewer protections.

What Can Be Done?

To stop the cycle of predatory lending and address its role in perpetuating the wealth gap, the government needs to step up its regulation of these industries. This means enforcing interest rate caps on payday loans, implementing stronger consumer protections for mortgage borrowers, and increasing transparency in lending practices. Additionally, expanding access to financial literacy education can help individuals make informed decisions and avoid falling into debt traps in the first place.

Predatory lending is not just a financial problem; it's a social and ethical problem that disproportionately impacts the most vulnerable segments of society. And when these vulnerable populations are trapped in debt, it only serves to widen the wealth gap, making it harder for them to achieve financial stability and climb the economic ladder. The exploitation of desperate people by predatory lenders is an example of the rich getting richer while the poor get stuck in a never-ending cycle of debt—and the government's failure to act only enables the system to perpetuate. The question is: When will we, as a society, demand that we stop profiting off the backs of the vulnerable?

Get Out There and Advocate

So, what's the big takeaway here? It's actually pretty simple, policy change is how we fix this mess. If we're going to address the wealth gap and create a more equitable society, it's going to take action—not just talking about it. From raising the minimum wage to ensuring fair labor rights, expanding social safety nets, and reforming the tax system, policy change is the key that unlocks the door to a more just and fair economy. And the best part? You don't have to be a policymaker or a high-powered lobbyist to make a difference. The change starts with you. Yes, you. Don't roll your eyes, I'm serious. You're in the driver's seat.

Remember the Power of the People. The idea that you, as an individual, can make an impact on the grand policy level might seem a little daunting at first. After all, when you're sitting on your couch watching the news, it's easy to feel like the political system is so far removed from your daily life that your voice won't matter. But let me tell you something: history is full of moments where people like you have made a difference.

Think back to the civil rights movement, the women's suffrage movement, or the fight for LGBTQ+ rights—in all of these, the spark for change came from ordinary people standing up and demanding more. And sure, they were met with resistance, some even facing personal hardship, but in the end, they changed the world. They didn't just accept the status quo—they fought for a better, more inclusive future. That's the power of advocacy, it's the force that shifts the tides of history. And it's not reserved for the powerful or the privileged. It's for all of us.

So if you're reading this and feeling like you've been waiting for someone else to fix things—wait no more. It's up to you.

Start Where You Are. Advocate in Your Own Backyard. Let's start small. You don't have to be standing in front of a crowd with a megaphone (although, if that's your thing, go for it). There are everyday actions you can take that will have a huge ripple effect.

1. Contact Your Representatives

Pick up your phone, send an email, or write a letter. I know, I know—contacting your elected officials might sound like a "throwaway" task, but it's more powerful than you think. Politicians often rely on constituent feedback to gauge public opinion. If a representative hears from 50 people about an issue, they're likely to pay attention. If they hear from 5,000? You've got their attention, and it can absolutely affect how they vote on legislation. They may not always agree with you, but that doesn't mean you should stop pushing for the changes you care about. After all, your voice matters just as much as anyone else's.

You don't even need to be overly formal about it—be polite, but let them know what's important to you. Tell them you want them to support a living wage, expanded labor rights, or tax reform. Ask them what they're doing to address the wealth gap. If they're not doing anything, ask why not? They work for you.

2. Support Organizations Fighting for Change

There are hundreds of organizations out there dedicated to addressing wealth inequality, pushing for living wages, fighting for tax fairness, and advocating for workers' rights. If you want to be a part of something bigger than yourself, find a local or national nonprofit that aligns with your values and support them. You don't have to start your own revolution (unless you really want to); these organizations are already doing the hard work. Whether it's through donations, volunteering, or spreading the word, your support can amplify their efforts.

Take groups like Fight for $15, The Economic Policy Institute, and The Center for American Progress—these organizations have been instrumental in pushing for legislative changes that aim to reduce the wealth gap. Find one that resonates with you, and become an active supporter. The more people who back these efforts, the stronger they get. And let's be real—money talks, so even a small donation or a share on social media could make a real impact.

3. Talk to Your Friends and Family

Okay, here's where the magic really happens—conversations. We all have that friend who rolls their eyes at every mention of taxes, who thinks the rich are "just smarter" or "worked harder" for their billions. We get it. People have different views, but the best way to change someone's mind is to talk it through—and sometimes, to challenge their assumptions with facts (without it turning into a shouting match, of course).

Start those conversations. Be the person in your circle who asks, "Have you ever thought about how much the wealthy pay in taxes compared to people making $50k a year?" Or, "Did you know that the federal minimum wage hasn't increased since 2009, even though the cost of living has shot up?" Don't assume your friends already know the facts or agree with you—educating others is a key part of advocacy. And who knows? You might change someone's mind—or at least plant a seed that can grow into a deeper understanding of how important these issues really are.

4. Participate in Protests and Movements

If you're feeling a little more bold, get involved in local protests or marches. There's power in numbers—and when you show up in person, it amplifies the message. Whether it's a local march for a higher minimum wage, a rally advocating for healthcare reform, or a protest calling for higher taxes on corporations, these movements send a powerful message to lawmakers and the public: We are here, we care, and we want change.

Plus, protests can be empowering and energizing! They give you a sense of community, where you can meet like-minded individuals who share your passion for social justice. If you're nervous about it, start small—attend a local town hall, participate in a peaceful protest, or even show up at a local event hosted by advocacy groups. You'll find your voice, and your presence can make a real impact.

It's Time to Get Comfortable with Being Uncomfortable. Let's get real for a moment, advocacy is not always easy, and it's not always comfortable. It's going to push you out of your comfort zone. You'll have to face resistance, face criticism, and sometimes face the fact that change doesn't happen overnight. It's going to take hard work, persistence, and patience. But here's the thing: it's worth it. The reward is not just about changing laws; it's about changing lives. It's about creating a society where hard work is rewarded fairly, where opportunity is within reach for everyone, and where wealth is not just concentrated in the hands of a few.

So, if you're tired of seeing the rich get richer while the rest of us are struggling to keep up, if you're frustrated by the growing gap between the haves and the have-nots, then start making noise. Use your voice to advocate for policies that support a more equitable economy. Call, write, protest, donate, and most importantly, speak up. This is your future, and it's time to make it count.

And hey—if you're going to yell at the TV, why not yell in favor of a living wage and fair taxes instead of just ranting about the latest reality show contestant? At least this way, you'll be screaming for something that actually matters.

Education Access & Reform

Education is often referred to as the great equalizer—the idea being that it's supposed to provide everyone with the opportunity to succeed, regardless of their background or circumstances. However, in the United States, the access to quality education is anything but equal. From pre-K through higher education, the opportunities available to students can vary widely based on where they live, their socioeconomic status, and their race. The reality is that the quality of education a student receives is often determined by their zip code—and that's a problem.

Think about it, your future shouldn't be decided by where you're born, but in the U.S., it often is. Children in wealthier neighborhoods attend schools with state-of-the-art facilities, experienced teachers, and a wide array of extracurricular activities. Meanwhile, students in low-income communities often face overcrowded classrooms, outdated textbooks, and schools that struggle to keep the lights on. The stark inequalities that exist within the American education system are not just unfair—they're morally indefensible. But, as with any major societal issue, the first step is to recognize the problem. The second step? Taking action to fix it.

The world is changing faster than ever before. Technology is evolving at breakneck speeds, global crises demand new forms of leadership, and our understanding of human potential is expanding. Yet, despite all these advancements, the education systems in many parts of the world—especially in the United States—are stuck in the past, shaped by outdated ideologies and historical structures that no longer serve the needs of our youth or the future of humanity. It's time for a radical rethinking of how we educate the next generation.

Let's explore why education access and reform are vital, delve into the systemic challenges that perpetuate inequality, and propose solutions that can help create a more equitable, accessible, and high-quality education system for all Americans.

A Tale of Two Schools

If you were to walk into a school in an affluent neighborhood, you'd likely see well-maintained buildings, advanced technology, small class sizes, and a variety of specialized programs. Teachers would likely have access to ongoing professional development, and students would have access to a full spectrum of extracurricular activities—from sports to arts to STEM clubs. The schools are often well-funded, thanks to local property taxes, which means these schools have the resources to offer a wide range of services and opportunities.

Now, if you were to visit a school in a lower-income neighborhood, the scene is often vastly different. You might find underfunded schools, crowded classrooms, outdated textbooks, and limited access to technology. Teachers might be overworked, underpaid, and struggling to provide the same level of attention to their students as those in wealthier districts. Without sufficient funding, these schools can't afford enrichment programs, counselors, or even basic supplies like paper and pens. In many cases, students don't have access to the same high-quality education that their wealthier peers do, simply because of the community they live in.

This disparity in education quality is deeply problematic because education is one of the most powerful tools for social mobility. When children from low-income families don't have the same educational opportunities as their wealthier peers, they are less likely to achieve economic success later in life. This sets off a vicious cycle—children in underserved schools struggle academically, which affects their future employment opportunities and financial stability. And when these children grow up, they often face higher levels of poverty, creating a never-ending loop of inequality.

Our current education systems are built on a foundation laid over a century ago. Created during the Industrial Revolution, these systems were designed to produce workers for factories, not visionaries or leaders of a rapidly evolving world. The curriculum is often outdated, focusing on rote memorization of facts instead of critical thinking, creativity, and problem-solving. The rigid, one-size-fits-all model ignores the diverse talents and aspirations of students, leaving them unprepared for the challenges they will face in a world that is already far beyond the limits of the education system.

Moreover, the current system is deeply inequitable. It perpetuates social and economic divides, ensuring that those who can afford private schooling receive a world-class education, while those in public schools are often left with insufficient resources, outdated materials, and underpaid, undervalued educators. As a result, the system reinforces existing power structures and keeps the wealthy, well-educated elite in power while leaving many young people struggling to reach their full potential.

Why Education Access & Reform Matter

Education is a lot like the seed that grows into a tree of opportunity, but it's only useful when nurtured with care. It's not just about memorizing facts for a test, cramming for exams, or passing through a series of academic hoops. In its truest form, education is the foundation upon which individuals can build a better future, regardless of their background. But to build that foundation, education needs to be strong, accessible, and equitable.

Too often in the United States, access to quality education depends not just on how hard you study but on where you live, how much money your parents make, or the color of your skin. The sad truth is that far too many students are not receiving the education they deserve, and that lack of access is a major contributor to the persistent cycle of poverty and the inability to climb the economic ladder.

Education is such a powerful tool for social mobility. Let's explore how it can break the cycle of poverty, and why reform is essential to create a fairer, more just society for all.

Education as a Ladder, Not a Wall

Picture this, a kid growing up in a lower-income neighborhood. Here schools are underfunded, teachers are overworked, and basic resources like books, computers, or extracurricular activities are luxuries. It's not just an inconvenient situation, it's a trap. This child is boxed in by circumstances beyond their control—high crime rates, food insecurity, or a lack of stable housing. Now, consider that without the chance to attend a quality school, this child might be stuck in the same situation for life.

That's where education steps in. Education can act as a ladder that helps children climb out of poverty. In a society that values equal opportunity, education is meant to provide every child, regardless of their background, with the tools they need to achieve success. This might look like:

Access to resources: Having textbooks that aren't dog-eared and taped together. Computer labs that actually work. Teachers who aren't spreading themselves too thin.

Supportive environments: Mentors, tutors, counselors—figures who genuinely care about the student's future. Also paying these teachers a fair wage so that they aren't experiencing a poor quality of life, leading to bringing a poor attitude or negative feelings into the learning environment.

Real opportunities: Programs that allow students to discover new interests, talents, or career paths they didn't know existed. While we are on the subject let's keep the arts in the school because everyone's talents aren't necessarily academic.

When children from disadvantaged backgrounds are provided with equal access to these opportunities, they are able to escape the confines of their circumstances. A quality education opens doors that might otherwise be closed. It can help an individual climb up the economic ladder, from a place where survival is the priority to one where thriving becomes possible.

But let's be real—if education isn't equal, how can we expect these ladders to be reachable? In many ways, we've been stacking the deck against the very kids who need education the most.

The point here is simple, without access to a high-quality education, poverty becomes a self-perpetuating cycle. But with education, that cycle is broken. Education provides the key to unlock a better life, one where students can not only escape poverty but thrive in ways they never imagined possible.

The Vision: A New Model of Education

We need a revolution in education—one that is rooted in the realities of the 21st century and responsive to the needs of the future. This is not just about updating the curriculum; it's about reshaping the very way we think about education. Here's how we can begin:

1. Integrate Technology and Innovation at the Core

The world is rapidly becoming more technological, and we must ensure our youth are equipped to thrive in this environment. Rather than viewing technology as an add-on, it should be woven into the fabric of the curriculum. This means teaching coding, digital literacy, artificial intelligence, and data science from an early age, alongside traditional subjects like math, science, and history. These skills will empower students to participate in and shape the future, not just adapt to it.

2. Expand Beyond Traditional Academics

Education shouldn't just focus on academic achievement—it must also prepare students for the real world. We need to expand the curriculum to include vocational training, apprenticeships, the arts, and sustainable practices. Vocational training in fields like renewable energy, sustainable agriculture, and green building can give students not just a job, but a meaningful career. We must also reimagine the arts and humanities, making them relevant to the challenges and opportunities of modern life.

Arts, literature, and music are more than just electives—they are essential to the human experience. Creativity and critical thinking are vital to solving the complex global problems we face, from climate change to social inequality. By integrating modern tools and technologies into creative fields, we can inspire the next generation of thinkers and doers.

3. Environmental Education: A Must for the Future

In an era of climate crisis, environmental education should be a cornerstone of every curriculum. We need to teach our children not only about the planet's fragile state but also about the solutions. From renewable energy to conservation, students must be empowered to take action on environmental issues, whether through scientific innovation, political advocacy, or community organizing. By embedding environmental literacy into every subject—from science to economics to art—we create a generation that understands the importance of sustainability and is ready to fight for a greener future.

4. Fostering Global Citizenship and Cooperation

The challenges of the future cannot be solved by individuals or nations acting in isolation. We must teach our students to think globally, not just locally. This means fostering empathy, cultural understanding, and collaboration across borders. Education must emphasize the importance of cooperation, not competition, and provide students with the tools they need to engage in global conversations around issues like peace, justice, and human rights.

5. Empowering Educators

The future of education depends on the people who teach it. Educators must be valued, respected, and compensated accordingly. Teachers are the heart of the educational system, and they need the resources, training, and autonomy to inspire and guide their students. Just as we expect our youth to be prepared for the future, we must also invest in the future of the teaching profession. This includes providing fair wages, ongoing professional development, and a voice in shaping educational policy.

6. Accessible and Affordable Education for All

Education is a fundamental human right. It should be accessible to everyone, regardless of their socioeconomic background. In a world of unprecedented wealth, there is no excuse for an education system that leaves people behind. We must work toward free or low-cost education systems that make learning a lifelong pursuit, not a privilege reserved for the few.

The Path to Better Jobs and a Better Life

We all know the saying, "Knowledge is power." It's a bit cliché, but it's true. The more you know, the more you can do—and the more you can earn. Higher levels of education are directly linked to better-paying jobs, and with the rise of the gig economy and the increasing reliance on technical skills, the importance of access to education has never been greater.

Consider that in the United States, the average earnings of someone with just a high school diploma are considerably lower than those of someone with a college degree. And the difference only widens as educational levels increase. A recent study from the U.S. Bureau of Labor Statistics found that people with a bachelor's degree earn about 60% more than those with just a high school diploma. In fact, those with a college degree have the opportunity to earn double what someone with only a high school diploma might earn over a lifetime.

In fact, education isn't just about what you know; it's also about who you know. College can be an incredible way to form relationships with professors, mentors, and peers who could open doors to career opportunities you might not have otherwise encountered. These social connections become part of the overall benefit of education—expanding your network and accessing opportunities you would not have had without it.

It's not just about the diploma or the degree itself—it's about what that degree represents. It represents dedication, discipline, and the ability to learn—qualities that are valuable in any career field. Whether you're heading into medicine, technology, business, or even the arts, a college degree signals to employers that you have the skills and perseverance to succeed. It's a stepping stone to careers with greater earning potential, benefits, and opportunities for advancement.

But here's where the real issue lies, education should be a pathway to earning potential, not a financial burden. Right now, access to higher education isn't guaranteed for everyone. In fact, it's often more like a luxury. And that's a huge problem. Which leads us to the next point.

Education Levels the Playing Field

One of the most profound impacts of education is its potential to level the playing field. The idea of social mobility—moving up from a lower class to a higher one—has been a cornerstone of the American Dream. But if your zip code determines your school's resources, then the game isn't fair. It's like starting a race with one runner in a shiny new pair of sneakers, while the other has to run barefoot on a gravel road.

Equal access to education means equal opportunities for all, regardless of the circumstances you were born into. It's not about giving everyone the same results, but about ensuring everyone has the same chance. When students from low-income families are provided with the same educational opportunities as those from wealthier families, the entire society benefits. Here's how:

More diverse talent pools: When students from all walks of life have access to education, we don't just get better individuals; we get a greater diversity of ideas, skills, and perspectives in our workforce.

Fostering innovation: A more educated population is also a more innovative population. Think about it: Some of the world's greatest thinkers came from humble beginnings. Without access to education, those minds might have never had the chance to shine.

Building strong communities: Education helps create communities where everyone contributes to the overall well-being of society, not just a select few.

Education reform isn't just about investing in schools, it's about addressing the broader inequities that exist in society. The gaps in wealth, racial inequalities, and access to healthcare all contribute to the disparities in educational outcomes. Tackling these issues head-on is essential if we are truly going to level the playing field.

Education's Role in Improving Health Outcomes

This might sound counterintuitive to some, but education is crucial to improving health outcomes. Studies consistently show that people with higher levels of education live longer, healthier lives. They have lower rates of chronic diseases, better mental health, and are more likely to engage in preventive care. But why?

Health literacy, the ability to understand and make decisions based on health information, is a major factor. When people are educated, they are better equipped to make informed health decisions—whether it's knowing when to seek medical attention, understanding how to maintain a balanced diet, or knowing the long-term effects of substance use.

Additionally, education is linked to better access to healthcare services. Educated individuals are more likely to have jobs with health insurance, which gives them the financial stability to take care of their health. They are also more likely to have the tools necessary to navigate complex healthcare systems.

Education's influence on health doesn't just stop at individuals, it extends to entire communities. Educated people are more likely to demand better healthcare services and advocate for healthier environments. They also tend to live in neighborhoods with better access to healthcare facilities, which means better outcomes for everyone.

Education Reform is Critical for Social Mobility

The point of all this is clear, education isn't just about book learning or test scores. It's about creating a pathway for everyone—no matter their background—to reach their full potential. Education has the power to break the cycle of poverty, increase earning potential, enhance social mobility, and improve health outcomes. But if we want to make these promises a reality, we need a system that's equitable and inclusive.

To build a society where every individual has the chance to succeed, we must prioritize education reform. That means providing equal access to quality education, addressing the structural barriers that disproportionately affect marginalized communities, and ensuring that everyone, regardless of their socioeconomic status, has a fair shot at achieving their dreams.

The future is in our hands. It's time to give every student the opportunity they deserve to climb the ladder to success, break free from the constraints of their circumstances, and thrive. And, just as importantly, we need to ensure that the ladder is tall, sturdy, and within reach of all.

Because the American Dream—the idea that anyone can succeed if they work hard enough—can only become a reality if we make education the cornerstone of that success. Let's ensure that ladder is there, and that no one gets left behind.

The Root Causes of Inequality in Education

As much as we like to believe that education is the great equalizer—a tool for lifting people out of poverty and providing opportunity—it's not always the case. In fact, the disparities between rich and poor schools are not only glaring but also persistent. Why? Because the root causes of educational inequality in the United States are systemic, deeply entrenched, and a little more complex than just "poor schools vs. rich schools."

From funding disparities tied to property taxes to racial segregation, and even the overwhelming burden of student loan debt, the challenges facing education are multi-layered, and tackling them will require significant overhaul and reform. But understanding these challenges is the first step in creating a more equitable and just education system for everyone.

Let's break down some of these deeply rooted challenges that have created an uneven playing field in education.

1. Funding Inequities: The Curse of Property Taxes

Let's start with the big one. How do schools get their money? The answer for most U.S. public schools is property taxes. Wait, property taxes? Yep, you heard that right. In the U.S., public schools are funded primarily by local property taxes. So, the wealthier the neighborhood, the more property taxes are generated—and the more money schools have to work with. Sounds good, right? Well, not so fast.

The problem lies in the geographic inequality of this system. In wealthy neighborhoods, property values are high, meaning schools in those areas can generate a lot of revenue. These schools have access to the latest technology, fully stocked libraries, well-maintained facilities, extracurricular programs, and even high teacher salaries to attract the best educators. In other words, rich kids get fancy classrooms and top-tier learning experiences.

Meanwhile, in low-income neighborhoods, where property values are lower, the opposite happens. Schools are often underfunded, and lack basic resources. If your school can't afford decent textbooks, let alone air conditioning (yes, it's a real problem), how are students supposed to thrive?

This funding gap has been called the "curse of property taxes" for a reason. It creates a two-tier system: the haves vs. the have-nots, and the haves —surprise!—tend to be in wealthier neighborhoods with higher property values. This funding structure isn't just an inconvenience, it's an outright inequality. The result? Stark differences in educational quality based on geography, and ultimately, social inequality.

So, what's the solution? Some advocate for reworking the funding formula so that every student has access to the same level of education, regardless of where they live. It might involve pooling state or federal funds to level the playing field—because, let's face it, children shouldn't have their future determined by their zip code.

2. Segregation and Racial Disparities: The Ghost of Brown v. Board of Education

Here's where things get a little uncomfortable. While Brown v. Board of Education (1954) famously declared that "separate but equal" schools were unconstitutional, the reality is that schools are still largely segregated today—not by law, but by de facto segregation. In other words, even though schools are no longer legally segregated, many students still attend schools that are essentially divided by race and income.

How does this happen? The answer is simple, but sad. Housing patterns and school district boundaries often align in a way that keeps schools racially and economically segregated. Historically, Black and Latinx communities were pushed into redlined neighborhoods with fewer resources. Today, those same communities are often trapped in lower-income areas with underfunded schools.

Now, it's important to note that segregation isn't just about race—it's also about income. Minority communities tend to be poorer, and poverty is often a powerful force behind these systemic inequalities. Wealthy communities are typically more racially homogeneous, so when they advocate for school funding, they tend to advocate for their own needs, leading to schools that are well-funded, predominantly white, and sometimes more racially homogenous.

The disparities go beyond just who sits in the classroom. Students in predominantly minority schools face significant challenges, including:

Fewer Advanced Placement (AP) courses or honors programs.
Higher dropout rates.
Discrimination or unconscious bias from teachers and peers.
Increased school suspensions and expulsions.

It's a cycle of disadvantage—when students aren't given the tools to succeed, they're more likely to drop out, struggle academically, or not go to college. And when they do go to college, they might face a system that has historically worked against them. So, racial disparities in education are not just a problem for the affected students—they impact the entire society, because we all lose out when potential is wasted.

Reform in this area could mean addressing both housing segregation and school district boundaries, and shifting the focus to creating equitable learning environments for all children, regardless of their race or income level.

3. Student Loan Debt: The Financial Burden of Higher Education

You did it! You worked hard in school, earned that degree, and were ready to jump into the workforce, right? Wrong. The average college graduate today is walking out the door with around $30,000 in student loan debt (though, honestly, it can be a lot more depending on the degree and institution). That's like buying a car you didn't need and then being stuck paying for it for the next 10–30 years. And the worst part? It's the students from lower-income families who carry the heaviest burden.

While wealthier families can afford to pay for college upfront or have the means to take out minimal loans, students from low-income backgrounds often face a starkly different reality. They rely on student loans to pay for school, which means they start their adult lives in a deep financial hole. And with the interest rates on student loans hovering around 4–7%, the debt can quickly spiral out of control. So much for that "investment" in their future.

The problem doesn't end once students graduate. Even if they do land a good job, that loan payment will eat into their salary, making it difficult to save for the future, buy a house, or invest in anything meaningful. It's like they're working for a paycheck that barely covers their bills, let alone allows them to thrive.

The impact of student loan debt extends beyond personal finances. For many students, the weight of debt forces them to delay major life decisions like buying a home or starting a family. And because those loans are often associated with a higher level of education, the debt burden disproportionately affects students from marginalized communities, who already face financial and structural barriers.

Reform is needed here too. We need to address the rising costs of higher education and the crushing weight of student loan debt. Student debt forgiveness programs, increased access to scholarships and grants, and more affordable tuition rates are all potential solutions. But ultimately, the goal should be to create an education system where students are not financially shackled by their pursuit of knowledge.

The Big Picture: It's All Connected

At the heart of the inequality in education is a web of interconnected systemic issues. The disparities in funding, segregation, and student loan debt all work together to maintain the status quo. It's like a puzzle with pieces that don't quite fit together, and as long as those pieces remain in place, the puzzle will never be complete.

In the end, reforming education isn't just about throwing more money at schools or passing laws; it's about fundamentally addressing the systemic roots of inequality—from funding disparities to racial segregation and the financial burden of higher education. If we can't fix these underlying issues, we'll continue to see the same problems perpetuated for generations to come.

But the good news? Change is possible. With the right reforms, we can create an education system that offers real equality of opportunity. Education is the key to breaking cycles of poverty, increasing social mobility, and empowering future generations. So, let's start with the tough conversations, challenge the status quo, and work toward a future where every child—no matter their background—has access to the education they deserve.

And who knows? Maybe one day, students will have the opportunity to graduate without the crushing weight of debt and walk into a world of opportunities, rather than a world of financial strain. Here's to that future!

Concrete Steps Toward Education Access & Reform

If you're feeling like education reform is a monumental task, you're not alone. The issues are big, systemic, and deeply rooted in American society. But here's the thing—they're not unsolvable. The path to improving education access is already paved with actionable steps that, if taken seriously and with a little political will, can make a world of difference for students of all backgrounds.

The good news? Education reform doesn't require a magical fix or some radical new invention. It requires clear action, policy changes, and a commitment to building a more equitable system. Here's how we can tackle the challenges head-on:

1. Advocate for Equitable Funding for Schools: Leveling the Playing Field

Imagine you're playing a game, but the rules say that kids in one team get a whole bunch of extra resources—better equipment, more practice time, and even a coach who gives them constant encouragement. Meanwhile, your team has to make do with old, broken gear and no support. You'd be a little annoyed, right?

That's the reality in education. Right now, the funding for public schools is largely dependent on local property taxes, meaning wealthy neighborhoods get more money for their schools, and poorer neighborhoods get... well, not so much.

This is the funding gap that creates the two-tier education system we currently see in America. It's like a lopsided game where only one team gets to play by the rules. But the solution doesn't need to be as complicated as rewriting the rulebook—we need to rethink how schools are funded.

What Can Be Done?

State-Level Funding Reforms: States should step in and provide supplementary funding to underfunded schools. It's time for states to ensure that every child has access to the same resources—whether they live in a high-income neighborhood or a struggling one. This could mean things like reducing class sizes, updating old textbooks, providing better technology, and even offering after-school programs to keep kids engaged and learning.

Federal Funding Boosts: Federal funding programs like Title I exist to provide extra support to schools that serve large numbers of low-income students, but these programs often fall short. More investment in Title I and other federal programs could give underfunded schools the resources they need to compete. For example, these funds could be used to hire additional teachers, offer tutoring programs, or improve school facilities.

Equity, Not Equality: It's not just about providing schools with the same amount of money—it's about providing schools with the right amount of money to meet the specific needs of their students. It's about creating a system that understands that not all schools are starting from the same place. As the saying goes, "It's not about giving everyone the same thing; it's about giving everyone what they need."

Why It Matters

When schools have the resources they need, students can thrive. And when students have the chance to succeed, we help break down the barriers that so often keep kids from marginalized communities from reaching their potential. If we can level the playing field by ensuring equitable funding, we will give every student—regardless of their background—the tools they need to succeed. That's the magic of reform, folks.

2. Address Student Loan Debt: Making Higher Education Affordable

Picture this: You've just graduated college, ready to take on the world, when you open your mailbox and find your first student loan bill. Suddenly, that degree that was supposed to be your golden ticket feels more like a ball and chain. Student loan debt has become the modern version of a "second mortgage"—only instead of buying a house, it's for paying for that degree you need to get a job in the first place.

In the United States, student loan debt has reached a staggering $1.7 trillion, and for many students, this debt is an almost insurmountable burden. The high cost of higher education makes college feel like an investment, but for many students, it's an investment they can't afford. The problem is particularly pressing for low-income students and students of color, who often take on more debt than their wealthier peers because they don't have the same access to resources or family support.

What Can Be Done?

Free Community College: One bold solution? Free community college for all students. Community colleges are often seen as the "second choice" after four-year universities, but they provide a great education at a fraction of the price. Making community colleges free would give students from low-income backgrounds a pathway to higher education without the crippling burden of student loans. It's the first step toward making college education truly accessible to everyone.

Income-Based Repayment: Not everyone can afford to pay off their loans at the same rate. Income-based repayment plans would ensure that students pay based on their income rather than a fixed monthly amount. If you're just starting out in your career and your paycheck is small, the last thing you need is to be hit with a hefty loan payment. Income-based repayment allows people to pay what they can afford, not what the loan servicer thinks they should be able to afford.

Student Loan Forgiveness: There's been a lot of talk about student loan forgiveness lately, and for good reason. One of the most promising solutions involves expanding student loan forgiveness programs, especially for people who work in public service jobs like teaching, social work, and nursing. Not only would this encourage more students to pursue careers that benefit society, but it would also offer much-needed relief from crushing debt.

Why It Matters

When students graduate without the cloud of debt hanging over them, they can make better decisions for their future. They're more likely to save for retirement, buy a home, or even start a business. They're also more likely to take risks and pursue career paths that might not have been possible if they were drowning in debt. This is how we create economic opportunity: by giving students the financial freedom to build a future without being held back by loans that never seem to end.

3. Ensure Affordable Access to Early Childhood Education: Starting Early, Starting Right

We all know the saying, "The early bird catches the worm." Well, when it comes to education, the "early bird" is often the student who has access to quality early childhood education—and that's a big worm.

The importance of early childhood education (from birth to age 5) cannot be overstated. Research shows that children who attend preschool or pre-K programs are more likely to graduate from high school, have better social skills, and even pursue higher education later in life. The skills they learn early on—like problem-solving, communication, and emotional regulation—create the foundation for academic success.

But not all families can afford preschool. While some parents may be able to send their kids to quality pre-K programs, others (particularly those from low-income communities) are unable to access this critical resource. In many cases, parents may have to choose between putting food on the table or sending their child to preschool.

What Can Be Done?

Expand Access to Subsidized Preschool: Offering free or subsidized preschool for families who can't afford it is one of the most effective ways to close the educational gap. By investing in early childhood education, we set children up for success from the very beginning. Universal pre-K would provide every child with the opportunity to gain foundational skills that will help them thrive later in life.

Increase Funding for Early Education Programs: Currently, funding for early childhood education is often a patchwork of state, federal, and private funding. We need to create a more coherent, consistent funding model that ensures every child has access to high-quality preschool programs. This can be done by increasing federal funding for early childhood education initiatives and incentivizing states to invest more in their own programs.

Why It Matters

Investing in early childhood education isn't just a nice-to-have; it's a game changer. The earlier we can provide children with the tools they need to succeed, the more likely they are to succeed later in life. Studies show that every dollar invested in early education returns several dollars in future economic growth. Not to mention, it breaks the cycle of poverty by giving every child, no matter their background, the foundation for academic and social success.

Education Is the Key to a More Equitable Future

Education is the great equalizer, but only if we make sure everyone has access to it. From equitable funding for schools to tackling student loan debt, ensuring affordable higher education, and improving access to early childhood education, we can create a system where every child has the opportunity to succeed.

By advocating for these reforms, we can break down the barriers that keep many children from achieving their full potential. And in doing so, we can build a future where education is truly a path to success for all Americans—no matter their zip code, their race, or their background.

So let's roll up our sleeves, get to work, and build a future where education opens doors, breaks down barriers, and helps every child thrive. After all, a better educated society is a stronger, more prosperous society—for everyone.

Innovate the Future of Education

The time has come for a bold and comprehensive global challenge—one that invites individuals, organizations, governments, and educational institutions to join forces in reshaping education for the 21st century. This challenge should be about finding innovative solutions to the problems facing education today, from outdated curricula to lack of access to quality teaching.

We need to challenge everyone—from students to educators, parents to policymakers—to think differently about education. What are the new tools, ideas, and systems we can create to prepare our youth for the future? How can we make education more inclusive, innovative, and relevant? How can we create new industries and jobs that are focused on renewal, sustainability, and the common good?

A Call to Action

This is a call to action for all those who care about the future of our planet, our communities, and our children. It's time for a radical shift in how we educate the next generation. Let's come together to build a system that is not only equitable and inclusive but also inspiring and forward-thinking. Let's provide our youth with the knowledge, skills, and passions they need to thrive in a world that is constantly changing.

We need visionaries, thinkers, activists, and doers to rise up and demand that our educational systems evolve. Let's collaborate to create a new paradigm—one where education is not just about learning the past but about building the future. Together, we can create a system that prepares every student for a life of purpose, innovation, and positive change.

The future of education is now—let's get to work.

Promoting Local Businesses

When we talk about tackling the wealth gap and creating more equitable economic opportunities, local businesses are often the unsung heroes. These small-to-medium-sized enterprises (SMEs) — from that quirky coffee shop down the street to the family-owned construction firm or local grocery store — are the backbone of vibrant, thriving communities. And when we support them, we're not just purchasing products or services; we're making an investment in the future of our own neighborhoods and economies.

Promoting local businesses is one of the most powerful ways to revitalize communities, create jobs, and redistribute wealth on a more grassroots level. By choosing to buy locally, support local entrepreneurs, and champion the small businesses that help shape the character of our communities, we can spark a cycle of growth and prosperity that lifts everyone up — whether they're entrepreneurs, employees, or consumers.

But what makes supporting local businesses so important, and how can we get involved in strengthening our community economies? Let's dive deeper into the topic and explore how small businesses can become a cornerstone in the fight against inequality.

Why Local Businesses Matter:
More Than Just a TransactionLocal businesses are more than just places where we buy things — they are engines of economic growth and catalysts for community development.

Job Creation and Economic Mobility

Local businesses are often the largest employers in small towns or urban neighborhoods. These businesses employ people who live in the community, contributing to a thriving local economy. The best part? Local jobs are often more accessible to people with varied levels of education and experience, from entry-level positions to skilled labor. Small businesses also tend to offer more personalized employment opportunities, where employees are treated as valued members of the team rather than just another number.

Local businesses also create a sense of economic mobility. By working in a family-owned business or a neighborhood café, an employee might gain skills and experience that can lead to upward mobility within the company or in another job down the line. These businesses are often more likely to provide mentorship, flexible schedules, and training programs that allow workers to build careers without needing to leave their communities.

Wealth Circulation within the Community

When you spend money at a local business, more of that money stays within the community. Unlike chain stores or online giants, which often funnel profits to corporate headquarters far away, locally owned businesses tend to reinvest earnings back into the community. This process is called the multiplier effect. For example, local businesses pay local taxes, hire local employees, and purchase from local suppliers—creating a ripple effect of economic activity that benefits everyone.

Studies consistently show that when consumers spend their money at local businesses, they contribute to higher tax revenues, better infrastructure, and improved public services. The result is a healthier, more prosperous community where people are more likely to thrive.

Cultural and Social Impact

Local businesses are often at the heart of a community's identity. They add character, flavor, and a sense of belonging that national chains can't replicate. Think about the neighborhood bookstore that's been a gathering place for years, or the locally owned ice cream shop that becomes a tradition for families. These businesses create a sense of pride, connection, and culture that binds people together.

Supporting local businesses also helps create a more diverse and resilient economy. Small businesses bring variety to the market by offering unique products or services that reflect the interests and values of the community. Unlike large chains that operate on a one-size-fits-all model, local businesses can innovate, adapt, and cater to the specific needs and desires of their customers.

How Can We Support Local Businesses?

Supporting local businesses is not just about visiting the neighborhood store once in a while or grabbing a coffee at the indie café. It's about becoming active participants in strengthening the community's economy. Here's how we can help:

1. Shop Local, Shop Small

The most direct way to support local businesses is by shopping locally. Whether it's your daily coffee, a birthday gift, or your groceries, choosing to spend your money at local stores, boutiques, or markets is a powerful act of support. Every time you make a purchase at a locally owned business, you're helping keep money within your community.

This can seem small on a case-by-case basis, but collectively, these purchases create a huge impact. According to studies, for every $100 spent at a local business, about $68 stays in the local economy, compared to only $43 when spent at a chain. This is because locally owned businesses are more likely to use local suppliers, hire local employees, and support local charities.

So, next time you're about to hit "buy now" on Amazon or head to the big-box retailer, ask yourself: Is there a local option? You might find that your local business offers a similar product, often with a more personal touch.

2. Encourage Local Entrepreneurship

Becoming an entrepreneur in your community is one of the most impactful ways to strengthen your local economy. But it's not always easy—especially in low-income or underserved areas where access to resources, capital, and mentorship might be limited.

To encourage entrepreneurship, invest in local startups, or mentor aspiring business owners. If you've got expertise in marketing, finance, or operations, share your knowledge. Crowdfunding campaigns can also be a fantastic way to get new businesses off the ground. Platforms like Kickstarter or GoFundMe allow people to pool resources to fund small business ventures that could otherwise struggle to gain traction.

Additionally, if you're able, you could also help by investing in local co-working spaces or supporting initiatives that provide funding and mentorship to young entrepreneurs, especially those from underserved communities. Encouraging the creation of new businesses increases job opportunities, helps cultivate new products and services, and brings fresh energy to the community.

3. Shop at Farmers' Markets and Local Artisans

Farmers' markets are the epitome of the local economy in action. When you shop at a farmers' market or support local artisans, you're directly contributing to the livelihoods of small-scale farmers, craftspeople, and food producers.

By choosing local over mass-produced products, you're promoting sustainability and supporting artisans who rely on small-scale production rather than factory farming or factory-based manufacturing. You're also reducing your carbon footprint, as products at a farmers' market typically travel a shorter distance than those in big chain stores.

4. Support Local Businesses Online

While physical stores have their charm, online shopping has become increasingly popular—and local businesses have caught up! Many local shops now have online stores, which means you can shop small no matter where you are. If you can't make it to your local bookstore, for example, you can still order their books from their website and have them delivered to your door.

Even larger companies like Etsy are paving the way for small businesses to reach a wider audience. By buying from independent sellers on platforms like Etsy, eBay, or locally owned e-commerce websites, you're still supporting small entrepreneurs, even if you're not walking into their brick-and-mortar store.

5. Spread the Word: Word-of-Mouth Marketing

Local businesses often don't have the advertising budgets that national chains do, which means they rely on word-of-mouth and customer loyalty to thrive. If you love a local business—whether it's a restaurant, a clothing boutique, or a service provider—share it with others. Leave positive reviews, share posts on social media, and tell your friends about your favorite spots.

It may seem small, but word-of-mouth referrals can do wonders for a small business, bringing in new customers who may have never heard of it otherwise. You can also encourage others in your community to share their favorite local spots to increase visibility for businesses that need a boost.

6. Get Involved in Local Business Associations

Many cities and towns have local business associations or chambers of commerce. These organizations bring together small business owners to support each other, share resources, and advocate for policies that benefit the local economy.

By becoming involved in or supporting these groups, you can help create a more collaborative business environment. These associations often organize community events, networking opportunities, and other initiatives designed to boost the visibility and success of local businesses.

The Ripple Effect of Supporting Local Businesses

Promoting local businesses isn't just a feel-good activity—it's a direct way to help reshape the economic future of your community. When we support local entrepreneurs, we're supporting job creation, economic diversity, cultural richness, and community resilience.

In a time when large corporations seem to dominate almost every aspect of our lives, it's more important than ever to reclaim our communities by investing in what makes them unique—our local businesses. Each dollar spent in support of a small business is a dollar spent on sustaining a community's identity, creating opportunity, and building local wealth.

So, the next time you're looking to make a purchase, ask yourself: Can I shop local? By doing so, you're not just buying a product or service; you're investing in the future of your community, creating a ripple effect that benefits everyone in the long run. When we all contribute to the success of local businesses, we're building a stronger, more resilient economy—one where everyone has the chance to succeed.

Corporate Greed and the Credit Card Rate Trap

Corporate greed isn't just about CEO bonuses or exploiting labor—it's also about the insidious ways major corporations manipulate systems to benefit themselves at the expense of smaller players in the economy. One of the most glaring examples of this is the credit card industry, where large corporations enjoy preferential treatment, while small businesses are left to shoulder the burden of ever-increasing fees and high interest rates.

The Two-Tiered System of Credit Card Rates

If you run a small business, you're likely familiar with the high costs of processing payments through credit cards. Credit card companies charge fees to merchants for every transaction, often a percentage of the sale plus a flat fee per transaction. While these rates are a standard part of doing business, they aren't the same for everyone.

Larger companies with significant buying power—think of the multinational corporations like Amazon, Walmart, or even big chain restaurants—are able to negotiate far lower rates. Why?

Because these companies process millions of transactions a day, and in the world of credit card processing, volume equals leverage. When a big company negotiates with a credit card processor, they can secure better terms, lower fees, and favorable conditions because they're offering a steady stream of revenue to the card companies. These companies are seen as high-value customers, and as such, they receive preferential treatment.

On the flip side, small businesses don't have the same bargaining power. They don't process enough volume to make negotiating terms worth the card companies' time. As a result, small businesses often face higher transaction fees—sometimes as much as 2%–3% of each sale, or more. For businesses with thin margins, those extra costs can be the difference between staying afloat or going under.

How This Amplifies the Wealth Gap

This disparity in credit card fees may seem like a small issue, but when you look at it through the lens of systemic inequality, the effects are far-reaching. By making it more expensive for small businesses to process payments, credit card companies are effectively hindering their ability to grow and thrive. Meanwhile, large corporations continue to benefit from preferential treatment and use their vast resources to further cement their dominance in the market.

This creates a vicious cycle:

Small businesses that are already struggling to compete with big corporations are forced to pass those extra costs onto their customers. This leads to higher prices, which often makes it harder for small businesses to attract and retain customers, especially when they're competing against giants with greater economies of scale and access to lower operating costs.

Big corporations, on the other hand, with their lower transaction fees and higher profits, continue to consolidate wealth. These companies are better equipped to weather economic downturns, expand their market share, and even avoid paying their fair share in taxes—all while small businesses are squeezed out of the market.

The end result? Fewer small businesses, fewer job opportunities for local communities, and an ever-growing concentration of wealth in the hands of a few powerful corporations. As more businesses fall to the wayside, the wealth gap between the haves and the have-nots only widens.

The Larger Picture: Corporate Influence and Economic Inequality

This is just one example of how corporate greed exacerbates the wealth gap. Credit card companies, just like other major industries, prioritize profits over the health of the economy and society. By designing systems that favor the rich and powerful—whether it's through preferential rates, tax loopholes, or favorable regulations—they contribute to a larger trend where wealth is concentrated at the top, and small businesses, communities, and workers bear the brunt of the inequality.

The reality is that when big companies pay lower fees and small businesses are burdened with higher costs, it's not just an issue of corporate pricing strategies. It's a clear case of structural inequality that perpetuates a cycle of wealth concentration. And as the gap between the rich and everyone else grows, the chances for economic mobility become slimmer for those on the bottom rung.

What Can Be Done?

To combat this, we need to advocate for policies that level the playing field. That means reforming the credit card industry to make fees more equitable across the board. It also means ensuring that small businesses have access to the same financial tools and benefits as larger companies. By breaking down the systems that artificially create these barriers to success, we can give smaller, community-based businesses a fighting chance and, ultimately, help reduce the wealth gap.

In the long run, creating a more just system means removing the corporate handouts and ensuring that the game is fair for everyone, not just the wealthiest players in the economy. As consumers, we can also support small businesses by consciously choosing where we spend our money—because, when we choose to support local over corporate, we can make a difference.

Community Investment

You've probably heard the saying, "It takes a village." But what if that village wasn't just a metaphor? What if we actually built villages, strong and resilient, where people from all walks of life had the tools, resources, and support to thrive? Well, this is the power of community investment. When we invest in our communities—whether through infrastructure, affordable housing, public services, or social programs—we're not just laying down bricks and mortar; we're laying the foundation for stronger, more prosperous futures. And the best part? Everyone gets to live in it.

Community investment is a lot like gardening. If you plant seeds, water them, and give them the right nutrients, you'll soon have a flourishing garden. But if you neglect the soil, don't water it, or plant your seeds in a desert, it's going to be a lot harder to grow anything, right? Same goes for communities. A community thrives when it is nurtured and supported, but it's up to us—whether we're residents, business owners, or local leaders—to do the nurturing.

So, let's take a look at how we can all get involved in building stronger community foundations and why it's so important to the fight for equity, economic opportunity, and a better quality of life for all.

What Does Community Investment Look Like?

To put it simply, community investment involves putting resources (money, time, energy) into projects and initiatives that improve the well-being of a community—now and for future generations. This can come in many forms, from creating accessible healthcare services to improving transportation systems, building affordable housing, investing in parks, or launching education programs that cater to specific needs.

Here are a few key areas where community investment can make a world of difference:

1. Building Infrastructure: Roads, Bridges, and Wi-Fi (Because We All Know That's Basically a Utility Now)

First things first—infrastructure. Without solid roads, reliable public transportation, and access to broadband internet, communities can feel like they're stuck in the 1950s (or worse, a bad episode of The Twilight Zone). Have you ever tried to navigate a pothole-ridden street or used Wi-Fi that cuts out every 30 seconds? It's like living in a sitcom—everyone's frustrated, no one's happy, and nothing gets done.

By investing in infrastructure, we're setting up the framework for economic growth and social connection. Reliable roads and public transit systems allow people to get to work, access essential services, and visit their friends without it feeling like an obstacle course. Meanwhile, expanding internet access is basically like opening the door to the modern world. With the internet, people can access education, work remotely, start businesses, and communicate across the globe. It's no longer just a luxury—it's essential.

Imagine a community where broadband reaches every home, public transit is efficient, and sidewalks are safe to walk on. That's not just convenient —it's transformative. It makes it easier for small businesses to operate, for students to learn, for parents to work, and for neighbors to connect. It creates a community where opportunity is accessible to all, regardless of zip code.

2. Affordable Housing: A Roof Over Everyone's Head

Nothing says "you're part of the community" quite like having a safe place to call home. Yet for far too many, affordable housing is like that illusive unicorn that everyone hears about but no one seems to find. With skyrocketing rents and a shortage of affordable homes, many families are stuck in a cycle of financial stress, constantly moving from one unstable living situation to another.

When we invest in affordable housing, we're not just putting up walls and roofs; we're providing a foundation for security, stability, and dignity. Affordable housing means families can stop worrying about eviction or being priced out of their neighborhoods. It gives people the space to build relationships, pursue careers, and raise children in environments that promote success. And the bonus? Stronger communities! When people have access to stable housing, they're more likely to contribute to the local economy, support local schools, and volunteer for neighborhood projects.

Want to make your community a more vibrant place? Start with investing in housing that people can actually afford. It's a game-changer. Seriously. Imagine everyone being able to live in a home they can afford, without having to choose between paying rent or buying groceries. That's the kind of future we should be working towards.

3. Public Services: From Parks to Policing (Yes, Both Matter)

A healthy community isn't just about economic investment—it's about social investment, too. We need to make sure that public services are robust and accessible for everyone. It's not just about having more parks, better schools, or more hospitals—it's about making these services equitable and accessible to all.

Let's talk about public parks, for instance. They're more than just green spaces for picnics (though, I'm not going to lie, a good picnic is pretty much one of life's great joys). Parks are places for exercise, community gatherings, and mental health. A nice stroll around a park can reduce stress, improve mood, and even inspire creativity. But if a community lacks green spaces or doesn't maintain the ones it has, well... that's a missed opportunity to improve the well-being of its residents.

And it's not just about parks. Think about other public services—libraries, after-school programs, mental health services, and even emergency response systems. Investing in these services means more accessible resources for people who need them. It means families don't have to scramble to get their kids into a safe after-school program or face long waits to see a therapist.

For example, have you ever walked through a neighborhood that felt alive with activity? Kids playing soccer, families grilling in the park, friends meeting at the community center for art classes. That's the kind of community you get when we invest in public spaces and programs that promote social interaction and well-being.

4. Social Programs: Helping People Help Themselves

Here's the thing about community investment, it's not just about creating physical spaces, it's also about investing in human capital—that is, people. For many communities, especially those affected by generational poverty, the key to overcoming the wealth gap lies in empowering individuals through education, healthcare, job training, and financial support.

Think about community outreach programs that provide job training, financial literacy workshops, or free healthcare screenings. These programs act like building blocks—giving individuals the tools they need to take care of themselves and their families. For instance, if you help someone develop new skills, you're not just improving their chances of landing a better job—you're investing in their long-term economic stability.

Let's be real, people love feeling supported. Just like how a little pep talk from a coach can turn an underdog into a champion, community investment can transform an entire population. Think of it as community cheerleading—except instead of pom-poms, we're holding out opportunities. Social programs are one of the best ways to make sure no one is left behind in the race to success.

How Can You Get Involved in Community Investment?

Okay, so now that we've explored why community investment is such a big deal, you're probably wondering, "What can I do to help?" Well, the good news is: a lot! Community investment doesn't have to be reserved for governments or large organizations—individuals can make a huge impact, too.

Volunteer Your Time: Whether it's helping out at a local food bank, tutoring kids after school, or lending a hand at a community garden, your time is valuable. Your effort could be the difference between someone getting the help they need or not.

Support Local Initiatives: Donate to or get involved with local nonprofits or community organizations that focus on improving education, healthcare, housing, or public spaces in your neighborhood. Sometimes, even a small donation can help fund critical programs that provide lifelines for those in need.

Advocate for Smart Policy: Community investment isn't just about what you do; it's also about who you support. Advocate for local government policies that prioritize funding for schools, affordable housing, healthcare, and other essential services. Don't underestimate the power of a well-timed letter to your city council!

Invest in Local Businesses: We've already talked about supporting local businesses, but this is part of the broader effort to invest in your community. Local businesses create jobs, stimulate the local economy, and enhance the overall vitality of your neighborhood.

Building for the Future

Community investment is like building a house. You don't just build the walls and call it a day—you invest in the foundation, the plumbing, the electrical wiring, and the design to ensure it stands strong for generations. A thriving community is built on more than just roads and buildings; it's built on opportunities, stability, and the well-being of its people. By investing in our communities, we're creating environments where people can grow, succeed, and contribute to the collective good.

So next time you walk down your street, remember: every investment you make, big or small, is a piece of the blueprint for a brighter future. Whether it's helping improve your neighborhood park, advocating for better schools, or supporting a local business, you're laying down a brick in the foundation for a stronger, more resilient community.

And hey, if that community happens to have Wi-Fi that actually works, even better.

Financial Literacy Programs

Money. We all need it, we all want it, but let's be real—most of us don't exactly get a manual on how to handle it. If you're anything like me, learning about finances felt like reading an ancient, foreign script as a teenager: confusing, intimidating, and littered with terms like "compound interest" and "credit scores" that seemed to belong in a highly specialized dictionary. But here's the thing: financial literacy isn't just for the Wall Street elite or the guy who knows exactly what stocks to buy on a Tuesday morning. It's for everyone.

Understanding how money works isn't just a nice skill to have—it's absolutely essential for building wealth and achieving financial freedom. In fact, financial literacy is one of the most empowering tools a person can have in their toolkit, whether they're making minimum wage or running a small business. And the good news is that it's never too late to learn.

So, how do we teach people to build wealth? By investing in financial literacy programs. These programs provide people with the knowledge, skills, and confidence to make informed financial decisions, set long-term goals, and, ultimately, build wealth. Let's dive into why this is so important, what it looks like in action, and how you can be part of the movement to make financial education accessible to all.

Why Financial Literacy Matters

Before we get into the how, let's talk about the why. The importance of financial literacy is simple: the more you know about managing money, the better you can make it work for you. When people understand how money flows—how to save it, invest it, and use it wisely—they're less likely to fall into debt traps, miss out on wealth-building opportunities, or feel hopeless when bills come in.

It's the difference between living paycheck-to-paycheck and having a savings cushion.

It's the key to understanding how credit works—and how not to wreck your score.

It's the foundation for building long-term wealth, from investing in the stock market to buying a home or starting a business.

Think about it like learning how to drive. If you've ever taken a road trip, you know that it's way more fun (and safe) when you actually know how to operate the vehicle. Financial literacy is like that driver's license to your financial future. Without it, you might still get from point A to point B—but you're more likely to end up in a few ditches along the way.

Breaking Down Financial Literacy

A financial literacy program isn't just about teaching people how to balance a checkbook (although, let's be honest, that's still a great skill to have). It covers a wide range of topics that build the foundation for sound financial decision-making. Here are some key areas these programs address:

1. Budgeting: Where Does Your Money Go?

Let's start with the basics, budgeting. If you're not budgeting, you're basically flying blind. Sure, you may have some idea of how much you earn, but without a budget, you'll never know where your money is really going. It's like trying to lose weight without tracking what you eat—you have no idea what's working or what's sabotaging you.

Financial literacy programs teach individuals how to create a realistic budget, one that's sustainable for their lifestyle. It's about understanding the difference between your needs (like rent, utilities, and food) and your wants (like that extra cup of artisanal coffee or the latest phone with the fancy camera). And it's not about denying yourself the good stuff—it's about balancing today's desires with tomorrow's goals. If you can set aside a little money each month for savings, and make sure you're not spending beyond your means, you're already ahead of the game.

2. Saving and Emergency Funds: The Safety Net You Didn't Know You Needed

Everyone should have a savings cushion—even if it's just a small one. It's that safety net that catches you when life throws you a curveball, like a medical bill, car repair, or—God forbid—your favorite Netflix series getting canceled (we've all been there). Financial literacy programs help people understand the importance of saving and how to set up an emergency fund.

When you have money set aside for the unexpected, you're not scrambling every time a bill or emergency arises. It means you don't have to rely on credit cards, loans, or borrowing from family. You can take care of the unexpected without it throwing off your entire financial plan. So, instead of living in a state of panic every time something breaks, you can sit back and say, "No worries, I've got this."

3. Debt Management: Getting Out and Staying Out

One of the most insidious wealth-stealers in this country is debt—particularly high-interest debt. Credit cards, payday loans, and student loans can feel like a weight around your neck. But financial literacy programs teach people how to manage debt, whether it's by consolidating loans, paying off high-interest balances first, or negotiating better terms with lenders.

Learning to manage debt is an essential part of financial freedom. It's not about denying yourself everything until the debt is paid off—it's about getting organized, making a plan, and sticking to it. For example, you may decide to pay down your credit card balance while still setting aside some savings. A little discipline goes a long way in making sure that debt doesn't control your life.

4. Credit Scores: Your Financial Report Card

Ah, credit scores. That mysterious number that determines whether you can get a loan for a house or a car, or even a decent rate on insurance. If you've ever stared at your credit score and thought, "What is this thing, and how do I make it go up?"—you're not alone. The good news is, financial literacy programs break down what makes up a credit score (payment history, credit utilization, length of credit history, etc.) and how to boost it over time.

Having good credit can be the difference between paying an extra $200 a month on a car loan or getting a better interest rate and saving that cash for your next vacation (or a small mountain of avocados, depending on your priorities). Understanding how credit works allows you to use it to your advantage, rather than letting it control you.

5. Investing: Making Your Money Work for You

Here's where the magic happens: investing. A lot of people think that investing is only for the super-rich or Wall Street brokers with expensive suits, but that's simply not true. Financial literacy programs demystify investing and teach individuals how to start building wealth—whether through stocks, bonds, mutual funds, or retirement accounts.

Think of investing like planting seeds. Sure, it takes time, but if you're patient and consistent, those little seeds grow into something much bigger over the years. When you invest your money wisely, you start building a nest egg that will continue to grow and compound, making your future self very happy indeed. (Trust me, your future self will thank you for those early investments).

Making Math Relevant

For many students, math class is a tedious chore, an abstract series of numbers, formulas, and equations that feel disconnected from the realities of daily life. For most, the lack of immediate relevance can lead to disengagement, frustration, and the all-too-familiar sentiment: "When am I ever going to use this?" For students who struggle to see the practical applications of the topics being taught—algebra, geometry, calculus—the typical response is either disinterest or resentment. But what if math could be reframed in a way that was engaging, practical, and directly applicable to students' futures?

One of the most powerful ways to capture students' attention and spark their interest in math is to tie it to something they care about—something they can see as valuable in their own lives. The world of global markets, investing, and personal finance is one area where the practical use of math becomes crystal clear. Imagine if students were taught how to read the markets, how to invest money wisely, and how to manage financial risk in the real world. Not only would this approach make math more relevant, but it could also ignite a new sense of purpose in students, motivating them to pursue higher education and lifelong learning.

The Disconnect Between Math and Daily Life

The traditional way math is taught often involves abstract concepts with little explanation of how those concepts will be used in the real world. For example, in high school algebra, students might spend months solving for x in equations with no clear explanation of why they are doing it or how it connects to any tangible outcomes. Similarly, geometry and calculus often remain theoretical exercises that students struggle to connect to their personal experiences or aspirations. Unless a student is interested in a career in engineering, physics, or a related field, it's easy to see why they might feel that the material is irrelevant to their lives.

Moreover, many students aren't exposed to real-world applications of math that could make it more engaging. They're rarely taught how math can be used to understand financial markets, run businesses, or manage personal finances—skills that are directly relevant to achieving financial security and independence. As a result, math is often seen as something to be endured for the sake of getting a diploma rather than as a tool that can unlock personal success in life.

A Shift in Focus: Financial Literacy and the Stock Market

One of the most compelling ways to make math engaging is to teach students how to use it in the context of financial literacy and investing. By introducing students to the world of global markets, stock trading, and personal finance, math takes on an entirely new dimension. Suddenly, students are not just manipulating numbers—they are learning how to apply mathematical concepts to real-world scenarios that have the potential to impact their futures.

Investing in the stock market, for example, involves a variety of mathematical concepts, including percentages, averages, compound interest, and risk assessment. These are all essential skills in understanding how wealth is built over time. If students were taught how to read stock charts, calculate the return on investment (ROI), understand how diversification works, and how to use tools like stock simulators and mock accounts, they would start to see the immediate relevance of math in their own lives. They could see the results of their decisions play out in real time, and that feedback loop would likely make math seem much more interesting and valuable.

Additionally, learning about financial markets teaches students to think critically about risk and reward. In the real world, investing is rarely straightforward—there are no guarantees, and the outcome of any decision depends on a multitude of factors. Teaching students about financial markets allows them to practice making decisions under uncertainty, weigh risks, and learn how to make strategic choices based on data and analysis. This is not only a valuable life skill but also a powerful motivator for learning math.

The Role of Mock Accounts and Simulators

A key tool in making math relevant and exciting is the use of mock accounts or stock market simulators. These platforms allow students to engage with real-world data without any financial risk. Platforms like Investopedia's simulator or apps like Robinhood (for real-world trading, with educational components) allow users to create virtual portfolios and experiment with buying and selling stocks. By providing students with an opportunity to simulate the experience of trading, they can learn how financial markets work and how mathematical concepts are used to navigate them.

Through mock accounts, students can track their "investments" over time, analyze their portfolios, and see firsthand how decisions based on mathematical principles—like compound interest or stock valuation—affect their outcomes. It's one thing to solve an algebraic equation on paper; it's quite another to see how your understanding of percentages, ratios, and growth rates influences a portfolio's performance in real time. This hands-on, experiential learning model has the potential to make math far more engaging and meaningful to students.

In addition, simulators and mock accounts allow for a safe space to make mistakes. In the real world, poor investment decisions can lead to financial loss, but in a virtual environment, students can experiment without the fear of real financial repercussions. This trial-and-error process can help them understand concepts like risk management, diversification, and the importance of long-term planning—skills that are essential for financial literacy.

Motivating Students to Pursue Higher Education

Integrating financial literacy and investing into the math curriculum could also help to motivate students to pursue higher education. Many students feel disconnected from the traditional academic pathway, seeing it as a set of arbitrary hurdles they must jump through in order to get a diploma. However, by showing students how the knowledge they gain in math class can be applied to the real world of finance, they may start to see the value in continuing their education.

Students who become interested in investing might be more motivated to pursue advanced studies in economics, business, or even mathematics. They might develop a desire to understand more about the global markets, delve deeper into the complexities of financial modeling, or learn more about risk assessment and quantitative analysis. If students see that higher education is not just about accumulating knowledge for the sake of knowledge, but rather about gaining practical skills that can be used to build wealth and achieve financial independence, they may be more likely to stay engaged in school and pursue post-secondary opportunities.

The Bigger Picture: Financial Independence and Empowerment

Teaching students about the financial markets is not just about making math class more interesting—it's about empowering them with the knowledge they need to navigate the financial landscape of the modern world. In an era of economic uncertainty, inflation, and mounting student debt, financial literacy is more important than ever. By introducing students to the basics of investing and personal finance, we can help them build a foundation for long-term financial success.

Furthermore, financial literacy promotes self-sufficiency and independence. When students learn how to make informed financial decisions—whether through investing, budgeting, or understanding credit—they are less likely to fall victim to financial pitfalls or make decisions that limit their economic mobility. In this sense, math becomes a tool not just for solving abstract problems but for securing a better future.

Math doesn't have to be boring or irrelevant. By reframing how we teach math—connecting it to real-world applications like financial markets and investing—we can make the subject far more engaging and meaningful to students. By introducing mock accounts and stock market simulators into the classroom, students can gain hands-on experience with financial concepts, learn how to make informed decisions, and see how math can directly impact their lives. In doing so, we can help foster a generation of financially literate, empowered individuals who are motivated to pursue higher education and build successful, independent futures.

Why Financial Literacy is for Everyone

The beauty of financial literacy is that it's for anyone, at any income level. You don't need to make six figures to benefit from it—you just need to understand the basics and apply them. Financial literacy is about empowerment: it helps individuals make choices that align with their values and goals, whether it's saving for a rainy day or investing for a comfortable retirement. It's about control, and who doesn't want a little more control over their money?

Moreover, financial literacy doesn't have to be boring or intimidating. It's not all spreadsheets and tax forms (although, let's face it, someone's gotta deal with the tax forms). With the right approach, learning about money can be fun, engaging, and even a little bit adventurous. Who knew that calculating compound interest could feel like cracking a code or getting a high score in a video game?

How You Can Get Involved in Financial Literacy Programs

So, you're sold on the idea. But how do you actually get involved in supporting financial literacy? Here's how you can take action:

Support Local Financial Literacy Initiatives: Look for programs in your community that teach financial basics. These could be workshops at libraries, online webinars, or even school programs designed to teach kids about managing money.

Volunteer: If you have financial knowledge, use it! Volunteer to teach others about budgeting, saving, or investing. Whether it's a local nonprofit, a community center, or a school, your expertise can help others build the financial confidence they need to succeed.

Advocate for Financial Education: Push for more financial literacy education in schools. Kids should be learning about credit scores, student loans, and basic investing before they even get their first job. After all, wouldn't it be great if future generations didn't have to spend years trying to understand how a 401(k) works?

Be a Role Model: Share your financial journey with others. If you've successfully paid down debt, built up an emergency fund, or started investing, talk about it. People learn from real-life examples, not just textbooks.

Building Wealth, One Step at a Time

In the end, financial literacy isn't about getting rich quick—it's about setting yourself up for long-term success. With the right knowledge, we can all build a solid financial foundation, and teach others to do the same. It's not about flashy cars or endless luxury vacations (though, sure, those things are nice)—it's about taking control of your financial future and setting yourself up for peace of mind.

So, let's put down the avocado toast, pick up a book on investing, and start building wealth the smart way. After all, it's your money—why not make it work for you?

Supporting Fair Employment Practices

Picture this, you're at work, grinding away on a project, hoping that your hard work will eventually lead to that coveted promotion. Then, you hear about a colleague who has somehow been promoted faster than a Wi-Fi signal at a coffee shop. You find out they've been skipping lunches to schmooze with the boss, and they're paid more for doing the exact same job. You start questioning everything, your productivity, your value, and possibly your entire career trajectory. Well, welcome to the world of inequity at work. It's not pretty, it's not fair, and it's something we need to change.

In a world where we spend roughly one-third of our lives working, shouldn't we all be able to expect fair pay, equal opportunities, and a safe, inclusive work environment? After all, work should be more than just a place where you punch in and punch out. It should be a place where people are respected, valued, and given equal opportunities to thrive.

That's where fair employment practices come in. It's about making sure that everyone, regardless of their gender, race, background, or who they know at the company barbecue, gets an equal shot at success. Fair employment practices aren't just a nice idea—they're essential to creating workplaces that are equitable, productive, and innovative. When we prioritize fair practices, we open the door to a workforce that's motivated, engaged, and ready to contribute at their best.

What Are Fair Employment Practices, Anyway?

Before we dive into the how of supporting fair employment practices, let's first take a step back and define what they actually are. Fair employment practices refer to policies and actions that ensure equal treatment of all employees, regardless of race, gender, age, religion, disability, or any other characteristic that's not related to job performance. At their core, these practices are about making sure that everyone has the same chance to succeed and be treated with respect.

Here's a breakdown of what fair employment practices can look like:

1. Equal Pay for Equal Work

The pay gap is real, and it's an issue that disproportionately affects women and minorities. Equal pay for equal work is a cornerstone of fair employment practices. Simply put, if you're doing the same job as someone else, you should be compensated equally, regardless of your gender, race, or any other characteristic that doesn't impact the work you're doing. Unfortunately, we're still battling the gender pay gap—women, particularly women of color, often earn less than their male counterparts for doing the same job. And that's not just an issue in the U.S.; it's a global problem. But that doesn't mean we have to accept it.

2. Non-Discriminatory Hiring Practices

Think about the last time you applied for a job. Did you feel like you had a fair chance at the role based on your skills, experience, and personality? Or did it feel like your resume might be collecting dust in a pile because of your gender or age? Non-discriminatory hiring practices are about ensuring that job opportunities are based solely on merit and qualifications, not assumptions or stereotypes. This includes writing job descriptions that are gender-neutral, using structured interviews to avoid bias, and employing blind recruitment where applicants' names and personal details (like age or race) are hidden until a later stage in the hiring process.

This is critical because unconscious biases (yes, we all have them) can influence hiring decisions, and they don't just affect who gets hired—they can also impact who gets promoted and who gets overlooked. Fair employment practices work to eliminate these biases.

3. Safe and Inclusive Workplaces

Everyone deserves a workplace where they feel safe, valued, and included. Unfortunately, workplace harassment and discrimination still exist in many industries, which can undermine employee well-being and productivity. Safe workplaces are those where employees don't fear discrimination, harassment, or retaliation. Employers must take proactive steps to foster inclusion, ensure zero tolerance for harassment, and promote diversity at every level.

An inclusive environment means making space for people of all backgrounds, cultures, identities, and abilities. And it's not just about being tolerant—it's about celebrating those differences. Think of it like a potluck: the more variety, the more delicious the spread. When different perspectives are brought to the table, we all benefit.

4. Accessible Opportunities for Advancement

There's nothing more frustrating than feeling like you've reached a glass ceiling, where no matter how hard you work, you're never going to get ahead. Fair employment practices include creating clear pathways for advancement, where every employee can see a roadmap for growth and is given the resources and mentorship to get there. Employees shouldn't feel like their opportunities for promotion are limited because of who they are, where they're from, or whether they "fit in" with the culture. Merit-based promotion policies and equitable professional development opportunities are key to ensuring that all employees, regardless of background, can grow and succeed within the company.

Why Should We Care About Fair Employment Practices?

Now that we've outlined the basics, you might be thinking, "Okay, sounds great. But why does this matter to me? I'm not an HR expert or a CEO— I'm just trying to get my paycheck and make it through another Monday without crying into my coffee." And hey, that's a fair point. But let me tell you why fair employment practices should matter to everyone—from the interns to the C-suite.

1. More Innovation

Diversity and inclusion are more than just buzzwords; they're drivers of innovation. When workplaces embrace diversity—whether it's cultural, racial, gender, or socioeconomic—they open themselves up to new perspectives, ideas, and solutions. Think of some of the most groundbreaking companies today, like Google, Apple, or Microsoft. What do they all have in common? A focus on diversity. When employees from different backgrounds come together, they bring unique insights that lead to better problem-solving and creativity. In short, diverse teams are better teams.

2. Higher Employee Satisfaction

Employees who feel like they are treated fairly and have the same opportunities for advancement tend to be more engaged and satisfied with their jobs. A fair workplace leads to less turnover, better morale, and a stronger sense of loyalty. When people feel valued, they put in more effort. And when employees are happier, that enthusiasm spreads across the organization—leading to a better overall work environment and increased productivity.

3. It's Just the Right Thing to Do

At the end of the day, fair employment practices are about treating people with respect and dignity. Everyone, regardless of their background, should be able to expect the same opportunities at work. When companies implement equitable practices, they show that they care about their employees as people—not just as workers. And this, in turn, helps to create a more just society overall, where everyone has a fair shot at success.

Let's be real, you don't have to be a saint to see the value in fair practices—it's good for business and good for society. When workplaces create environments of inclusivity and opportunity, everyone wins.

How Can You Support Fair Employment Practices?

Okay, so now that you're convinced that fair employment practices are essential for an equitable society, you're probably wondering, "How can I contribute to the cause?" Well, lucky for you, there are plenty of ways to get involved—whether you're a leader in your organization or just an employee who wants to see change.

1. Advocate for Change at Work

If you're in a position of influence—whether as a manager, HR specialist, or leader—advocate for policies that promote fairness and equity. Review your hiring and promotion practices to ensure they're free of bias and that opportunities for advancement are open to everyone. Make sure your company has diversity and inclusion initiatives, and don't be afraid to call out unfair practices when you see them.

2. Be an Ally

Even if you're not in charge, you can still be an ally to your coworkers. If you see someone being treated unfairly—whether it's based on gender, race, or any other factor—speak up. Support those who might be overlooked or marginalized, and help create an environment where everyone feels heard, seen, and valued.

3. Educate Yourself and Others

Becoming an advocate for fair employment practices starts with education. Read up on issues like unconscious bias, pay equity, and workplace discrimination. Share what you learn with others, and engage in conversations that challenge assumptions and promote inclusivity.

4. Support Companies with Fair Practices

When choosing where to work or what products to buy, consider supporting companies that have a strong commitment to fair employment practices. Look for companies that are recognized for their efforts in diversity and inclusion. These organizations are not only doing the right thing, but they're also likely to have stronger employee retention and productivity—making them great places to work.

Building a Better Workplace, One Fair Practice at a Time

By supporting fair employment practices, we're not just helping workers feel more valued; we're creating a stronger, more innovative workforce that can propel companies—and society—forward. It's about equal opportunity, respect, and opportunity for growth for all. So, the next time you find yourself in the office (or on Zoom, let's be real), remember: We're all in this together. Let's make sure everyone has a seat at the table and the chance to rise.

And if you ever hear someone complaining about unfair practices at work, tell them, "Hey, don't just vent—be the change you want to see." The workplace of the future is fair, equitable, and just, and with a little effort from all of us, we can get there faster than you can say "promotion!"

Engaging In Philanthropy

Giving Back to Close the Gap

Let's talk about a word that has a lot of power, but sometimes carries a heavy aura of "I'm not rich enough for that" or "I don't have enough to give." That word? Philanthropy. But here's the thing: philanthropy isn't just about writing a check for millions of dollars (although, if you happen to be a secret billionaire, feel free to make your next donation go big). It's about giving back to the community, supporting causes that matter, and getting involved in ways that can help close the gap—whether that's the wealth gap, opportunity gap, or access gap.

The good news is, you don't have to be a millionaire to make a difference. Philanthropy comes in all shapes and sizes: big and small, personal and corporate, money and time. If you have a little spare cash, or even just a few hours on the weekend, you can still engage in philanthropy and help tackle systemic issues that perpetuate poverty and inequality. So, let's explore how giving back can do far more than make you feel warm and fuzzy—it can be a transformative tool for social change. And yes, even you can be part of the change.

What is Philanthropy, Anyway?

Philanthropy, in its simplest form, means "the love of mankind". But in today's world, it's mostly associated with donating money or time to support a cause. Now, you might be thinking: "I'm not exactly Bill Gates or Beyoncé with a fortune to give away. Does philanthropy even apply to me?"

Short answer: Yes. Long answer: Absolutely, yes.

While large-scale donations are the first thing that comes to mind for many people when they think of philanthropy, giving doesn't have to mean giving away millions. Philanthropy is also about investing in your community, empowering others, and using your time, talent, and voice to help bridge the gap between the haves and the have-nots.

Monetary Donations: The classic route—sending a check, giving to charity, crowdfunding for a cause, etc. While money is great, it's not always the only thing that's needed.

Time and Skills: Volunteering your time, whether it's mentoring a young person, teaching financial literacy in underserved communities, or working at a food bank, is just as valuable as giving money—sometimes even more so.

Advocacy: Using your voice to raise awareness for social issues, advocate for systemic change, or encourage others to get involved is a form of philanthropy that can create widespread impact.

Corporate Philanthropy: Companies that donate to causes, or give employees paid time off to volunteer, are engaging in philanthropy on a much larger scale. So, if you're lucky enough to work for a company that offers volunteer hours or charity matches, take advantage of that—it counts!

Why Philanthropy Matters in Closing the Wealth Gap

Okay, so now you know philanthropy can be a lot more than just a check with a lot of zeros. But how does it close the wealth gap?

In simple terms, philanthropy helps redistribute resources, opportunities, and services to the people who need them most. It's like when you and your friend are sharing a pizza and you're trying to split it evenly, but they took the last slice of pepperoni and you're stuck with only cheese (how dare they). Philanthropy, in this case, is giving your friend some of your cheese slices to make things right. Just kidding—what we really mean is that philanthropic efforts, whether they involve donating to food programs, building homes, or supporting education, serve to level the playing field.

Let's face it, in a world where the wealth gap is as wide as the Grand Canyon, we need all hands on deck to close it. Think about it: the top 1% in the U.S. own more wealth than the entire bottom 90%. Let that sink in for a second. Closing that gap is going to take more than just one person donating a pile of money. But when individuals, communities, and organizations work together, even small donations and efforts can add up, creating a collective force for change.

How Can You Get Involved in Philanthropy?

Now that you know why it matters, you might be wondering, "How can I help, and where do I even begin?" Don't worry, we've got you covered. Whether you've got a little spare change or just a lot of heart to give, there's a way for you to get involved. Here's how:

1. Support Organizations That Focus on Economic Equity

A great starting point is to donate to or partner with organizations that are tackling systemic inequality. Many nonprofits are working directly on addressing issues like poverty, education inequality, and job access. By supporting these organizations—whether financially or through volunteerism— you can help them expand their reach and continue the work they're doing.

For example, if you want to make an impact on the wealth gap, you could donate to organizations that support financial literacy, help people gain access to education, or provide career training for underserved populations.

A few examples of impactful organizations:

United Way: They focus on providing education, financial stability, and health to the most vulnerable populations.

Kiva: A micro-lending platform where you can help entrepreneurs in low-income communities build businesses and, eventually, wealth.

Teach for America: A nonprofit aiming to close the educational gap in underserved communities, which is directly tied to long-term wealth inequality.

2. Volunteer Your Time

You don't need a ton of money to be a philanthropist. If you're not in a position to donate, consider giving your time and skills. Volunteer at local food banks, shelters, or mentorship programs. Whether it's helping people learn how to budget, distribute resources, or teach a job skill, your time can make a world of difference.

The truth is, time is the one resource we all have (whether we admit it or not). So, if you can give up a couple of hours each month to teach financial literacy at a local school, or if you can spend a Saturday helping build affordable housing, you're making an impact. Plus, let's be honest—helping others feels pretty good. It's a win-win.

3. Use Your Voice to Advocate for Change

You know how people love to talk about the weather? Well, you can leverage that love for conversation and talk about more impactful things, too. Advocacy is a key part of philanthropy. Raising awareness about the wealth gap and advocating for policies that support greater economic equity is a powerful way to contribute. If you're passionate about closing the wealth gap, use your platform—whether it's social media, your community group, or even your family dinner table—to talk about how we can create fairer, more equal systems.

Join advocacy groups that are pushing for change. Speak out on behalf of people who don't have the same opportunities as you. That could mean advocating for better labor rights, improved access to healthcare, or better funding for education. The point is, the more people who are educated and aware of the issue, the greater the chances that systemic change will happen.

4. Small Acts Matter Too

Okay, this is the feel-good part: even small acts of kindness can be considered philanthropic, especially when they add up. Maybe you're not in a position to donate thousands of dollars, but you can buy coffee for a colleague, help a neighbor, or donate gently used clothes. These are all ways of contributing to a culture of kindness, and they have a ripple effect. Good deeds beget more good deeds. It's like passing the torch—one kind action at a time.

Think of philanthropy as a snowball effect—your small contributions might seem insignificant at first, but as more people join in, the momentum grows and makes a bigger impact.

Philanthropy for All

Philanthropy is for everyone—not just the super wealthy or the people with bottomless bank accounts. It's a powerful tool that anyone can use to help close the wealth gap, whether you're donating money, time, skills, or advocacy. By giving back, you're not only helping individuals who are struggling, but you're also contributing to a better, more equitable society.

So, the next time you think about philanthropy, don't let the misconception that "I'm not rich enough" hold you back. Because every little bit counts. Whether you give a dollar or a few hours of your time, you're doing your part to make the world a little bit better. And honestly, that's what the world needs more of these days: people who care enough to act.

Go ahead—be the change you want to see. After all, a generous heart can be as valuable as a generous check.

Voting And Civic Participation

Let's talk about something that's both incredibly powerful and, if we're being honest, can sometimes feel like the world's most complicated online shopping experience, voting and civic participation. Whether it's casting your ballot, attending a local council meeting, or simply signing a petition, participating in the democratic process is one of the most direct ways you can influence the course of society and help close the wealth gap.

Now, I know, you might be thinking, "Voting? But my one vote doesn't really matter, right? I'm just one person in a sea of millions." Well, buckle up—because I'm about to show you how voting, engaging in your community, and staying civically active can be a total game changer when it comes to building a fairer, more just world.

The Power of Your Vote: It's Not Just a Sticker

First things first, let's talk about voting. It seems simple enough: you show up to the polls, cast your vote, and then you get a nifty little "I Voted!" sticker to wear proudly. But don't let that sticker fool you—voting is serious business, and it's your opportunity to shape the future of the country. One vote might feel like a drop in the ocean, but when you multiply it by millions of people who share your vision for a more equitable world, it's a tidal wave of change.

The reality is, elections matter. They shape policies around education, healthcare, taxation, labor rights, and even the minimum wage—all of which directly influence the wealth gap. You might not have control over the fortune of a corporate CEO, but you do have control over who you elect to make decisions on your behalf.

Candidates shape policies, and policies shape the lives of everyday people. Your vote can determine whether your community gets funding for affordable housing, whether workers get better wages, or whether corporations are taxed fairly. These policies have a direct impact on closing the wealth gap and addressing income inequality.

Now, I know what you're thinking. "But all those politicians, they just say the same things every time, don't they?" Ah, yes. The classic campaign speech of promises and catchy slogans. Here's the thing though, you get to decide which promises matter most. Voting is a chance to choose leaders who will actually work on closing the wealth gap, pushing for policies that support economic equity and opportunity for all, especially for those who've been left behind by the system. Your vote is your voice. And guess what? Voices matter—they can turn the tide of history.

Don't Just Vote—Get Involved

Okay, so you've cast your ballot, and you're feeling pretty good about it. But voting alone isn't always enough to make lasting change. If you're really serious about amplifying your voice, you've got to go beyond just voting once every few years. Civic participation is an ongoing process, and the more you engage with it, the more impact you'll have.

Here are a few ways you can get involved:

1. Attend Local Government Meetings

Don't think of civic participation as something that happens only during election season. Local government meetings are where a lot of the real work gets done. You might be surprised by how much influence local governments have on issues like zoning laws, affordable housing policies, and public services—all of which have an outsized impact on people living in lower-income communities.

And let's be real, sometimes these meetings are more entertaining than you might expect. Who doesn't love a good drama about parking regulations or local tax breaks for businesses? (Okay, maybe that's just me—but you get the idea.) The point is, by attending and participating, you can get a seat at the table where decisions are being made. When local government makes decisions about how resources are distributed, those decisions ripple outward—affecting everyone in the community.

2. Get Involved in Grassroots Movements

Sometimes, the best way to amplify your voice is to join forces with like-minded people. Grassroots movements are where real change begins—whether it's advocating for universal healthcare, fighting for living wages, or pushing for fair housing policies. Getting involved in grassroots movements is a fantastic way to connect with others, stay informed, and build solidarity around common causes.

These movements are often fueled by people who care deeply about social justice, and they rely on the power of the people to hold elected officials accountable and create lasting change. Whether it's signing petitions, attending marches, or just raising awareness on social media, grassroots activism can have a huge impact on policy decisions—and that can help close the wealth gap over time.

3. Advocate for Policy Change

Okay, here's where it gets juicy: advocacy. You don't have to be a politician or a famous activist to advocate for change. Speaking up about issues you care about, and using your voice to push for better policies that promote economic equality can do wonders in moving the needle on closing the wealth gap.

For example, if you're passionate about income inequality, you can advocate for progressive taxation, or raise awareness about the importance of a living wage. If education access is close to your heart, there's always room to lobby for better funding in schools, or for greater access to higher education for marginalized communities.

The good news? You don't have to do this alone. There are already advocacy groups doing this work—labor unions, civil rights organizations, and think tanks—and they're always looking for people who want to lend their voice to the cause.

Voting + Civic Engagement = Change

Let's break it down into an easy formula:

Voting: You choose the leaders and policies that reflect your values.

Civic Participation: You engage with your community and local government, pushing for better policies and accountability.

Advocacy and Grassroots Movements: You fight for the change you want to see, alongside others who share your vision.

It's a pretty powerful combination, don't you think?

Here's the thing about voting and civic participation—they're like money in the bank when it comes to building a fairer, more just society. When you participate in the democratic process, you not only influence decisions but you also empower others to do the same. It's about using your voice to ensure that the policies being enacted serve everyone, not just those with the loudest voices or deepest pockets.

But, Really...Does My Vote Matter?

Okay, I get it—you're still asking: "But does it really matter? I'm just one person!"

Well, think of it this way, your vote is like a grain of sand on the beach. A single grain might seem insignificant, but when you get millions of grains together, you get a massive, powerful force. One vote doesn't change the world on its own, but collective action does.

To give you a bit of perspective, in the 2018 midterm elections, nearly 117 million Americans voted. That's a lot of people speaking up for what they care about. And trust me, that power doesn't go unnoticed. Politicians and policymakers take note when citizens show up in big numbers. It sends a message: We care about these issues.

When millions of people vote for leaders who prioritize economic fairness, racial justice, and access to opportunity, change happens. It's that simple.

Your Voice Is Your Power

So, what does all of this mean? It means that your voice matters. Voting, civic participation, and advocacy are the tools you can use to fight for a fairer, more equal society. They're not just privileges—they're your right as a citizen, and they're some of the most powerful weapons in your arsenal when it comes to closing the wealth gap.

Remember, you are not powerless. The wealth gap might seem massive, but with enough people using their voices, showing up, and advocating for change, we can bridge it. It might not happen overnight, but every vote, every meeting attended, and every letter written to your representative is a step in the right direction.

So, take a deep breath, vote like your future depends on it (because it does), and keep participating—because, in the end, it's not just about casting your ballot. It's about casting a vision for a better world. And that's the kind of thing worth showing up for.

Let's amplify our voices and make the change we all want to see. And hey, don't forget the sticker. It's kind of a perk.

Raising Awareness

Raising awareness isn't about shouting from the rooftops or posting dramatic, "we need to talk about this NOW" rants on social media. While those can be fun (and occasionally therapeutic), truly raising awareness is about sparking meaningful conversations that get people thinking, discussing, and—dare I say it—acting. After all, awareness is the first step toward action, and sometimes, all it takes is one conversation to plant the seed that grows into a whole movement.

So, how do we go about sparking these conversations? And how can we make sure they actually lead to change, rather than just another awkward silence at the dinner table when someone mentions income inequality? Let's dive in.

1. Start Small, Start Local: Conversations Begin at Home

Think about your closest circle—whether that's family, friends, or coworkers. You might feel like the issues of wealth inequality are too big to discuss over dinner or during a casual coffee break. But here's the thing: conversations often start small. You don't need to give a TED Talk to get the ball rolling—a simple question or observation can spark a deeper discussion.

Imagine sitting at brunch with friends, and someone mentions how expensive it is to buy a home in the city. Instead of nodding in agreement and returning to your avocado toast (which, let's be honest, probably cost more than your entire grocery bill last week), turn that observation into a conversation. Ask, "Do you think it's fair that so many people can't afford to live in the places where they work?" This question might seem simple, but it opens the door to a much bigger discussion about wealth distribution, access to affordable housing, and the growing gap between the rich and everyone else.

The key here is to approach the conversation with curiosity, not judgment. You don't need to be the expert—just someone who's genuinely interested in exploring the issue. It's like inviting people into a discussion, rather than preaching to them. Make it an open-ended conversation where everyone feels welcome to share their opinions without fear of being shut down. And hey, even if you're just talking over pizza—those discussions are still important. Sometimes, the most powerful ideas come from the most unexpected places.

2. Use Social Media for Good (But Keep It Real)

Alright, I can already hear you thinking, "Social media? Isn't that where people just argue about pineapple on pizza?" Yes, social media can be a dumpster fire sometimes, but it also has the potential to be a powerful tool for raising awareness and spreading ideas. Done right, it can connect you with others who share your values, give you access to information, and allow you to amplify important messages.

But before you dive into posting about wealth inequality and the need to close the wealth gap, let's keep it real: authenticity is key. People don't want to be hit over the head with guilt-inducing statistics every time they scroll through their feeds. Instead, share stories, personal experiences, or thought-provoking questions that can start a conversation without feeling like you're forcing an agenda.

For instance, post something like, "I just learned that the top 1% of Americans own 40% of the wealth in the country. Can you believe that?" and follow it up with a question like, "What do you think we can do to change this?" Keep the tone conversational, approachable, and relatable. No one wants to feel like they're being lectured, but most people are open to genuine conversations—especially when they're framed in a way that invites dialogue, not debate.

You can also share articles, infographics, or videos that make the topic accessible. Social media is a great tool for breaking down complex issues like the wealth gap into bite-sized pieces of information that people can digest and discuss. Remember, you're not out there to win an argument—you're just trying to open people's eyes to something they might not have thought about before.

And if things get heated in the comments section? Remember to stay calm, take a deep breath, and keep it respectful. Not every conversation is going to be a home run, but sometimes, just planting that seed is enough to get someone thinking.

3. Support The Conversation Starters

Supporting authors, journalists, and podcasters who are courageously raising awareness about the growing wealth gap is vital to fostering the change we so desperately need. These individuals are not afraid to challenge the status quo or to question the systems that perpetuate inequality. Through their work, they spark critical conversations and shed light on issues that many would rather ignore.

By tackling tough subjects—whether through investigative reporting, insightful storytelling, or powerful commentary—these voices are pushing society to confront the realities of economic disparity. Their efforts create spaces where discussions about the need for systemic change can thrive, allowing the public to better understand the connections between wealth inequality, social justice, and economic opportunity.

In a world where the rich continue to accumulate more wealth while the working class struggles, it is these bold individuals who offer a fresh perspective on how to address these imbalances. Their knowledge, passion, and willingness to stand up to the powerful make them invaluable contributors to the fight for a fairer society.

Perhaps it's time to recognize their potential beyond the written word or the airwaves. These authors, journalists, and podcasters could play an instrumental role in reshaping our policies, offering fresh outlooks in advisory or political positions. Their ability to challenge the system with thoughtfulness and integrity positions them to make a real difference in the creation of fairer, more equitable laws and systems.

If we are to truly make change, it is crucial that we amplify their voices and provide them with the platforms and positions they deserve. They are the ones who have started the conversations and have the knowledge to see them through to meaningful solutions.

4. Educate Yourself, So You Can Educate Others

You know what they say—you can't pour from an empty cup. If you want to raise awareness, you need to know what you're talking about. Becoming informed isn't just for your benefit—it makes you a better advocate for change. When you understand the underlying causes of the wealth gap, the history behind it, and the current policies that are perpetuating it, you'll be able to have more effective, nuanced conversations.

That doesn't mean you need to get a Ph.D. in economics (unless you want to, in which case, more power to you). It just means taking the time to learn about things like income inequality, wealth distribution, and economic policies that affect the people at the bottom of the income ladder. A simple Google search or a few clicks on news websites that focus on social issues can give you a lot of valuable insights that you can then share with others.

Plus, educating yourself can be fun! There are tons of documentaries, podcasts, and books that break down these complex issues in an engaging way. If you're not sure where to start, check out titles like "The Spirit Level" by Richard Wilkinson, or "Capital in the Twenty-First Century" by Thomas Piketty. And for something lighter but still insightful, tune into podcasts like "The Indicator from Planet Money"—they'll teach you about economics in less time than it takes to finish your coffee.

Knowledge is power, my friend. And the more you know, the better equipped you'll be to raise awareness and help others understand the issues at hand.

5. Be a Bridge, Not a Wall

When you start these conversations, it's tempting to get passionate and dive right into the deep end. But let's be real: people don't respond well to being attacked or guilt-tripped. If you want to truly spark change, your goal should be to build bridges, not walls.

Not everyone is on the same page when it comes to social issues, and that's okay. You're not going to change someone's mind with a single conversation—but you can plant a seed. If you approach these topics with empathy and understanding, you'll be far more likely to keep the conversation flowing. Listen as much as you talk. If someone disagrees with you, don't just brush them off. Instead, ask them to share their perspective and find common ground. For example, you might say, "I get where you're coming from, but here's why I think we should make sure everyone has access to quality healthcare. Do you think there's a way to do that without hurting the economy?"

The goal is to open minds, not force people to think exactly like you. Be patient, be kind, and let the conversations develop naturally. You never know when you'll say something that causes someone to stop and go, "Huh, I never thought of it that way before."

6. Humor Is Your Secret Weapon

And finally—let's talk about humor. I know, I know, wealth inequality isn't exactly a laughing matter (unless, of course, you're talking about the sheer absurdity of the ultra-wealthy hoarding billions while regular folks are struggling). But humor is a powerful tool when it comes to opening people up to difficult topics.

You don't need to make light of the situation, but a well-timed joke or witty observation can help make the conversation feel less heavy. Think of it as a way to disarm tension and make the topic feel more approachable. People are far more likely to engage in a conversation if they feel like they're having an honest, open dialogue rather than being lectured or scolded.

For example, you might say, "It's crazy to think that some people are working multiple jobs just to make ends meet—meanwhile, Jeff Bezos is launching rockets into space. I mean, I get wanting to escape the planet, but does it have to be with all the money?"

A little bit of humor can make the conversation feel less confrontational, and it can even help dispel any resistance to the topic. Just remember to keep it light, not dismissive, and always be respectful.

Start the Conversation, Keep It Going

Raising awareness is one of the most powerful tools you have in the fight against the wealth gap. Conversations are the spark that ignite the fire of change, and even if it feels like your efforts are small, they make a difference.

So, don't be afraid to talk about the issues that matter—whether over coffee, on social media, or in your local community.

It's not always about having all the answers or winning every debate. It's about starting the conversation and keeping it alive. Ask questions. Share stories. Be open to different perspectives.

And above all, keep the conversation going. The more people talk about wealth inequality, the more likely we are to see meaningful change.

Who knows? That one conversation you have today might just inspire someone else to take action tomorrow. And, in the end, that's how we bridge the gap—one conversation at a time.

Building Coalitions

When it comes to tackling big, complex issues like closing the wealth gap, it's easy to feel like David facing Goliath. The challenges are massive, the systems entrenched, and the gap between the haves and have-nots seems impossible to bridge. But here's the good news: you don't have to do it alone. In fact, you shouldn't.

Enter coalitions—those magical things where people who might not even agree on everything come together to tackle a common cause. It's like the Avengers for social change: different backgrounds, different skills, but all united by the same goal: fighting for a more just and equitable society. If you're thinking, "Okay, that sounds good in theory, but how do I get involved?" don't worry, we're about to break it down.

1. Why Coalitions Are Key

First, let's take a step back. Why are coalitions so effective when it comes to addressing the wealth gap? The short answer is: because power in numbers. In fact, they're one of the most powerful tools for social change.

When we come together, we can pool resources, amplify voices, and share expertise in ways that individual efforts simply can't match. A coalition isn't just a group of people who happen to agree on a single issue; it's a partnership that brings diverse perspectives and collective strength to the table. For example, community groups, labor unions, activists, academics, and politicians may not always see eye to eye on every little thing, but when they join forces, they have the power to push for real change that impacts people on the ground.

Think about the civil rights movements, labor movements, and environmental campaigns throughout history—many of them were successful because different groups (often with varying focuses) saw the need to collaborate. They realized that the issue—whether it's economic inequality, worker rights, or climate change—was bigger than any one group. And that's where the magic happens: collective action.

So, when it comes to closing the wealth gap, building coalitions is one of the most effective ways to rally the resources, support, and momentum needed to push for systemic change.

2. Finding Common Ground: The Art of Collaboration

You might be wondering, "Okay, but if coalitions are made up of diverse groups, how do we even begin to work together?" Great question. Building a coalition isn't about everyone agreeing on everything. That's the beauty of it—diversity of thought is actually a strength.

For example, one group might focus on economic policy reform, while another may work on education access, and yet another might be focused on housing rights. But here's the thing: all of these issues are interconnected. If we want to close the wealth gap, it's not just about raising the minimum wage (although that's crucial)—it's also about creating opportunities for education, investing in communities, ensuring affordable housing, and so much more. These issues don't exist in silos, so why should our efforts to address them?

The key to building a successful coalition is to focus on shared values and goals. What's the end goal? In this case, it's a more equitable society where economic opportunities are accessible to all. Once you identify that common goal, it becomes easier to align efforts, even if the path forward looks different for each group.

For example, a labor union might focus on advocating for better wages and benefits, while an education-focused organization may work to expand access to vocational training and higher education. Both are working toward the same outcome: increasing economic mobility and reducing inequality. When you look at it this way, the potential for collaboration is huge.

3. Finding Your People: How to Start Building Your Coalition

Let's say you're ready to jump in. You're all fired up about fighting the wealth gap and want to build a coalition. How do you start? Networking—in a word. But don't think of it as traditional networking (you know, the kind that involves awkward handshakes and trying to remember the person's name after 30 seconds). Instead, think of networking as a collaborative process, where you're seeking out people who are equally committed to the cause. Look for organizations, groups, and individuals who share your values and passion for reducing the wealth gap.

Here are some tips for getting started:

Start local: Look around your community. Who's already working on the issues you care about? Local grassroots organizations, community groups, labor unions, or even schools and universities can be great places to start. The best coalitions often begin in local communities where the need is most urgent.

Reach out to like-minded people: If you know someone who's active in social justice or economic equity, reach out to them. Start a conversation. Invite them to collaborate. They might know others who can add value to the cause.

Get creative: Coalitions don't always have to be formal organizations. If you can't find a pre-existing group that aligns with your goals, start your own. Maybe it's just a handful of people meeting regularly over coffee or Zoom to brainstorm ideas for action.

Leverage social media: You'd be surprised how many grassroots groups and organizations are active online. Twitter, Instagram, Facebook, and LinkedIn are great places to find and engage with others who are passionate about economic justice. Use hashtags like #EconomicJustice, #WealthGap, #FairWages to find communities already talking about these issues.

4. The Power of Diverse Voices: Why the More, The Merrier

One of the greatest strengths of a coalition is the diversity of voices it brings together. Think about it: when people from different walks of life come together to work toward a common goal, you get a rich, multifaceted perspective on the issue. A coalition that includes students, workers, activists, and policymakers can approach the wealth gap from all angles—education, policy reform, community investment, labor rights, and more.

That diversity leads to better ideas and more creative solutions. For example, people with personal experience in poverty might bring insights that others—like those who have never experienced that level of economic struggle—might miss. A teacher can speak to the challenges students face when it comes to affordable education, while a community organizer can offer insight into how local policies affect families struggling to make ends meet.

But remember—don't make it about "one size fits all." There's no magic bullet to fix the wealth gap, but by listening to and amplifying a broad range of voices, you're ensuring that you're working toward solutions that are more holistic and inclusive.

And yes, sometimes the dynamics can get complicated—different groups might have different priorities or ways of working. But here's where the magic of collaboration comes in: when you're all committed to the same larger goal, it's amazing what you can accomplish, even if the path looks a little winding.

5. Real Change Takes Time: Stay in It for the Long Haul

It's easy to get discouraged when change feels slow. But when you're working with a coalition, remember that big victories take time. Building momentum, influencing policy, shifting public opinion—none of it happens overnight. Think of it like planting a tree. At first, you just see a seed. Then a sprout. And then, after years of tending, the tree starts to bear fruit.

Real, lasting change comes when coalitions stay committed, even when progress feels like it's inching forward. Consistency is key. Showing up, having difficult conversations, continuing to advocate for policies that close the wealth gap—these small actions, done collectively, build up over time. That's how movements grow into transformational change.

6. Celebrate Success, Big and Small

Finally, remember to celebrate the wins—even the small ones. In any long fight, it's important to acknowledge progress, no matter how incremental it might seem. Maybe you successfully lobbied for an increase in the local minimum wage. Or perhaps you helped organize a community event that raised awareness about wealth inequality. Those are big wins, and they deserve to be celebrated!

But even smaller successes—like connecting with new coalition members, sharing new resources, or starting important conversations—are worth recognizing too. Every step forward is a step closer to the goal.

Together, We Can Close the Gap

Building a coalition to address the wealth gap isn't about perfection; it's about persistence, partnership, and collective action. You might not have all the answers, but by bringing together people with different skills, experiences, and perspectives, you'll create a force for change that's bigger than any one individual.

So, gather your allies, build those bridges, and get to work. After all, when it comes to fighting the wealth gap, the more the merrier. The true power lies in working together, and if we can unite for this cause, there's no limit to what we can achieve.

Even the smallest effort can spark a movement. Who knows? You might just be the one who gets this whole coalition thing rolling. Let's close that gap together.

Healthcare

Access to Affordable Healthcare

Healthcare in the United States is often a topic that gets people's blood pressure rising—even before they step foot in a doctor's office. Let's face it: we've all heard the horror stories—huge medical bills, surprise charges for out-of-network care, the kind of stress that makes you wonder whether your doctor has been secretly moonlighting as a magician, conjuring up the latest bill out of thin air. As a country, we seem to have mastered cutting-edge medical technology, but when it comes to affordable healthcare, we often stumble, tripping over our own high premiums, deductibles, and confusing insurance jargon.

And while it may seem like an issue that only affects the unlucky few, healthcare costs in the U.S. are a huge burden for millions of families. They affect not just the sick, but everyone—from the young and healthy, to the elderly, to small business owners who struggle to offer health insurance to their employees. Healthcare is not just a medical issue; it's a financial one, a societal one, and yes, a moral one. It's about life expectancy, community health, and ensuring that people aren't forced to choose between seeing a doctor or paying for their children's college tuition.

In this chapter, we'll explore the fundamental question of why access to affordable healthcare is so crucial, how the current system isn't working, and what we can do to fix it—together. If you're wondering whether it's really worth the effort, think about this: the answers to these questions could be the key to not only saving lives but improving quality of life for millions of people in the U.S.

The Financial Burden: Healthcare in the U.S.

Let's kick things off with a bit of reality check: healthcare in the United States is expensive. Like, expensive-expensive. You don't need to check the news to see this; just check your wallet after a trip to the ER for a sprained ankle or a routine physical. The numbers are staggering: in 2022, the U.S. spent nearly $4.3 trillion on healthcare, which equates to about 18% of the country's GDP. This is the most of any country in the world. And yet, many Americans still can't afford basic medical care. In fact, approximately 30 million Americans were uninsured as of 2022, and tens of millions more were underinsured—meaning they have coverage, but still face overwhelming out-of-pocket costs that prevent them from seeking care.

Why? Because the system is designed to leave people in a bind. For the uninsured or those with high-deductible plans, the cost of medical treatment can be catastrophic. Let's break this down in simple terms: if you need surgery and you don't have insurance—or you're underinsured—the bill could easily reach tens of thousands of dollars. And if you can't pay that bill? Well, now you're in medical debt, which, according to a study by the Kaiser Family Foundation, affects nearly one in four Americans. This medical debt can be worse than a bad breakup—it can follow you around for years, destroy your credit, and make you feel like you're trapped in a never-ending cycle of financial insecurity.

But it's not just the uninsured who suffer. Even people with insurance often face sticker shock when they try to get medical treatment. High deductibles, surprise out-of-network charges, and co-pays make accessing care far more expensive than it needs to be. Even with "affordable" plans, you may find yourself paying a few hundred bucks just to see a primary care doctor. Oh, and don't forget the additional costs for medications. According to a recent study, prescription drug prices in the U.S. are among the highest in the world. In fact, Americans pay, on average, more than 250% of the price for the same drugs in other countries. Yeah, that'll make you think twice before picking up that painkiller prescription.

Why is healthcare so expensive in the U.S. in the first place? It's a fair question, and one that doesn't have a simple answer. But there are a few main reasons why the cost of healthcare has ballooned over the years.

1. The Profit Motive in Healthcare

One of the primary drivers of high healthcare costs in the U.S. is the profit-driven nature of the system. Unlike many other countries that treat healthcare as a public good or basic human right, in the U.S., healthcare is a multi-trillion-dollar industry, driven by for-profit motives. Hospitals, insurance companies, pharmaceutical companies, and medical device manufacturers all have a vested interest in keeping the system as expensive as possible.

This profit motive creates an environment where healthcare costs are artificially inflated. For example, the U.S. spends a huge portion of its healthcare dollars on administrative costs. In fact, the U.S. healthcare system is one of the most administratively burdensome in the world, with hundreds of different insurance providers, each with its own rules, networks, and paperwork. That's a lot of overhead—and it costs a lot of money.

Meanwhile, drug prices are often sky-high because pharmaceutical companies are incentivized to charge as much as they can. The U.S. is the only developed nation that allows drug companies to set their own prices. As a result, the cost of life-saving medications like insulin can rise dramatically, leaving people who need it scrambling for affordable alternatives or—worst case—skipping doses altogether. The financial incentives for pharmaceutical companies often stand in direct opposition to the needs of the public. A $200 price tag on a pill doesn't help anyone except the people at the top of the corporate ladder.

In essence, healthcare in the U.S. is treated like a commodity rather than a service. It's treated as something that can be maximized for profit, not something that should be universally accessible and equitable. And therein lies the problem.

2. The Fragmented Nature of the System

Unlike other countries with a more centralized system, the U.S. has a patchwork of private insurers, government programs like Medicare and Medicaid, and employer-provided plans. This fragmentation creates inefficiencies. It's like having five different subway lines that don't connect properly, causing delays, confusion, and extra costs. Patients and providers alike end up spending excessive time and energy navigating the system to get the care they need.

The complexity of the system results in administrative waste—time and money that could be better spent on actual patient care. It also results in confusion. One person's insurance might cover something, while another's won't. And even when insurance covers a service, patients often find themselves hit with surprise bills for things they didn't even know were out-of-network.

There's no coherence between the parts, and the result is a system that's difficult to navigate and incredibly expensive. With the system divided among so many players, it becomes easy for the costs to spiral out of control. And guess who gets stuck in the middle? The people who need care the most—the patients.

3. Lack of Price Transparency

In many other industries, you can get an estimate before you make a purchase. Want to buy a car? You can compare prices and get quotes from different dealers. Need a new fridge? You can check prices at multiple stores before making a decision. But when it comes to healthcare, transparency is often nonexistent. You go to the doctor, you get a test, and then—surprise!—you get an unexpected bill that might be five times what you thought it would cost. A routine X-ray could cost $1000 or $5000, depending on where you go. But you won't know until you get the bill in the mail months later.

Price transparency is a simple solution to this issue. If people could see and compare prices for services and prescriptions upfront, they could make more informed decisions. It might even encourage hospitals and doctors to lower their prices in a competitive marketplace. Price transparency could reduce the shock of surprise medical bills and create a more consumer-friendly healthcare market.

While some private companies are pushing for transparency, there's resistance from big players who benefit from the status quo. That's why advocates for healthcare reform must continue to push for greater price transparency in order to give patients the power to make informed choices.

The Cost of Delay: Why Access Matters

Let's say you've been feeling under the weather for a while. Maybe it's just a cold, or maybe it's something more serious, but you can't afford to see a doctor, so you decide to wait it out. Sound familiar? You might think you're saving money, but in reality, you could be making the situation worse. Preventative care—the kind of care that detects problems before they become serious—is far less expensive than treating an emergency.

For example, let's take diabetes. Early detection and treatment of type 2 diabetes can cost a few hundred dollars in doctor's visits and medication. But if left untreated, the complications—things like heart disease, kidney failure, blindness, and even amputations—could cost tens of thousands of dollars to treat. And guess what? This doesn't just affect the person with diabetes; it affects the healthcare system and, by extension, society as a whole. Those costs are passed on to everyone, in the form of higher insurance premiums, taxes, and healthcare fees. It's like an ever-expanding game of Jenga—each time a person forgoes preventative care, the whole system becomes a little more precarious.

By making healthcare more affordable, we could prevent the need for expensive emergency room visits, lengthy hospital stays, and costly surgeries.

And the best part? We'd be improving the overall health of society. When people have access to the healthcare they need, when they need it, they can get better sooner and contribute to the community in more meaningful ways.

What's Working Elsewhere?

Lessons from Around the Globe

We don't have to reinvent the wheel. In fact, we have a wealth of examples from other countries that show how universal healthcare can work without bankrupting the system. Let's take a look at a few:

1. Canada's Single-Payer System

In Canada, healthcare is publicly funded through taxes and is available to all citizens, regardless of their income or employment status. The system is simple: you go to the doctor, you receive care, and you don't get a bill. No deductibles, no co-pays, no surprise charges.

Canada spends about half as much per capita on healthcare as the U.S., yet its citizens live longer and experience better health outcomes. How do they do it? By keeping the system streamlined, eliminating profit motives, and negotiating drug prices through bulk purchasing. Canada also invests in preventative care, which reduces long-term costs.

2. The UK's National Health Service (NHS)

The NHS in the UK provides comprehensive healthcare to all citizens, free at the point of use. Funded through taxes, the NHS has proven to be a highly effective and efficient system—providing high-quality care while keeping costs relatively low. The system focuses on preventative care and emphasizes access to primary care doctors, reducing the burden on hospitals and emergency rooms.

Although the system has its challenges—long waiting times for some services—overall, it provides a model for healthcare that prioritizes access and equity over profits. With strong public support, the NHS continues to provide care for millions of Britons, and its funding comes from a more progressive tax structure.

3. Germany's Health Insurance System

Germany operates a universal healthcare system that's based on a combination of public and private insurance. Everyone is required to have insurance, but there's a choice of public or private plans, depending on income and employment status. The public system is funded through employer and employee contributions, and costs are regulated by the government to ensure affordability.

Germany's system is highly effective in ensuring that everyone has access to care. With an emphasis on quality and efficiency, Germany spends much less than the U.S. on healthcare while achieving comparable health outcomes.

Why Universal Healthcare?

When it comes to healthcare, there's one fundamental question that tends to spark passionate debates: Should healthcare be universal? In simpler terms, should the government ensure that everyone, regardless of income or employment status, has access to health coverage?

The short answer: Yes. But let's unpack this a little.
The Case for Universal Healthcare

The idea of universal healthcare—where everyone has access to the same high-quality care, regardless of their financial situation—isn't some radical, pie-in-the-sky dream. It's a practical and proven model that works in many other developed countries around the world. Nations like Canada, the UK, and

Sweden have implemented universal healthcare systems, and their citizens are healthier and happier for it.

Here's why we should be advocating for it:

Health Equity: In a universal healthcare system, health outcomes aren't determined by your income. Whether you're a millionaire or a minimum-wage worker, everyone gets the same level of care. This leads to healthier, more equitable communities. The current system in the U.S., on the other hand, often forces low-income people to choose between healthcare and other basic needs, like food or housing.

Lower Costs for Everyone: It might sound counterintuitive, but universal healthcare actually saves money in the long run. By pooling resources, the government can negotiate lower prices for healthcare services and prescription drugs, cutting administrative costs, and eliminating the profit-driven motives that make healthcare in the U.S. so expensive. Right now, the U.S. spends more on administrative costs than most other countries spend on their entire healthcare systems.

Better Health Outcomes: Studies show that countries with universal healthcare have better overall health outcomes, including higher life expectancy, lower infant mortality rates, and fewer preventable deaths. A single-payer system allows doctors to focus on patient care, rather than dealing with the red tape of insurance claims.

Reducing Financial Strain: Under a universal healthcare system, people won't have to choose between seeking medical treatment and paying for other essentials. No one should have to worry about going bankrupt because they needed a simple procedure. By removing financial barriers to care, universal healthcare makes it possible for people to live healthier, more secure lives.

Better Insurance Coverage: The Key to Universal Access

While universal healthcare is a great goal, it's not an overnight fix. However, there are steps we can take in the meantime to improve insurance coverage and make healthcare more affordable for everyone. In many ways, the current insurance system can be improved by focusing on three key areas:

Expanding Medicaid and Subsidies: In the U.S., Medicaid provides health insurance for low-income individuals. Unfortunately, not every state has expanded Medicaid under the Affordable Care Act (ACA), leaving millions of people without access to affordable insurance. By expanding Medicaid nationwide, more people could gain access to necessary healthcare services, reducing disparities in care and improving health outcomes.

Reducing High Deductibles and Out-of-Pocket Costs: One of the biggest barriers to accessing care for many people, even those with insurance, is high deductibles and co-pays. In some cases, patients are required to pay thousands of dollars before their insurance even kicks in. By capping out-of-pocket costs and lowering premiums, we can make health insurance more accessible and ensure that people actually use their benefits instead of avoiding necessary care due to cost concerns.

Allowing for More Competition in the Marketplace: When insurance companies have limited competition, they can raise prices without much consequence. Encouraging more insurance providers to participate in the marketplace, along with offering a public option that allows people to buy into a government-run insurance program, could drive down costs and increase choice for consumers. A competitive marketplace also fosters innovation, creating more tailored options for individuals and families.

Lower Prescription Drug Costs: The Elephant in the Room

If you've ever had to fill a prescription, you know how quickly the costs can add up—especially if you need medication for a chronic condition. But did you know that the U.S. pays some of the highest prices for prescription drugs in the world? The price of a medication in the U.S. can be several times higher than in countries like Canada or the UK, where governments negotiate drug prices on behalf of their citizens.

There's no reason why we should be paying so much more for the same medication. By allowing Medicare and private insurers to negotiate directly with pharmaceutical companies, we could reduce prices and make medications more affordable for everyone. For instance, in 2022, the Biden administration passed legislation to allow Medicare to negotiate the prices of certain prescription drugs—a move that will save taxpayers billions of dollars in the long term. Expanding this ability to negotiate could drastically lower the prices of life-saving medications, making healthcare even more affordable for the public.

What You Can Do: How to Advocate for Change

So, now that we've laid out the case for universal healthcare, better insurance coverage, and lower prescription drug costs, the question is: What can you do to make it happen? After all, no one likes to feel powerless. Fortunately, there's plenty you can do to push for change.

1. Get Informed:
The first step is to educate yourself. Understand the issues, the statistics, and the stories of people who are affected by the current healthcare system. The more you know, the better equipped you'll be to advocate for change.

2. Contact Your Representatives:
One of the most effective ways to make your voice heard is by contacting your elected officials. Tell them that you support universal healthcare and want to see improvements to the system. Write letters, make phone calls, and attend town halls. Politicians are more likely to act when they know their constituents care about an issue.

3. Support Policies that Promote Access:

Support candidates and policies that aim to reduce healthcare costs, expand insurance coverage, and create a more equitable healthcare system. Pay attention to local and national elections and vote for leaders who prioritize healthcare reform.

4. Advocate for Transparency:

One of the biggest problems with the current system is the lack of transparency around healthcare prices. Advocate for policies that require hospitals and insurers to disclose prices upfront, so people aren't caught off guard by surprise bills.

A Healthier Future for All

Access to affordable healthcare is not just a lofty ideal—it's a fundamental human right. It affects not only the lives of individuals, but the health and well-being of entire communities. By advocating for universal healthcare, improving insurance coverage, and lowering prescription drug costs, we can create a system that prioritizes health over profits, fairness over bureaucracy, and life over death.

Improving access to affordable healthcare isn't just about reducing financial strain; it's about giving people the opportunity to live healthy, fulfilling lives. Because when people are healthy, they can thrive. And when they can thrive, society as a whole thrives. It's a win-win.

So, let's get to work. Let's make sure that healthcare in the U.S. is something everyone can afford, and that no one has to choose between their health and their financial future. After all, we're all in this together. And that's a good place to start.

Mental Health Awareness & Support

"It's okay not to be okay."

If you've spent any time on the internet in recent years, you've probably seen this phrase plastered across memes, t-shirts, and Instagram posts. It's a good sentiment. It's a reminder that mental health struggles are a normal part of life, and it's important to talk about them. But there's a small catch: it's a lot easier to say it than to believe it, especially in a culture that still tends to treat mental health issues with a cocktail of stigma, avoidance, and a healthy dose of misunderstanding.

For too long, mental health has been treated like the ugly step-sibling of physical health. We know the importance of looking after our bodies. We know that we should go to the doctor for regular check-ups, that we need sleep and nutrition, and that we need exercise to keep things running smoothly. But when it comes to our minds? Not so much. It's still somewhat taboo to talk about feeling anxious, depressed, or overwhelmed. In fact, many people are more comfortable admitting they have a cold than saying they're struggling with a mental health challenge.

Mental health is health. It's as crucial as any other part of your well-being, and it has the power to affect every aspect of your life. If your mental health is off, it can bleed into your relationships, your job, your physical health, and even your ability to enjoy life.

The problem is, mental health care has often been treated as an afterthought—a luxury or something to be dealt with only when things get really bad, when someone hits rock bottom. And that, my friend, is where we're doing it wrong.

Why Mental Health Awareness & Support Matters

At the core of improving mental health is a simple idea, when people feel better mentally, they do better in all areas of life. It's not just about preventing tragedy or saving lives (although, of course, that's crucial). It's also about unlocking human potential, fostering resilience, and creating a society where people are equipped to thrive.

The Prevalence of Mental Health Issues in America

Mental health issues are more common than you might think. According to the National Institute of Mental Health (NIMH), one in five U.S. adults experiences mental illness each year. That's nearly 50 million people. Anxiety disorders alone affect around 40 million adults, and depression affects over 17 million. If you've ever had a stressful day, or if you've dealt with grief, trauma, or a challenging life transition, you're not alone. These are normal human experiences—what's not normal is when people feel like they can't talk about them or get the help they need.

And yet, despite this widespread prevalence, mental health remains an underserved area of healthcare. Only about 40% of those with mental health conditions receive the treatment they need. This is a tragedy on multiple levels. Untreated mental health issues can lead to a cascade of problems, including substance abuse, job loss, homelessness, crime, and even suicide. And for those who do seek help, accessing proper care can be difficult, expensive, and complicated.

What makes this all the more frustrating is that mental health treatment is not some fringe, touchy-feely thing—it's about real, tangible outcomes. A healthy mind supports physical well-being, improves work performance, enhances relationships, and even impacts a person's ability to contribute to society as a whole. Simply put, when we invest in mental health, we're investing in the quality of life for everyone.

The Cost of Ignoring Mental Health

So, let's zoom out a little bit. When we fail to address mental health in a meaningful way, the consequences ripple through society. The personal costs are obvious—individuals who struggle with untreated mental health issues are more likely to experience chronic physical health conditions, job instability, relationship breakdowns, and a lack of overall well-being. But the societal costs? They're even steeper.

For example, untreated mental health conditions are a major factor in the cycle of poverty. Individuals with mental illnesses are more likely to experience unemployment or underemployment, and they often face additional barriers to securing housing, education, and healthcare. They're also at higher risk for substance use disorders, which in turn put additional pressure on social services and the criminal justice system.

Crime: Mental health is closely tied to issues such as substance abuse, homelessness, and violence. While the vast majority of individuals with mental illness are not violent, untreated mental health issues can contribute to behaviors that result in interactions with the criminal justice system. In fact, studies show that people with untreated mental illnesses are disproportionately represented in jails and prisons. Improving mental health support can be a key strategy for reducing crime and improving community safety.

Unemployment & Economic Productivity: People with untreated mental health conditions often struggle to maintain consistent employment. Mental illness can impact concentration, decision-making, and interpersonal relationships—core skills needed for success in any job. By investing in mental health services, we can improve workforce participation, reduce absenteeism, and enhance overall productivity. Everyone benefits when people are able to work at their best.

Health Costs: Mental health issues can exacerbate physical health problems. For example, untreated depression has been linked to a higher risk of heart disease, diabetes, and other chronic conditions. By addressing mental health earlier, we could significantly reduce healthcare costs related to these physical conditions.

Simply put, investing in mental health isn't just a kindness to individuals—it's an investment in society as a whole. Healthier minds contribute to healthier bodies, better jobs, stronger communities, and lower societal costs.

How to Improve Mental Health Support: Actionable Steps

The good news is that there are clear, actionable steps we can take to improve mental health awareness and support. While there's no quick fix, there are systemic changes and individual shifts in attitude that can make a huge difference.

1. Increase Funding for Mental Health Services

One of the most pressing needs in the U.S. is a significant increase in funding for mental health services. Despite the fact that mental health disorders are among the leading causes of disability in the country, mental health services are often underfunded and overburdened. A report from the National Alliance on Mental Illness (NAMI) found that state mental health agencies received 30% less funding per capita in 2018 than they did in 2009, despite the increased need for services.

The Funding Gap:
The problem isn't just that there isn't enough money—it's also about how the money is allocated. Many community mental health programs face budget cuts, and there's a general lack of investment in preventative care. It's far cheaper to provide accessible mental health services upfront, preventing crises before they occur, than it is to deal with the aftermath of untreated mental health problems.

Increasing funding for mental health is a no-brainer. More funding means more professionals in the field, shorter wait times for therapy, better resources for schools, workplaces, and community centers, and more research into innovative treatments. The government can play a critical role in shifting funding priorities to reflect the actual needs of the population. After all, it's much cheaper to treat someone's mental health early than it is to address the complex web of issues that arise from untreated illness.

2. Reducing the Stigma Around Mental Health

In many ways, stigma is the silent killer of mental health. When people feel like they'll be judged or misunderstood for seeking help, they're less likely to reach out for support. This is especially true in cultures or communities where mental health struggles are seen as a personal weakness or something to hide.

In fact, a study from the American Psychological Association found that nearly 40% of Americans who experience a mental health issue do not seek treatment because of stigma.

We've come a long way in the fight to reduce stigma around mental health. Celebrities, athletes, and politicians are beginning to speak out more openly about their own struggles. But the work is far from over. We need to continue to challenge the idea that seeking mental health support is a sign of weakness. It's a sign of strength to admit that you need help. Just as no one would hesitate to go to the doctor for a broken bone, no one should hesitate to seek therapy for emotional pain.

To fight stigma, we need to normalize conversations about mental health. Schools, workplaces, and healthcare providers need to openly talk about mental well-being as an integral part of overall health. Let's make mental health care as routine as brushing your teeth.

Practical Tips for Reducing Stigma:
Educate the public about mental health and its prevalence.
Encourage open conversations about mental health, whether in schools, workplaces, or communities.
Use positive language around mental health. Instead of saying "crazy" or "insane," use terms like "mental health struggles" or "emotional challenges."
Support people who are open about their mental health journeys. Share stories of hope and resilience.

3. Integrating Mental Health into General Healthcare Systems
Right now, in many places, mental health care operates in a silo, separate from physical health care. You might visit a general practitioner for a check-up and receive a referral to a therapist or psychiatrist, but the two systems often don't communicate well with each other. This fragmentation can lead to gaps in care, confusion for patients, and missed opportunities for early intervention.

What we need is a more integrated system, where mental health is treated as part of overall health care. This would involve training all healthcare providers—general practitioners, nurses, and even pharmacists—on how to recognize the signs of mental health issues and how to provide initial support or refer people to appropriate services.

This integration should also extend to insurance coverage. Mental health care should be covered just as comprehensively as physical health care. The Affordable Care Act made strides in this direction by requiring insurance companies to cover mental health services, but the reality is that many plans still have high co-pays or limited coverage for mental health treatment. We need to ensure that mental health care is not just accessible but affordable for everyone.

4. Promoting Prevention and Early Intervention

Prevention is always better than cure—and this is especially true when it comes to mental health. Early intervention can reduce the severity and duration of mental health problems, and can prevent conditions from escalating into major crises.

Preventative mental health care can take many forms. Mental health education in schools, stress management programs in workplaces, and community programs that promote emotional well-being. When people learn to identify signs of stress, anxiety, or depression early, they're more likely to seek help before things get out of hand.

A Brighter, Healthier Future

Mental health awareness and support are not just "nice-to-haves." They are essential to the well-being of individuals, families, and communities. Improving access to mental health services, reducing stigma, and integrating mental health care into general healthcare systems will help create a society where everyone can thrive, not just survive.

As a society, we have the opportunity to foster a culture of compassion, support, and understanding. When we take care of our mental health, we take care of our future. So let's commit to the work ahead: let's make mental health a priority for everyone. Because the truth is, when we're all mentally well, we all rise together.

Remember, It's okay not to be okay—but it's even better to talk about it, and it's absolutely okay to get help. So, let's start the conversation. Let's break the stigma. And let's build a healthier, happier world for all.

Improving The Care, Treatment, & Funding For The Disabled & Elderly

"We don't stop playing because we grow old; we grow old because we stop playing."

That quote, attributed to the legendary George Bernard Shaw, reminds us that aging—and by extension, growing older with disabilities—shouldn't be a death sentence for joy, purpose, or activity. But for many elderly people and individuals with disabilities, the harsh reality is that society has a tendency to make their later years feel less like a golden age and more like a battleground for dignity, independence, and basic care. The struggle is real, but the good news is, it doesn't have to be this way.

Imagine, for a moment, a world where the elderly and disabled are not seen as burdens or afterthoughts. A world where every senior has access to quality healthcare, every person with a disability can navigate the world with dignity, and every family doesn't have to sacrifice their life savings just to ensure their loved ones are well-cared for. A world where the words "affordable" and "care" aren't seen as oxymorons. That's a world worth building—and it starts with all of us.

The reality we face today, however, is far from ideal. The elderly and disabled populations, though deserving of the best we can offer, often fall victim to a fragmented, inefficient, and underfunded healthcare system. As we face an aging population (the number of U.S. adults over 65 is projected to more than double by 2060), it's critical that we reevaluate how we treat, support, and care for these individuals. It's time to rethink the systems that are in place, upgrade the care options available, and—yes—ensure that it's all affordable.

Let's explore how we can improve the care, treatment, and funding for the elderly and disabled, creating better healthcare systems and living situations for them. We'll break down the challenges they face, highlight potential solutions, and explore how investing in these areas can create a more equitable society for all.

The Current State of Care for the Elderly and Disabled: A Snapshot

Imagine you're trying to get from point A to point B in a race, but the course is filled with obstacles—stairs, narrow hallways, and confusing signposts, and you're told that the clock is ticking, so you better hurry. That's the reality many elderly and disabled individuals face when navigating the labyrinth of healthcare, home environments, and societal expectations. In theory, we live in an advanced, enlightened society, yet for many, particularly those who are aging or living with disabilities, the world just isn't built for them. And navigating this maze can feel a lot more like a game of "Chutes and Ladders" where the chutes come a little too often, and the ladders are just out of reach.

We currently live in a world that's not designed for aging bodies or disabilities. Let's start with the basics, the home. Your home, whether you own it, rent it, or are merely visiting, was likely designed with the assumption that the people living there are relatively able-bodied and free of significant physical limitations. Now, picture someone in a wheelchair trying to navigate a hallway narrower than their chair. Or an elderly person with shaky hands trying to balance on one foot while reaching for a towel in a shower with no grab bars. The struggle is real.

Take Susan, for example. Susan is 72, and she's lived in her cozy suburban home for nearly 40 years. It's familiar and comfortable—until one day, after a fall, she finds herself facing the reality that her home was never designed for someone with arthritis and balance issues. Her bathroom? It's basically a slip-and-slide, complete with a tub that requires Olympic-level flexibility just to step into. And don't get her started on the stairs—Susan is now at a point where even moving between floors feels like an expedition in the Himalayas. The thing is, she doesn't want to leave. She wants to stay in her home, surrounded by her garden and her decades of memories. But when every day becomes a battle against her own home, "aging in place" can feel more like "aging in peril."

Home modifications are not just about safety and mobility; they are about preserving the dignity and independence of individuals with disabilities and the elderly. Being able to live in one's own home, maintain a sense of autonomy, and avoid institutionalization is essential for quality of life. However, when the financial means to make necessary modifications are lacking, the emotional and psychological toll of this limitation can be significant. The inability to live comfortably in one's home can lead to feelings of helplessness, isolation, and depression, all of which negatively impact overall health.

The issue isn't just architectural, though. Our entire society's infrastructure isn't built with the elderly and disabled in mind. In public spaces, sidewalks often have uneven surfaces, public transportation lacks accessible features, and there's a constant battle with things like public restrooms that are more "public" than "restroom" for someone in a wheelchair. Did you know that in a 2019 survey, three out of four public spaces in cities across the U.S. failed to meet the needs of people with disabilities? Even something as simple as "going to the store" becomes a full-fledged challenge for many people.

As people with disabilities and the elderly experience illness, injury, or a decline in health, they often require home modifications to maintain independence and safety. Modifications such as wheelchair ramps, widened doorways, stairlifts, or bathroom adaptations are often necessary for people with mobility impairments. However, these modifications are costly, and many government assistance programs do not provide sufficient funding to make these adjustments.

The costs of home modifications can vary significantly depending on the type and extent of the changes required. A simple wheelchair ramp may cost a few thousand dollars, but a full bathroom renovation for accessibility can cost tens of thousands. For individuals living on fixed incomes, these expenses can be prohibitively expensive, forcing them to either live in unsafe or uncomfortable conditions or delay necessary modifications until a crisis occurs. In some cases, individuals may be forced to move out of their homes entirely and into assisted living facilities, which, as discussed earlier, can be unaffordable.

Healthcare: A Disjointed, Fragmented Puzzle

Now, let's move on to healthcare. You've heard it before: "The system is broken." For elderly and disabled individuals, it's more like "the system is a jigsaw puzzle with a few key pieces missing." Trying to get comprehensive care when you're elderly or disabled is like trying to assemble IKEA furniture without instructions—you just have a bunch of random parts, and you're hoping something eventually clicks.

Here's a scenario that happens far too often. Margaret, a 68-year-old woman with both diabetes and early-stage dementia, goes to the doctor for a routine check-up. The doctor treats her high blood sugar but doesn't seem to pay much attention to her cognitive decline. Why? Because diabetes is the immediate problem, while dementia is, sadly, often seen as something "just part of getting old." As a result, Margaret gets the care she needs for her physical health, but her mental health—the thing that could make or break her quality of life—gets sidelined.

Here's the crux of the problem, elderly care is often siloed. A person with complex health issues, like someone who is both elderly and disabled, needs a holistic care plan. Instead, they're bounced from specialist to specialist, all of whom have their own narrow focus, creating a fractured care experience. You might have an eye doctor, a cardiologist, a neurologist, and a podiatrist—but none of them are talking to each other, so you're left with a care experience that's as effective as a group project where no one communicates.

Let's talk about the elephant in the room, money. Oh yes, the cost of care. It's a topic no one really enjoys, but it's the cold, hard truth of navigating life as an elderly or disabled individual. According to AARP, nearly 60% of people aged 65 or older spend more than $3,000 annually on out-of-pocket medical expenses, and that's before factoring in the cost of long-term care or specialized equipment (like wheelchairs, home health aides, etc.). And for those with disabilities, the picture is even grimmer.

Many people, family members in particular, are often forced into a financial bind just to provide basic care. Take Tom and Judy, who are both in their late 60s. Tom's mother, an Alzheimer's patient, requires constant care. Judy's sister, who has cerebral palsy, needs regular physical therapy and personal care assistance. Between the two of them, they're managing caregiving duties that require not just time but money, and lots of it. The cost of professional in-home care, medical supplies, and specialized therapies means they're constantly dipping into their retirement savings. In some cases, families are even forced to sell their homes just to cover expenses. All of this, of course, is happening while Tom and Judy are themselves aging and trying to manage their own health issues. It's like trying to juggle while riding a unicycle on a tightrope.

And this financial burden doesn't just fall on families, it also falls on society as a whole. Medicare and Medicaid programs, while crucial, are chronically underfunded and often fail to meet the needs of the most vulnerable. This leaves many individuals to rely on patchwork solutions, like sharing caregiving duties with siblings, neighbors, or hiring cheap, often undertrained, home health aides who may not have the proper training or support.

In many countries, people with disabilities and the elderly are often given a set monthly income from the government, designed to support them as they navigate the challenges of living with chronic health conditions, mobility issues, or aging. These funds, though crucial for survival, often fail to meet the evolving needs of individuals over time. In most cases, the amounts provided are fixed, meaning they do not increase to keep pace with inflation, rising costs of living, or escalating healthcare expenses. This issue becomes even more pronounced when individuals face increased costs due to home modifications needed for accessibility or medical treatments related to illnesses and injuries. Furthermore, these fixed incomes fail to consider the essential aspect of quality of life, which is critical for maintaining dignity and mental well-being as individuals age or deal with disabilities.

For most people, a steady increase in income is essential to meet the rising costs of daily life. Whether it is the increased price of groceries, utilities, housing, or transportation, inflation is a constant factor that erodes the purchasing power of a fixed income. For people with disabilities and the elderly, who are already living on limited budgets, these rising costs can create severe financial strain. Fixed incomes, often derived from government assistance programs such as Social Security Disability Insurance (SSDI) in the United States, or similar programs in other countries, may be adjusted periodically for inflation, but the increase is typically modest and often insufficient to keep up with actual cost increases. For example, in 2023, Social Security beneficiaries in the U.S. saw a cost-of-living adjustment (COLA) of 8.7%. While this was one of the highest adjustments in years, it still fell short of keeping pace with the sharp increases in housing costs, energy prices, and food inflation, particularly in urban areas where many elderly or disabled people are forced to live due to the proximity of essential healthcare services. For people on fixed incomes, these rising costs mean less disposable income for anything beyond basic needs.

The mismatch between fixed government income and the real cost of living places a tremendous burden on the elderly and those with disabilities, forcing them to make difficult choices about what they can afford. Some may cut back on essentials like food, healthcare, or transportation, leading to a lower quality of life. Others may face a higher risk of financial instability, potentially leading to homelessness or an inability to access critical healthcare services.

Healthcare costs have been rising consistently, and government assistance programs often do not provide enough financial support to cover these expenses. Medicare, for example, covers a substantial portion of healthcare costs for Americans aged 65 and older, but it does not cover everything. Many prescription drugs, especially specialized medications, are not fully covered by Medicare, and the out-of-pocket costs for these medications can be astronomical. People with disabilities who are eligible for Medicaid may face similarly high costs, depending on their specific situation and the state they live in.

For individuals on fixed incomes, the high costs of prescriptions, doctor visits, physical therapy, and medical procedures can lead to a serious financial dilemma. They may find themselves forced to choose between buying necessary medications and paying for food or utilities. This situation can lead to poorer health outcomes, as people may skip doses, delay treatments, or avoid seeing a doctor altogether in order to preserve their limited financial resources.

Additionally, the need for long-term care can be a significant strain. Nursing homes, assisted living facilities, or in-home care services are often prohibitively expensive, and government programs like Medicaid may cover some of the costs, but not all. For many elderly individuals, paying for such services out-of-pocket is simply not an option. The reality is that many seniors face an increasing likelihood of living in poverty as they age, unable to afford the care they need to maintain their health and well-being.

Given the clear evidence that fixed monthly incomes for people with disabilities and the elderly are insufficient to meet their needs, it is essential that governments reconsider their approach to financial support. A more dynamic, responsive system of support is needed—one that accounts for the rising costs of living, healthcare, and the additional financial demands that come with aging or living with a disability.

The Erosion of Quality of Life

While financial hardship is the most obvious consequence of insufficient government assistance for people with disabilities and the elderly, the erosion of quality of life is equally significant. Quality of life encompasses more than just the ability to pay for basic necessities; it also includes the ability to engage in meaningful activities, maintain social relationships, and enjoy personal fulfillment. For those living on fixed incomes, these opportunities are often out of reach.

Many elderly people and individuals with disabilities face significant isolation due to limited mobility, lack of financial resources, or the inability to participate in social or recreational activities. Without the financial means to travel, attend events, or participate in community activities, they may become isolated from friends and family. This isolation can contribute to a range of mental health issues, including depression and anxiety, which are prevalent among both elderly and disabled populations.

Moreover, the stress of financial instability can take a toll on mental health as well. The constant worry about how to pay for healthcare, medications, housing, or even food can cause anxiety and exacerbate existing health conditions. The loss of hope for improvement or for a better quality of life can lead to feelings of despair, further diminishing a person's mental and emotional well-being.

Discrimination against the elderly and disabled is a major issue that goes unnoticed by many. In the case of disabilities, the barriers are visible—whether it's the lack of wheelchair-accessible ramps or the constant battle for accessible parking spaces, people with disabilities face daily struggles just to get from point A to point B. For the elderly, however, discrimination is more subtle. It's the assumption that someone over 70 can't possibly know what's best for them anymore, or that they have nothing left to contribute to society. In reality, many older adults continue to play vital roles in their communities. They mentor younger people, share their vast knowledge, and volunteer. But when society pushes them aside, we lose the valuable contributions they offer. It's like tossing away a classic novel because it's "too old," without realizing that the wisdom it contains might be more relevant than ever. For the elderly, the problem is less about discrimination but more about a society that frequently overlooks them altogether.

In fact, we often forget that older adults and people with disabilities are contributors to society—they volunteer, they mentor, they provide valuable knowledge and perspective. But their ability to contribute is often stymied by poor healthcare options, inaccessible living situations, and the lack of affordable services.

I recently read a study where a group of 80-year-olds was asked if they wanted to "remain active in the workforce." The answers ranged from "Absolutely, I still have plenty of energy!" to "

Yes, but only if I can nap in the afternoon." Which, frankly, sounds like a perfectly reasonable request from someone who's earned it.

The Benefits of Improved Care and Support for the Elderly and Disabled

So, why should we care? What do we stand to gain by improving care for the elderly and disabled? Well, more than we might think.

A Better Quality of Life

First and foremost, improving care means better quality of life for elderly and disabled individuals. It means that they can live with dignity, respect, and autonomy. Rather than being forced into a system of care that's subpar or inaccessible, they can thrive in environments that meet their needs—whether that's in their own homes, assisted living, or skilled nursing facilities. A happier, healthier senior or individual with a disability isn't just a more fulfilled person; they're also more engaged with their community, more productive, and more likely to experience better mental health.

Financial Savings for Families and Society

Investing in better care and treatment also leads to financial savings. Properly funded healthcare systems and preventative measures can reduce the burden of chronic conditions, emergency room visits, and long-term care costs. A person who has access to proper medical care for their condition—whether it's physical therapy, counseling, or social services—can remain more independent for longer, reducing the need for more expensive care options down the road. Moreover, improved care for the elderly can allow seniors to stay in their homes, which is often cheaper than institutionalized care.

Families won't be drained financially, and society as a whole can save resources by preventing avoidable hospitalizations or institutionalized care. Long-term, it's not just an investment in individuals—it's an investment in the stability of society as a whole.

A More Inclusive Society

By improving care and accessibility, we also create a more inclusive society. Disability and aging are not "other" categories—they are an inevitable part of the human experience. By providing better infrastructure, healthcare, and services, we signal that these individuals are valued members of society, deserving of the same opportunities, respect, and dignity as anyone else. An inclusive society benefits everyone, not just those directly impacted. When we create systems that work for the elderly and disabled, we end up creating systems that work for everyone—systems that are more flexible, adaptable, and supportive of all people, regardless of age or ability.

How to Improve the Care, Treatment, and Funding for the Elderly and Disabled

Now that we've established why it's important, let's take a look at the concrete steps we can take to make these changes happen. From policy reforms to personal shifts in behavior, there's a lot we can do to improve the lives of elderly and disabled individuals.

1. Increase Funding for Elderly and Disability Care

The first step in making any kind of meaningful change is funding. Governments at both the state and federal levels need to invest in programs that provide care for the elderly and disabled. This includes:

Funding for Home Modifications: Direct funding or low-interest loans for home modifications could be made available to individuals with disabilities and the elderly, enabling them to make necessary changes to their living environments without facing financial ruin.

More funding for home healthcare services: Many seniors and individuals with disabilities prefer to live at home, but home health aides are often underfunded, overworked, and in short supply. Investing in these services would give individuals more options for remaining at home longer.

Affordable long-term care: We need to expand affordable long-term care options, whether it's in-home care or residential care. Medicaid and Medicare, which serve the elderly and disabled, must be adequately funded to cover the full range of services these individuals need.

Support for family caregivers: Many families bear the brunt of caregiving responsibilities, often without financial support. We need to provide funding for respite care and direct financial assistance to family caregivers, helping to ease the financial strain and stress.

Inflation-Proofing Benefits: Government assistance programs could be indexed to inflation more regularly, ensuring that income adjustments more closely reflect the actual cost of living. A more frequent and substantial cost-of-living adjustment (COLA) could help maintain the purchasing power of fixed incomes.

2. Improving Access to Healthcare Services

Access to healthcare is another critical area that needs improvement. We need to:

Healthcare and Prescription Support: Governments could increase funding for healthcare programs, expand coverage for prescription medications, and provide more comprehensive coverage for long-term care. This could reduce the financial burden on elderly and disabled individuals, allowing them to access the care they need without sacrificing other essentials.

Integrate healthcare systems: Create a more holistic approach to care by integrating healthcare services for the elderly and disabled. This means providing coordinated care that addresses both physical and mental health needs, as well as social services like housing and employment support.

Expand telehealth: Telehealth services should be expanded and made more accessible to elderly and disabled individuals, particularly in rural or underserved areas. Many seniors or disabled individuals have difficulty traveling to appointments, so virtual visits can provide a crucial lifeline to care.

Improve accessibility: Healthcare facilities need to be fully accessible to those with disabilities. This means investing in things like ramps, elevators, and wheelchair-accessible rooms, as well as training medical staff to be more sensitive to the needs of elderly and disabled patients.

3. Designing Accessible Communities

For seniors and disabled individuals, the world outside their homes can often be just as inaccessible as their homes. To fix this, we need to:

Create universal design in communities: This could include everything from accessible public transportation to sidewalks and public spaces that are wheelchair-friendly. Universal design isn't just about meeting the needs of people with disabilities; it's about creating spaces that work for everyone.

Support aging in place: We need to help individuals age in place by providing accessible housing options, home modifications, and community-based services that allow people to live independently for as long as possible.

4. Combatting Stigma

One of the biggest barriers to improving the care and treatment of the elderly and disabled is stigma. Both groups are often marginalized or ignored. It's crucial that we work to reduce this stigma by:

Increased Social Support: Expanding access to social programs that promote community engagement and mental health support could help mitigate the social isolation that often accompanies financial insecurity. Investments in local community resources, including transportation, caregiving, and social programs, would improve the quality of life for these populations.

Normalizing aging and disability: These aren't fringe issues—they're part of the human experience. The more we talk about aging and disability openly, the more we'll shift societal attitudes.

Education and advocacy: We need to raise awareness about the needs of the elderly and disabled, particularly when it comes to healthcare and housing. Advocacy organizations, politicians, and communities can all play a role in highlighting these issues and pushing for change.

A Future Worth Building

People with disabilities and the elderly face a variety of challenges, many of which are compounded by insufficient government support. Fixed monthly incomes that do not adjust for inflation, rising healthcare costs, or home modifications create significant financial strain, limiting individuals' ability to live comfortably or access essential care. Furthermore, the lack of financial resources often leads to a diminished quality of life, characterized by isolation, poor health outcomes, and emotional distress.

The reality is, we need systemic reform to address the needs of the elderly and disabled. Aging-in-place solutions need to be more affordable, accessible, and, frankly, better designed. Healthcare systems need to be integrated, with professionals communicating and coordinating care for the whole person, not just the individual ailments. And we need to stop treating the elderly and disabled as "other"—isolated, forgotten—and start recognizing them as valuable members of society.

Until that happens, we'll continue to face an uphill battle. And while it might seem overwhelming at times, the good news is that the conversation has started. Reform is on the horizon, and every voice—yours included—adds to the momentum for change. Whether it's advocating for better home accessibility, supporting universal healthcare models, or simply acknowledging the worth of older and disabled individuals, every step toward reform brings us closer to a more equitable society for all. And let's face it, at some point, we're all going to be on the receiving end of these systems, so it's in all of our best interests to make sure they work. So, let's fix the course. Remove the obstacles. Because, as we all know, life's marathon is tough enough without someone trying to trip you up along the way.

When we improve the care, treatment, and funding for the elderly and disabled, we're not just helping these individuals—we're helping everyone. We're creating a world that values people of all ages and abilities, a world that believes in dignity, respect, and compassion for all. It's not just about providing better healthcare; it's about building a more inclusive society where every person has the opportunity to live a full, meaningful life.

The good news is, change is possible. With increased funding, improved access to services, better infrastructure, and a shift in attitudes, we can build a society that truly supports our elderly and disabled populations. And in doing so, we'll build a society that benefits all of us.

So, let's get to work. The future of our loved ones—and our own future—depends on it.

Big Pharm Big Problem

Greed, Abuse, and the American People

Pharmaceutical companies are the titans of the healthcare industry—juggernauts that control much of the world's drug supply, from life-saving treatments to everyday medications. They're the ones who decide what pills you pop, what syrups you swallow, and what injections you endure. The world of Big Pharma is vast, powerful, and, in some cases, downright unaccountable. But what's the cost of this power? How much have these companies been willing to exploit the American public in their relentless pursuit of profit? Well, let's dive into the world where billions of dollars are made off of ailments, where people suffer for corporate greed, and where governmental policies sometimes serve as mere roadblocks to even more lucrative schemes.

The Price of a Pill

Pharmaceutical companies make their money by selling medications to the public. But here's the catch—those prices aren't determined by production costs, research, or even the complexity of the drug. No, the prices are often determined by what the market will bear. And the American market? It bears a lot. This isn't necessarily a surprise—after all, when you've got a monopoly on a life-saving drug, you can charge whatever you want. And that's precisely what happens.

Take the case of insulin, for example. A drug that's been around since the 1920s and literally saves the lives of millions of diabetics has seen its price skyrocket in the U.S. over the past few decades. In 1996, the price of insulin was about $21 per vial. By 2016, that same vial cost upwards of $275. And for what? Is the drug any different? Not really. It's still the same insulin, largely produced by the same companies, like Eli Lilly, Novo Nordisk, and Sanofi. These are the giants that control the insulin market, and they've repeatedly raised prices despite making absurd profits from it.

In fact, Eli Lilly alone made a profit of $12.5 billion in 2022. Meanwhile, the average American insulin user spends about $1,000 a year on the drug. And for many, that's just for the basics—if you need more specialized insulin, the price can double, triple, or more. The reason for this price hike is part greed and part market manipulation. Insulin is sold as a "lifesaving" drug, and since diabetics have little choice but to buy it, the companies can raise prices without losing customers. This practice has been described by critics as price gouging—and they've got a point. Just like a vendor selling bottled water at a concert for $8, the pharmaceutical industry knows there's a captive audience that will pay whatever is necessary to stay alive.

The Opioid Crisis: A Case Study in Corporate Corruption

But insulin isn't the only place where Big Pharma has come under fire for gouging the public. If you want a textbook example of pharmaceutical greed, you need to look no further than the opioid crisis—the crisis that continues to ravage communities across the United States and has claimed the lives of hundreds of thousands of people. In the late 1990s, pharmaceutical companies, most notably Purdue Pharma, began aggressively marketing OxyContin, a powerful painkiller that was advertised as a "safe" alternative to other opioids. The drug was pitched as non-addictive, despite being a highly addictive substance.

Purdue Pharma knew full well that its drug was dangerous. Studies and internal reports revealed that OxyContin was easily abused, but the company downplayed these risks, lobbied for doctors to prescribe it widely, and pushed it as the solution to America's "pain problem." By 2007, Purdue had already paid a $600 million settlement for misleading advertising, but that wasn't nearly enough to stop the flood of opioid prescriptions that followed. It wasn't until 2019 that Purdue filed for bankruptcy under the weight of lawsuits from states and local governments, but not before they made billions of dollars off addiction and death.

Between 1999 and 2019, over 500,000 people died from opioid overdoses, and opioids contributed to more than half of all drug-related deaths in the United States. Meanwhile, companies like Purdue and Johnson & Johnson—two of the biggest players in the opioid game—walked away from this tragedy with some of the largest settlements in history, totaling billions of dollars. Yet, despite the settlements, Purdue's executives largely escaped criminal charges. The company's former president, Richard Sackler, was one of the few who wasn't personally penalized for his role in the opioid epidemic. Instead, the Sackler family, who owned Purdue, has kept most of their wealth and even gained a reputation for philanthropy, donating to museums, universities, and hospitals.

If there's one thing that's clear from the opioid crisis, it's that for many pharmaceutical companies, the bottom line has always come before the well-being of American citizens.

The Price of "Innovation"

Now, Big Pharma often defends its inflated drug prices by pointing to the enormous costs of drug development. Sure, there are costs associated with research, clinical trials, and the long approval process required by the FDA. Developing a new drug isn't exactly cheap. But here's where things get murky. According to a 2019 study by the House of Representatives Ways and Means Committee, the average cost of developing a new drug is approximately $1 billion—which sounds impressive. But the problem is, companies rarely spend that much. Instead, they spend a large portion of their budgets on marketing and lobbying, with some estimates suggesting that up to 40% of pharmaceutical companies' revenues are spent on advertising.

Consider the case of Humira, one of the world's top-selling drugs. Humira, which treats conditions like rheumatoid arthritis and Crohn's disease, generated about $20 billion in annual sales for its maker, AbbVie. Despite being on the market for over two decades, Humira is extremely expensive—$5,000 per month or more, depending on the dosage. And why is it so expensive? Because AbbVie holds a near-complete monopoly on the drug, largely thanks to aggressive patenting and a series of legal battles that delayed the release of cheaper generics. Even though the drug has been around since 2002, AbbVie has found ways to extend its exclusivity through patent "evergreening"—making small tweaks to the drug to ensure they don't lose their monopoly.

AbbVie has raked in billions on Humira and avoided competition for years. Yet, despite their massive profits, the company continues to argue that they need high prices to fund "innovation"—even though their research and development expenditures don't match their claims. According to some analysts, companies like AbbVie spend more on lobbying and marketing than they do on actual research for new drugs.

Political Influence and the Abuse of Policy

Perhaps the most insidious aspect of Big Pharma's influence is its ability to manipulate governmental policies to its advantage. Pharmaceutical companies spend billions each year on lobbying, ensuring that they have a seat at the table when it comes to health policy. In 2020 alone, the pharmaceutical industry spent more than $350 million on lobbying efforts. That's right—$350 million to make sure their interests are well-represented in Congress. This is more than the oil and gas industry, and it's nearly double what the tech industry spends.

One example of Big Pharma's political influence can be seen in the Medicare Part D program, which was enacted in 2003. Part D was designed to provide prescription drug coverage to seniors, but a major flaw in the law is that it explicitly prohibits the government from negotiating directly with drug manufacturers over prices. Why? Because pharmaceutical companies lobbied hard for this provision, arguing that it would stifle innovation and lead to fewer new drugs. The result? Seniors and taxpayers are stuck with much higher drug prices than they would be if the government had the ability to negotiate.

There's also the matter of direct-to-consumer advertising (DTCA), which is largely illegal in most countries but is commonplace in the U.S. In fact, Americans are the only people in the world who see TV ads for prescription drugs. It's all part of the strategy to push medication, often for conditions that may not even require a pharmaceutical solution. From ads for antidepressants to erectile dysfunction pills, Big Pharma spends billions on advertising aimed at getting people to ask their doctors for specific drugs. This leads to a cycle of over-prescribing and drives up healthcare costs.

But it doesn't stop there. Pharmaceutical companies have also been known to fund political campaigns, contributing large sums of money to lawmakers who support their agenda. This influence is particularly evident in the Food and Drug Administration (FDA), the agency tasked with ensuring drug safety and efficacy. A revolving door exists between the FDA and the pharmaceutical industry, where former pharmaceutical executives take high-ranking positions within the FDA, and vice versa. This raises serious concerns about the agency's ability to regulate effectively.

The Death of Generic Drugs

In the ideal world, after a drug's patent expires, cheaper generic versions should flood the market, giving consumers access to affordable alternatives. But in the real world, Big Pharma has developed creative ways to keep generics out of the picture. Companies often engage in practices like pay-for-delay, where they make deals with generic drug makers to delay the release of cheaper versions. This keeps prices high and profits flowing. A famous example is the EpiPen debacle, where Mylan, the maker of the EpiPen, raised prices by more than 500% between 2007 and 2016. At the same time, they worked hard to keep generic versions off the market. The result? A $600 pen that was once affordable became a financial burden for many families.

The practice of evergreening is another tactic where companies make minor changes to existing drugs—whether it's a new dosage form, a new delivery system, or even just a new combination drug—to extend their patents. This delay tactic keeps generics at bay and allows the company to continue charging exorbitant prices.

Big Pharma's greed and manipulation of the American healthcare system is a complex, multifaceted issue, and the examples above only scratch the surface. From price gouging of life-saving medications to exploiting vulnerable populations through the opioid epidemic, the pharmaceutical industry's pursuit of profit often comes at the expense of public health and well-being. And with billions of dollars spent on lobbying, advertising, and political contributions, the industry has the power to shape policies that benefit its bottom line—while leaving consumers to foot the bill.

The American people are paying the price, not just in terms of money, but in terms of health outcomes. Next time you pop a pill remember, you're not just swallowing medicine, you're also swallowing the enormous influence of one of the most powerful industries in the world. And it's not just your health that's at risk—it's your pocketbook, too.

Curtailed by the immense power and influence of large pharmaceutical companies, addressing the issue of their potential exploitation for extreme personal gain at the expense of citizens and governing bodies requires a multi-pronged approach. These companies, while providing essential medications and innovations, have sometimes been criticized for prioritizing profits over people. Practices such as inflating drug prices, aggressive lobbying, and the prioritization of shareholder returns over public health are examples of how the pharmaceutical industry can, at times, exploit the system.

So how can we address and mitigate this issue?

Strengthen Regulation and Oversight:
Holding Big Pharma to Account

Let's be honest—regulation often gets a bad rap. It's like the broccoli of the policy world: not exciting, not exactly a crowd-pleaser, and not something that everyone is jumping up and down to endorse. But when it comes to holding the pharmaceutical industry accountable for its pricing and practices, regulation is not only necessary, it's the unsung hero of the whole system. Think of it as the necessary bouncer at a nightclub, ensuring that Big Pharma doesn't sneak in too many overpriced cocktails and push people out the door while still making sure the party (i.e., access to medications) can go on.

So, how do we get it right? Well, let's break down the key areas where regulation can be tightened up, beefed up, and generally given a turbo boost to ensure that pharmaceutical companies don't get too comfortable with their power.

Regulatory Agencies: Empowering the Watchdogs

We've all heard the term "the fox guarding the henhouse," and it's usually a metaphor for situations where the people or institutions tasked with protecting the public aren't exactly inclined to do so. Nowhere is this more pertinent than in the realm of healthcare. The U.S. Food and Drug Administration (FDA) and the European Medicines Agency (EMA) were created to keep an eye on pharmaceutical companies, ensuring that drugs are safe and effective before they reach consumers. But sometimes, these watchdogs can seem a bit, well, sleepy.

The problem? Underfunding, political pressure, and sometimes even industry influence can weaken their ability to act effectively. So, what can be done? Let's start with empowering regulatory agencies to do their job:

Independence: Regulatory agencies must operate free of industry influence. The FDA, for example, has faced scrutiny for being too cozy with the very companies it's supposed to oversee. Part of fixing this lies in ensuring that regulatory bodies remain independent from the companies they regulate, with stricter limits on conflicts of interest, especially in leadership roles.

Increased Funding: If you've ever wondered why your local police department doesn't have enough resources to keep your neighborhood safe, or why your public school seems underfunded, you can bet the same thing happens with regulatory bodies. Without adequate funding, agencies like the FDA or EMA are limited in how they can investigate drug safety, track adverse reactions, or monitor market behavior. Governments must allocate more funds to these bodies so that they can properly vet the drugs being introduced and make sure safety isn't compromised in favor of profit.

More Transparency: Transparency in the approval process is key. Right now, some pharmaceutical companies are not always forthcoming with data. They might, for example, downplay negative results from clinical trials or overstate the benefits of a drug in their marketing. Regulatory bodies need to enforce transparency by ensuring that all clinical trial results are made public, and that any potential side effects are clearly communicated. In an ideal world, when a company submits a drug for approval, the public should be able to easily see the clinical trial data, including all the good, the bad, and the ugly.

Price Controls and Transparency: Making Big Pharma Open the Books
Now, we get into the juicy stuff—price control. Here's the thing: there's no reason why essential medications should be treated like luxury handbags, jacked up to ridiculous prices just because the market can bear it. We've all seen those headlines about life-saving drugs priced at astronomical rates. For example, the price of insulin, a drug that's been around for nearly a century, has tripled over the last 20 years. It's as if the pharmaceutical industry got together and decided, "Hey, why not make people pay more for something they literally cannot live without?" It's a prime example of corporate greed creeping into healthcare, and it's high time we do something about it.

Reworking the Patent System: No More Evergreening
Pharmaceutical patents exist for a reason. They reward companies for their innovations and give them exclusive rights to market new drugs. But, just like a lot of other things in life, it's all about balance. You want to reward innovation without giving companies an indefinite monopoly on life-saving treatments.

This is where patent reform comes in—specifically, we need to curb the practice of "evergreening," which is a sneaky trick companies use to extend patent protection on drugs that are close to expiring. Evergreening is the pharmaceutical equivalent of buying a new car and then adding a spoiler, painting it a different color, and claiming it's a completely new model. This lets the company extend the exclusivity period on the drug for several more years, keeping prices high while preventing cheaper generic versions from entering the market.

To stop this, the system needs to be reformed so that patents are granted only for genuinely new innovations. It also means ensuring that generic drugs (which offer the same medical benefits at a fraction of the price) can come to market more quickly when patents expire.

The Role of Global Cooperation in Regulation

Pharmaceutical companies are global entities, and the effects of their pricing practices stretch far beyond national borders. In fact, one of the most frustrating things about pharmaceutical pricing is the vast discrepancy between the cost of the same drugs in different countries. In the U.S., for example, drugs can be vastly more expensive than they are in Canada, the U.K., or other countries with price regulations. This isn't just a U.S. problem—it's a global issue.

International cooperation in drug regulation could help combat this. Countries could agree to align their pricing standards, making it more difficult for pharmaceutical companies to charge astronomical prices in wealthier nations while offering drugs at lower prices in poorer countries. By coordinating price-setting mechanisms or sharing data on pricing structures, governments could prevent pharmaceutical companies from exploiting price differences across borders.

The Long-Term Vision: A More Equitable System

If we can successfully strengthen regulatory oversight, improve price transparency, and implement fairer pricing systems, the pharmaceutical industry will no longer be able to manipulate the system for extreme profit. This won't just result in more affordable drugs—it will also ensure that the health of the public takes precedence over profit margins.

Now, we're not saying that regulation will solve all of the pharmaceutical industry's issues overnight. It's going to take years of work, political will, and public pressure to implement some of these changes. But, if we want a future where people aren't bankrupting themselves just to get the medicine they need, this is the road we have to travel. A better, fairer healthcare system for all is within reach—but only if we commit to making regulation work for everyone, not just for those at the top.

Making Regulation Work for the People

The pharmaceutical industry, with all its power and influence, doesn't have to be a force of greed and exploitation. By strengthening regulation and oversight, we can create a system that prioritizes public health and fairness over corporate profit. This means empowering regulatory agencies, pushing for price transparency, rethinking patent laws, and creating global standards that hold pharmaceutical companies accountable.

And while it may seem like an uphill battle, the truth is that each step we take to strengthen these regulations is a step toward a future where essential medications are affordable and accessible to all. After all, nobody should have to choose between paying for their medication or paying for their rent. By making these changes, we can ensure that everyone gets a fair shot at good health—without the pharmaceutical industry breaking the bank.

Implement Fair Pricing Mechanisms:

The Pursuit of Reasonable Costs and Greater Access

The pharmaceutical industry's pricing practices have often seemed like a bad magic trick: the kind where you're left wondering how you got fleeced so quickly and how you didn't even see it coming. One minute you're getting a life-saving prescription, and the next, you're wondering if you need to sell a kidney (yours, not theirs) to afford it. High drug prices have become a national crisis, one that hits patients in their wallets and their well-being. So, how do we fix it? We need to get creative, and there's one surefire way to start: fair pricing mechanisms.

Let's dive into what these mechanisms are, why they're needed, and how they can be used to bring prices down, improve access, and balance the scales of pharmaceutical power. Spoiler alert: it's going to involve some strategic negotiations, global collaboration, and a whole lot of transparency.

Public-Private Partnerships: Negotiating for Fairer Prices

In the world of healthcare, we often talk about the public sector (government-run programs) and the private sector (pharmaceutical companies) as if they were oil and water. They seem to coexist, but rarely do they mix without some level of friction. The public sector wants affordable medications for the people it serves, while the private sector is, let's face it, in business to make a profit. But here's the thing: these two sectors need each other, and when they work together, we can see a significant shift in how drug pricing works.

Public-private partnerships are a powerful tool for addressing this issue. These partnerships leverage the negotiating power of government-run healthcare systems, such as Medicare in the U.S. or the National Health Service (NHS) in the U.K., to secure better prices for life-saving medications. By pooling the buying power of millions of patients under one banner, governments can negotiate directly with pharmaceutical companies to secure lower costs. Think of it like bulk buying at a warehouse store: the more you buy, the cheaper each individual item costs.

Why This Works:

Negotiating Leverage: Pharmaceutical companies are businesses, and businesses like volume sales. The more a government can guarantee the purchase of a particular drug, the more negotiating leverage it has to drive down the price.

Better Access: By negotiating with drug manufacturers, governments can secure discounts, rebates, or even outright price reductions, making medications more affordable for everyone. This is particularly critical for life-saving treatments such as insulin, cancer therapies, and heart medications, where price hikes have often resulted in unnecessary hardship.

Public Health Savings: Ultimately, paying less for medication means governments can allocate more resources elsewhere—such as preventive care, mental health services, or improving access to healthcare in underserved communities. By lowering the cost of pharmaceuticals, governments can stretch their healthcare budgets further, ensuring better care overall.

In some countries, the NHS has been doing this for years. In the U.S., however, the government has not been able to negotiate directly with pharmaceutical companies on drug pricing (thanks to a law that prohibits Medicare from doing so). This leaves private insurance companies and patients to bear the full brunt of these high prices. It's high time that the U.S. followed in the footsteps of countries like Canada, where public-private partnerships help ensure that life-saving drugs are affordable and accessible.

Price Transparency: Show Us the Receipts

There's an old saying that goes something like, "If you can't explain it, you shouldn't be selling it." Well, pharmaceutical companies sure could use a little more transparency in their pricing. Right now, the costs associated with drugs—especially life-saving ones—are often shrouded in mystery. When a medication is priced at $500 a pill, it's hard not to wonder: what exactly is behind that number? Is it all justified? How much is going to R&D (research and development), and how much is going to the CEO's bonus?

Price transparency laws are a crucial step toward exposing the true cost of medications. By requiring pharmaceutical companies to disclose a breakdown of drug prices—ranging from R&D costs to marketing expenses to distribution—governments can create a more transparent system where everyone understands why a drug costs what it does.

Why Transparency Matters:

Accountability: When pharmaceutical companies have to publicly disclose how they arrive at the prices of their drugs, it forces them to be accountable for their pricing practices. If they can't justify an exorbitant price, the public and lawmakers can demand changes.

Empowering Consumers: Transparency doesn't just benefit governments; it benefits consumers too. If you're a patient trying to figure out how to afford your medications, knowing how much the company is actually charging for each part of the process can help you make informed decisions. Patients will also be able to spot instances where the pricing isn't aligned with the actual production cost, potentially leading to lower prices.

Competition: When companies disclose their costs, it creates an environment where competition can flourish. If one company reveals that it only takes them $50 to produce a drug that another company is charging $500 for, suddenly, consumers and other companies alike have an incentive to demand fairer prices. This could lead to more competitive pricing in the marketplace, which ultimately benefits everyone.

Countries like France and Germany have already implemented price transparency in their healthcare systems, and it has helped keep drug prices in check. It's time for the U.S. to catch up, don't you think?

International Price Comparisons: A Global Push for Fair Pricing

The price of drugs can vary significantly depending on where you live. In the U.S., a vial of insulin can cost upwards of $500, while in Canada, it's often a fraction of that. The reason for this discrepancy is largely due to different healthcare systems and government-negotiated prices. But what if we could level the playing field by using international price comparisons as a guide?

Global price comparisons could be an effective way to benchmark the cost of drugs in one country against the cost in others. If a drug is priced dramatically higher in the U.S. than in Europe or Canada, policymakers can use those international prices as a reference to negotiate lower rates domestically.

Why International Price Comparisons Matter:

Global Standards: If countries agree to use global price comparisons to set pricing standards, pharmaceutical companies will be forced to offer more reasonable prices across the board. No longer could they get away with charging wealthy countries like the U.S. exorbitant prices while offering cheaper rates in developing nations. Prices could be better aligned across borders, making access to essential medications more equitable worldwide.

A Fairer Market: Global price comparisons will encourage competition on a larger scale. By creating a system where pharmaceutical companies can't play one country against another, countries can ensure they're getting a fair price for life-saving drugs. Essentially, this creates a more level playing field for healthcare systems worldwide, where every patient gets access to affordable medications, regardless of their country's wealth.

Precedent from Other Countries: Countries like the U.K. and Australia have already adopted price comparison methods in their healthcare systems. These countries negotiate drug prices with manufacturers based on the prices they see in other markets, creating a more balanced approach to pricing.

While global price comparisons aren't a magic bullet (there will still be some variation based on local factors), they can go a long way toward ensuring that prices are fairer, more consistent, and more accessible.

How These Pricing Mechanisms Can Reshape the System

All of these strategies—public-private partnerships, price transparency, and international price comparisons—work together to create a healthcare system that puts patients first. Right now, the pharmaceutical industry seems to operate with a "take it or leave it" attitude, pushing prices higher and higher without regard for the consequences. But with the right pricing mechanisms in place, we can shift the power dynamic.

Imagine a system where prices are more transparent, pharmaceutical companies are held accountable, and governments have the leverage to negotiate better prices for everyone. Patients would no longer have to make impossible decisions about whether they can afford their medication or pay their bills. Instead, they could focus on getting better, without the constant anxiety of rising prescription costs.

And it's not just about saving money—it's about saving lives. By making medications more affordable, we ensure that people can access the treatments they need without fear of financial ruin. This is the ultimate goal: creating a world where public health is prioritized over private profits. When pharmaceutical companies put the health of people first, rather than focusing solely on their bottom line, everyone wins.

The Road to Fair Pricing is Paved with Collaboration

It won't be easy to dismantle the entrenched systems of profit-making that have shaped the pharmaceutical industry, but it's far from impossible. By embracing fair pricing mechanisms—such as public-private partnerships, price transparency, and international price comparisons—we can move towards a future where the cost of medication is not an insurmountable barrier to health and well-being.

This isn't just about keeping Big Pharma in check; it's about creating a healthcare system that works for everyone, not just those who can afford to pay top dollar. The tools to achieve this are at our disposal—now it's up to governments, businesses, and consumers to work together to make this vision a reality. After all, health is a universal right, and everyone deserves a fair shot at it. So, let's make sure that, from now on, the only thing that goes up is life expectancy—not drug prices.

Reinforce Anti-Trust and Competition Laws:

The Fight Against Pharma's Monopoly Game

Imagine walking into a grocery store, only to find that the one company selling all the bread in town also has a monopoly on every other essential food item. The prices are outrageous, the selection is limited, and, worst of all, they can raise the prices whenever they want because, well, they're the only game in town. You've got to eat, so you pay—no choice. Sounds like the beginning of a dystopian novel, right? But for millions of people, this is the grim reality of the pharmaceutical industry today. The lack of competition—whether through price-fixing, monopolies, or market manipulation—has turned the drug market into a rigged game where the only ones winning are the pharmaceutical giants.

So, what can we do to fix this? Enter: anti-trust laws and competition reinforcement. These laws are the legal equivalent of a referee at a wrestling match, making sure that everyone plays by the rules. If a company is trying to corner the market, we need to step in and say, "Not so fast, pal." Let's explore how these legal mechanisms work, why they're so crucial in ensuring fair play, and how they can shake things up in the pharma world.

Investigating Price-Fixing and Collusion: The Shadowy World of Pharma Price-Gouging

In an ideal world, pharmaceutical companies would compete to offer the best drugs at the most affordable prices, and patients would benefit from healthy competition. But in reality, sometimes, companies don't compete—they collude. Price-fixing is one of the dirtiest tricks in the pharmaceutical playbook. It's when companies secretly agree to set drug prices at artificially high levels, leaving patients to foot the bill while the companies pocket the profits.

A Price-Fixing Scandal in the Making

If you've ever heard about a generic drug scandal, you know exactly what this looks like. For example, in 2016, it was revealed that several major pharmaceutical companies were collaborating to hike up the prices of life-saving medications like epinephrine (used for severe allergic reactions) and heart medications. The conspiracy involved companies agreeing to raise the prices of certain generic drugs at the same time—essentially inflating the prices through mutual back-scratching.

This is not just "bad business"; it's outright fraud. The whole point of anti-trust laws is to prevent this kind of manipulation, but enforcing these laws requires active monitoring, investigations, and swift penalties. When price-fixing occurs, we're not just talking about greedy executives—this is a public health issue.

How Anti-Trust Laws Can Help:

Investigations into Collusion: Governments need to actively investigate when there's suspicion of price-fixing or other forms of collusion. This means keeping an eye on major players in the market and ensuring they're not secretly coordinating price hikes or stifling competition.

Punishments for Price-Gougers: When companies are caught price-fixing, the penalties should be severe—including hefty fines and, in some cases, the possibility of criminal charges. Let's face it: a slap on the wrist just doesn't cut it when people's lives are at stake. Pharmaceutical giants need to be held accountable for manipulating the system for profit.

Breaking the Silence: Whistleblowers—whether from within the industry or from patients themselves—are often the key to exposing these shady practices. Anti-trust authorities need to offer incentives to encourage people to come forward and reveal collusion or unethical business practices.

Breaking Up Monopolies: The Tyranny of the Single Seller

The term monopoly usually conjures up the image of a board game where one player manages to control everything. And if you've ever played Monopoly the board game, you know it can be downright miserable when one player owns all the property and refuses to trade. Well, when it comes to the pharmaceutical industry, the stakes are much higher than the meager sums of money in your Monopoly bank.

The True Cost of a Pharma Monopoly

When a single company controls a life-saving drug, it can do whatever it wants with the price. Take insulin, for example. A small handful of companies have dominated the global insulin market for decades. Because of the lack of competition, these companies have raised prices relentlessly—often with little to no justification for the hikes.

This is what happens when a monopoly runs amok:

Limited Choices: Patients can't "shop around" for a better price because there's often only one manufacturer offering the drug.

Skyrocketing Prices: When there's no competition, prices can increase with little to no resistance. The monopolist knows that people will pay—because they have no alternative.

Stifling Innovation: If a company knows that it's the only one providing a critical drug, why bother innovating or improving it? The lack of competition can stifle progress.

This is why breaking up monopolies is critical. Anti-trust laws must be used to challenge pharmaceutical giants that engage in monopolistic practices and prevent smaller companies from entering the market.

How Anti-Trust Laws Can Help:

Splitting Up Giants: In extreme cases, when a single company has an overwhelming hold on a drug market, the government may need to break them up—splitting the company into smaller entities that can compete with each other. A little friendly competition could go a long way in driving prices down.

Preventing Anti-Competitive Mergers: Pharmaceutical companies are always looking to acquire competitors. A company could buy up a smaller player or patent rights to prevent a cheaper generic version from reaching the market. Anti-trust laws can prevent these anti-competitive mergers by blocking or undoing acquisitions that threaten market competition.

Encouraging Market Entry: Governments can make it easier for startups and smaller companies to enter the market. Whether through streamlining the approval process for generic drugs or providing incentives for innovative biotech firms, reducing barriers to entry increases competition and drives prices down.

Creating a Level Playing Field: Competition and Fairness for All

Now, you might be thinking, "But what if breaking up the monopolies and investigating price-fixing makes things worse? What if it just causes chaos in the industry?" Fair question. It's true that regulating an industry as complex as pharmaceuticals requires a careful balance. However, healthy competition is a good thing—it benefits everyone. Here's how:

Lower Prices: The more competition there is, the less power any single company has to set outrageous prices. When consumers have multiple options, companies are forced to compete on price, quality, and service. Lower prices on life-saving drugs could translate into millions of lives improved or even saved.

Increased Innovation: Healthy competition encourages companies to invest in new treatments, improve existing ones, and develop cheaper alternatives. In the absence of a monopoly, pharmaceutical companies will have to innovate to stay ahead of their competitors—leading to better drugs and more affordable options.

Better Access: A competitive market creates a greater variety of treatment options, improving accessibility for people across different income levels. When multiple companies are fighting for market share, they'll be more likely to find ways to reduce costs and make treatments available to a wider population.

Why We Need to Act Now

The pharmaceutical industry is one of the most powerful sectors in the world. But with great power comes great responsibility—and when that power is unchecked, it can lead to exploitation and inequality. By reinforcing anti-trust laws and making sure that monopolies and price-fixing don't run rampant, we can level the playing field.

The path forward requires vigilance, strong enforcement, and a commitment to fairness. No company, no matter how big, should have the power to set prices that leave patients struggling to afford basic medications. We need to create a system where competition thrives, prices are transparent, and patients—not profits—are the priority.

Let's make it clear, the pharmaceutical game needs a serious rulebook update. We can't let the big players keep playing monopoly with people's lives. We deserve a fair market, where the health of citizens isn't for sale, and where companies compete to make the world healthier—not wealthier.

Encourage the Development of Generic Drugs:

The Heroic Underdogs of the Pharmaceutical World

Let's face it—sometimes, we're all a little tired of the big names getting all the glory. Whether it's in sports, fashion, or the pharmaceutical industry, it's easy to get swept up in the hype of the dominant players. In the pharmaceutical world, the brand-name drugs are the superstars—the Beyoncé and LeBron James of medicine. But here's the thing: Just because someone's wearing a fancy label doesn't mean they're the only ones who can deliver. Enter generic drugs—the under appreciated, lower-cost alternatives that are often just as good as the name-brand versions, but with one huge advantage: They're cheaper!

So why don't we see more of them? What's holding back these generic heroes from taking center stage and saving consumers from outrageous drug prices? Let's break it down, because it turns out, generics are the unsung heroes of the pharmaceutical industry—and they deserve a whole lot more love.

What Are Generic Drugs, and Why Do They Matter?

First, a little pharmaceutical 101. A generic drug is essentially a copy of a brand-name drug that has the same active ingredients, strength, dosage form, and route of administration (e.g., pills, injections, etc.). The key point here is that generic drugs are bio equivalent—meaning they work the same way in your body as their brand-name counterparts.

So, what's the difference? Well, the biggest distinction is in the price. Generic drugs tend to be significantly cheaper than their branded versions—sometimes up to 80-85% less—but this doesn't mean they're any less effective. No, you're not sacrificing quality for cost. You're just skipping the marketing fluff and fancy packaging, and that, my friends, is where the savings come in.

Why Are Generics So Important?

Now, you might be wondering, "If generics are cheaper and work just as well, why aren't they the default choice?" Well, as with many good things, there are some roadblocks standing in the way of their wider adoption. But before we dive into the obstacles, let's take a moment to celebrate the good stuff about generics:

They Save Money: The biggest, most obvious benefit. The cost savings associated with generics are staggering. Think about it—if every person in the U.S. switched from a brand-name drug to a generic, the healthcare system could save billions of dollars. And when you're talking about something as expensive as prescription medications, a billion here and a billion there can make a huge difference. Plus, those savings don't just help individuals. They help entire healthcare systems cut costs, too.

They Increase Access: When medications are cheaper, more people can afford them. Generics make life-saving drugs accessible to a wider population, especially in lower-income communities or countries with limited resources. This means that people who otherwise might have to go without treatment can now get the medication they need to survive, thrive, and live healthier lives.

They Promote Competition: Generics level the playing field. With more options on the market, pharmaceutical companies can't just hike up prices without anyone noticing. When generics enter the scene, they introduce much-needed competition to the market—driving prices down for everyone, including those still buying the brand-name version.

They Free Up Resources: With lower drug costs, patients don't have to worry about choosing between paying for their medication and paying for other necessities like rent or food. It's a huge win for public health when more people can afford their medications without compromising their well-being.

So, What's Holding Generics Back?

Ah, here's the rub. It's all well and good to sing the praises of generics, but the road to widespread adoption isn't without its speed bumps. So, why aren't generics the clear winner, here? Let's take a look at some of the barriers:

1. The Regulatory Approval Process

Getting a generic drug onto the market is no small feat. Sure, the active ingredient in the generic version is the same, but the manufacturer still has to go through a rigorous approval process with agencies like the FDA to ensure that the drug meets safety and efficacy standards. It's not enough to just show up with a bottle of pills and say, "Hey, we made this cheaper version of X drug." The approval process involves a lot of paperwork, testing, and time.

And even when a generic is approved, the process can still take years for widespread availability. During this time, patients might have to pay higher prices for the brand-name version while waiting for generics to hit the shelves.

2. Lack of Public Awareness

Despite their advantages, many people still don't realize the benefits of generics. Thanks to years of clever marketing by big pharma, the general public often associates brand-name drugs with superior quality. This is where a little education can go a long way. We need to shift the narrative and help consumers understand that generics are not only safe but are, in many cases, the smarter choice for their wallet and their health.

How Can We Overcome These Barriers?

Now that we know the challenges, let's look at how we can overcome them and give generics the standing ovation they deserve.

1. Speed Up the Generic Approval Process

Governments and regulators should streamline the approval process for generics. One of the simplest ways to make generics more widely available is to make the regulatory process faster and more efficient. That means cutting down on unnecessary delays, providing more resources for generic drug applications, and reducing the time it takes for these drugs to hit the market. The sooner generics are approved, the sooner patients can start saving.

2. Strengthen Anti-Evergreening Laws

It's time for regulators to take a closer look at evergreening and take action against companies that use minor modifications to extend patents. Pharmaceutical companies should only be able to hold exclusive rights to a drug for a reasonable period of time—after which the market should be open to generics. It's a common-sense fix that can lead to lower prices and increased competition.

3. Promote Public Education and Awareness

We need to launch public awareness campaigns that educate people on the benefits of generics. From billboards to social media posts to TV ads, we should be telling people that generics are safe, effective, and, most importantly, affordable. It's all about shifting the public mindset from "brand-name is best" to "generic is just as good, and way cheaper!"

4. Support Manufacturers Who Play Fair

Lastly, government and public health organizations should support pharmaceutical companies that prioritize the development of affordable generics. Whether through tax incentives, grants, or public contracts, these companies need to be rewarded for producing affordable medications that benefit society at large. This helps increase supply and drive down prices even further.

Generics: The Unsung Heroes of Healthcare

When you look at the pharmaceutical landscape, it's easy to get overwhelmed by the giants—those multi-billion-dollar companies with their shiny advertising campaigns and glittering stock portfolios. But the truth is, the real champions in the world of medicine are often the ones working quietly in the background, helping to bring down costs and make healthcare accessible to all.

So the next time you walk into your local pharmacy and see that generic version of a drug on the shelf, don't just grab the brand-name out of habit. Take a moment to appreciate the generics—those humble, yet powerful, agents of change. Because, in the end, they're doing more than saving you money—they're helping to save the entire healthcare system from spiraling out of control.

And hey, they're the ones who deserve the standing ovation.

Enforce Stronger Ethical Guidelines in Pharmaceutical Marketing:

No More Snake Oil, Please

Let's be honest, there's something deeply unsettling about the way some pharmaceutical companies market their drugs. It's almost as if they've perfected the art of persuasion to a point where you start wondering if you're buying medicine or enrolling in a pyramid scheme. The glossy ads, the over-the-top promises, and the slick language that makes you think, "This drug could cure everything from heart disease to a bad hair day!" But here's the kicker—it's all designed to make you buy, whether you need the drug or not. And that's where things get murky.

Pharmaceutical Marketing: The Fine Line Between Helpful and Harmful

Pharmaceutical marketing is supposed to serve a noble purpose, educate healthcare professionals and the public about life-saving medications. But somewhere along the way, the lines blurred, and now, pharmaceutical companies spend billions to convince you that you need drugs you may never have considered, even if you're perfectly healthy (and that little sniffle you've had for two days would probably go away on its own anyway).

Direct-to-consumer (DTC) advertising—the kind you see during prime-time TV, featuring a jubilant couple walking hand-in-hand on the beach, as a narrator tells you all about the wonderful benefits of a drug that might be slightly dangerous if you have a history of heart conditions—has turned the pharmaceutical industry into a marketing machine more focused on persuasion than on patient well-being. It's a little like those late-night infomercials that sell you a "revolutionary" mop that's guaranteed to clean up every spill in your kitchen while somehow turning your floor into a slip-resistant, non-stick surface.

It's great, right? Until you read the fine print, may cause dizziness, nausea, loss of appetite, and a sudden urge to invest in a second mop.

The Case for Banning Direct-to-Consumer Advertising

You've seen those TV ads for prescription drugs: a person sitting in a sun-dappled field of daisies, smiling brightly, while the narrator rattles off a laundry list of potential side effects that could include everything from mild nausea to sudden onset of "severe death" (okay, maybe I'm exaggerating on the death part, but you get the drift).

While these ads might seem harmless, they serve a far more insidious purpose: they inflate demand for drugs that may not be necessary for most people, causing patients to insist on prescriptions from their doctors. The result? Well, for one, it often leads to over-prescription of certain drugs, which drives up healthcare costs and puts unnecessary pressure on the healthcare system. And two, it can lead to unneeded treatments being administered, sometimes with harmful side effects.

Here's a fun fact, the U.S. is the only developed country that allows these kinds of direct-to-consumer ads for prescription drugs. That's right, while countries like the U.K., Australia, and Canada are far more cautious, we've been sold the idea that we can decide which medication is right for us, thanks to some perfectly coordinated ad campaign.

Now, don't get me wrong—information is good. But just like you wouldn't trust your plumber to give you medical advice, you probably shouldn't trust a 30-second commercial to do the same.

The Arguments for a Ban:

It Fuels Over-Prescription: When people see an ad for a drug, they often think, "Hey, that sounds like me!" But doctors, trained in understanding the nuances of human health, aren't swayed by clever marketing. Instead, they make decisions based on your medical history, diagnostic tests, and professional guidelines—not a pharmaceutical company's sales pitch. By allowing DTC ads, we encourage people to ask for drugs that might not be necessary for their condition, simply because they saw a promising, shiny commercial.

It Increases Costs: Ads don't come cheap. Pharmaceutical companies pour millions into advertising campaigns, but guess who gets to pay for that? We do! These costs are inevitably passed on to consumers, driving up the price of drugs. If we banned DTC advertising, that money could be spent on actual research, or better yet, passed on as lower prices for consumers. You know, just a thought.

It Distorts Risk and Benefits: A lot of these ads focus heavily on the benefits of a drug, but gloss over the potential risks. They may show a smiling, energetic person who's now cured of their chronic condition, but rarely do we see that same person after they've spent weeks suffering from side effects. A more responsible approach would be to provide a balanced view—showing both the possible benefits and the potential risks—rather than pretending that all meds are a miracle cure with no consequences.

Tighten Marketing and Lobbying Rules: Why Less is More (Sometimes)

You know how some people have that one friend who's always trying to sell you something, whether it's skincare products or multi-level marketing opportunities? We've all been there. One minute, you're at a BBQ, enjoying a burger, and the next thing you know, your friend is telling you about the life-changing powers of the latest "wellness" tea. You try to politely steer the conversation in another direction, but no—she's relentless.

Now, imagine that on a larger scale, with millions of dollars behind it and a target audience made up of vulnerable patients who are simply trying to manage their health. This is where pharmaceutical companies really rack up the points—through aggressive lobbying and marketing that shape the policies and regulations that affect us all.

The pharmaceutical industry spends millions of dollars each year to lobby lawmakers and influence healthcare policies. This doesn't just mean pushing for policies that benefit patients—it also often involves securing favorable conditions for themselves. Let's be real, lobbyists are often paid to help companies keep their profits high—even if it means keeping drug prices sky-high, prolonging patents, or avoiding regulations that could lead to cheaper alternatives. And this, folks, is where we run into issues. If we allowed these companies to write the rules, they'd just keep writing themselves a bigger and bigger check.

Stronger lobbying rules could help limit the influence pharmaceutical companies have over lawmakers, ensuring that healthcare policies reflect the best interests of patients and not just the bottom line of some drug company CEO. Transparency in how much companies are spending on political donations and lobbying efforts would go a long way in making sure that these policies are fair, rather than catering to the highest bidder.

What Can We Do About It?
Ban Direct-to-Consumer Advertising: It's time to follow the lead of other countries and put an end to DTC pharmaceutical ads. Sure, some argue that it gives people more control over their health choices, but we've seen how it can mislead people into seeking unnecessary treatments. Instead, let's focus on

better education and public health campaigns that can provide real, honest information without the sales pitch.

Implement Stricter Marketing Rules: The days of pharmaceutical companies running wild with their unrestricted marketing budgets should be over. Let's push for transparency and accountability. Stronger regulations on advertising and clearer restrictions on what can and cannot be said in drug ads would keep companies from making over-hyped claims and misleading patients.

Cap Lobbying Expenditures: We should limit how much pharmaceutical companies can spend to influence legislation. It's about time we get rid of the revolving door between Capitol Hill and Big Pharma and ensure that healthcare policy is made with public health, not profits, in mind.

A World Without Snake Oil (Or At Least Less of It)

Imagine a world where pharmaceutical companies were held to the same ethical standards as any other business: where marketing wasn't about selling a product, but about informing people in a transparent and truthful way. Picture ads that focused on honesty and patient well-being—ads that didn't gloss over the risks or overpromise the results. We'd all be a lot better off. And, maybe just maybe, healthcare could become a little less about the bottom line and a little more about the greater good.

So, let's put the focus back on healthcare and not on buying our way to better health through slick advertising and shady lobbying. Because, in the end, it's not about the money. It's about real solutions for people who need them.

Empower Consumers and Healthcare Providers:

The Power of Knowledge (and a Little Transparency)

So you find you're at your doctor's office, and the diagnosis is in. Maybe you're dealing with a chronic condition, or perhaps you're just in for a routine checkup. Whatever the reason, the doctor hands you a prescription and sends you off to the pharmacy to pick up your meds. But here's the twist—you have no idea how much it's going to cost. You just assume it's covered by insurance or that the price will be somewhat reasonable. After all, how much could a little bottle of pills cost? It's not like they're made of gold... right?

Then you get to the pharmacy, hand over your prescription, and the pharmacist hands you a receipt that might as well be written in hieroglyphics. You squint at it, confused by the price. Your heart sinks as the pharmacist says, "That'll be $300, please." What? For something you need to live?

Now, imagine if you had full transparency on medication prices, from the get-go. Imagine knowing what your meds would cost before you even set foot in the doctor's office or pharmacy. What if you could easily compare prices, ask about cheaper alternatives, and make an informed decision on the best course of treatment for you—and your wallet?

That's the power of empowering consumers and healthcare providers. It's about giving people the tools, information, and transparency they need to make better health decisions. And yes, we know—"healthcare" and "empowerment" are words that don't always go together. But it's time to change that.

Public Awareness Campaigns: Knowledge is Power (and Possible Savings)

Imagine if you could get a primer on the costs of drugs before you walked into the doctor's office. Public awareness campaigns could arm you with information about drug prices, the real costs of certain treatments, and the potential harms of over-prescribed medications. The truth is, most people are in the dark about how much drugs actually cost. For example, did you know that generic drugs can be up to 90% cheaper than their brand-name counterparts? 90%! That's like finding out your favorite brand of coffee can be swapped for something just as good—and 10 times cheaper. Who wouldn't take that deal?

The thing is people aren't being told about generics. Doctors often don't mention them because they may not get the same kind of financial incentive from prescribing them. Pharmacists may not have the time or inclination to mention cheaper alternatives. That's where public awareness campaigns come in. Think of it as a mini "guidebook" to better decision-making. These campaigns could highlight:

Price comparisons: If you know that a certain brand-name drug costs $300, but the generic version costs only $30, you might be more inclined to ask for the cheaper version.

The true value of medications: Sometimes, you don't need the most expensive medication to get the same results. For example, high cholesterol can often be managed just as well by a cheaper statin as it can by a pricier one.

How to ask the right questions: Educating patients on how to have a conversation with their doctors about drug costs. It's not about being confrontational but about being informed. Ask questions like, "Is there a cheaper option?" or "Can we try a generic?"

And guess what? Public awareness campaigns don't have to be dull and boring. They can be engaging, funny, and relatable. Think of your favorite funny TV commercials or meme-worthy internet ads, but for medications. Information doesn't have to feel like a lecture—it can feel like a helpful chat from a friend, maybe even with a bit of humor to lighten the mood.

Transparency in Healthcare: More Than Just a Buzzword

We've all been there: You ask the pharmacist how much your prescription will cost, and they give you that look—the kind that says, "It's not my fault you didn't bring a trust fund with you."

Wouldn't it be nice if you didn't have to ask at all? Transparency in healthcare is the dream of a lot of patients, and it's something we should be actively working toward. Imagine a world where you could easily compare drug prices—just like you compare prices for things like airline tickets or concert tickets. You wouldn't settle for paying $500 for a flight to a nearby city when you could get it for $200 on a different airline, right? So why should we settle for astronomical drug prices when we know there's a cheaper alternative?

With transparency in healthcare, patients could:

Compare prices across pharmacies: You know how when you shop online for a product, you can see which store offers it at the best price? The same principle could apply to medication. Sure, pharmacies are busy places, but it would be great if you could compare the costs of your prescriptions with a quick online tool, ensuring that you're not getting charged more than you need to.

Know the true cost breakdown: Have you ever wondered why your $10 prescription ends up costing $50 at the pharmacy? Transparency laws could require pharmaceutical companies to disclose the true costs of their drugs, from R&D costs to marketing expenses, so you know exactly where that price tag is coming from.

Understand insurance involvement: Sometimes, the cost you're paying is influenced by your insurance plan, copays, and deductibles. If insurance companies had to provide more clarity around how they're influencing drug prices, patients could understand if they're getting a good deal or if they're being taken for a ride.

Transparency in healthcare doesn't just help patients make better decisions—it can help doctors make more informed decisions too. If doctors could compare prices easily, they might be more likely to recommend cost-effective treatments and steer patients toward affordable options. The result? Better health outcomes and a less stressed-out bank account.

Promote Preventive Care: A Little Health Maintenance Goes a Long Way

Let's face it—healthcare costs are ridiculous. You know what's even worse? Not only do they hurt your wallet, but many of the conditions that require expensive medications are preventable in the first place. So why not spend less money on meds and more on staying healthy?

Promoting preventive care is like the old saying, an ounce of prevention is worth a pound of cure. If you're exercising, eating well, and getting regular check-ups, you're less likely to develop chronic conditions that need expensive, lifelong medications. Now, we're not saying you have to become a marathon runner or start doing juice cleanses (please, no one needs to hear about your cleanse diet). But things like eating more vegetables, getting enough sleep, quitting smoking, and keeping your stress levels low can make a massive difference in how much medication you need.

Medications are not a substitute for a healthy lifestyle. If we prioritize health education and preventive measures, we can cut down on the number of people who need to rely on high-cost drugs. This is where public health initiatives can play a major role—through campaigns that educate people on the benefits of exercise, healthy eating, and mental well-being. You know, the kinds of things that cost us a lot less than chronic disease management.

Empowering consumers and healthcare providers isn't just about giving people more information; it's about giving them the tools they need to make better, more informed decisions. When people know what they're getting into—whether it's understanding the prices of medications, knowing that generics exist, or realizing that prevention is more cost-effective than treatment—they can take control of their own healthcare and reduce the grip that pharmaceutical companies have over their wallets.

And it doesn't stop there. Empowerment can help create a ripple effect—where consumers push for better transparency, where doctors get more involved in cost-conscious care, and where the healthcare system shifts from being reactive to proactive. So let's embrace the power of knowledge, transparency, and preventive care, and turn the tide on this overpriced, over-medicated world we've found ourselves in.

After all, when we're in charge of our health, we're not just better off financially—we're healthier too. Now that's a prescription we can all get behind!

Create Stronger Partnerships Between Public Health and Research:

Innovation, Collaboration, and a Better Future

When you think about drug development, you might picture a group of brilliant scientists huddled in a lab, working long hours on their next big breakthrough—a pill that could cure cancer, or a vaccine that could save millions of lives. While that image is partly true, what's less obvious is that this innovation doesn't always come from the biggest pharmaceutical companies with the most profit-driven motives. Sometimes, the breakthrough you've been waiting for comes from a humble government-funded laboratory, or even a nonprofit organization. And that's where stronger partnerships between public health and research really start to shine.

But why should public health and research be more closely intertwined? Well, it's simple, when public funding fuels medical research, it takes the profit-driven incentives out of the equation. You're not just trying to create a drug that will make shareholders a fortune; you're focused on the public good, on advancing science for everyone. And let's be real—doesn't that sound a whole lot more noble than squeezing every last cent out of people who need life-saving treatments?

Let's break it down in a way that's fun, inspiring, and packed with real potential.

Public Funding for Drug Research: From the People, For the People

Let's take a trip down memory lane—back to the days when the government funded some of the most important medical advancements in history. Did you know that many of the foundational breakthroughs in modern medicine, like the development of insulin or the HIV/AIDS antiretrovirals, were funded by public institutions before being adopted by the private sector? These weren't the flashy, profit-driven drugs pushed by Big Pharma. They were products of public-funded research that changed the lives of millions. Public investment in drug research isn't just a nice idea; it's critical to the future of medicine.

Why? Because public funding is not motivated by the same profit margins that drive private pharmaceutical companies. Public institutions can prioritize health outcomes over revenue. This model fosters more collaborative, innovative, and inclusive science, instead of pushing products into the market that are based on whether they'll turn a handsome profit. In short, it's like having a dinner party where the goal is to feed as many guests as possible, rather than making sure the host gets the biggest slice of the pie.

Take the National Institutes of Health (NIH) in the U.S., for instance. The NIH has poured billions into drug research and development, funding projects that would never see the light of day if left to profit-driven companies. It's a great example of how public funding can pave the way for innovations that would otherwise be too risky or unprofitable. We need more of this—public money fueling public health.

This could be a game-changer in creating affordable medicines. When governments fund the research, the result can be open-sourced knowledge or, better yet, a decreasing reliance on patents and monopolies that usually come with new drug discoveries. This democratizes innovation, ensuring that new treatments reach as many people as possible, at prices that make sense for everyone. And yes, I mean everyone—from the person in a wealthy country to those in lower-income regions.

Open-Source Drug Development: Collaboration Is Key (And It's a Lot More Fun Than You Think)

Let's talk about open-source drug development for a second. Now, before you imagine a group of lab-coated scientists in a dark, dusty basement somewhere doing science for the greater good, let's clear this up. Open-source doesn't mean unregulated or chaotic. It's about sharing knowledge freely—kind of like how open-source software allows programmers to share code for everyone to benefit from, with no corporate lock-ins or proprietary constraints. Open-source drug development is all about collaboration—between governments, nonprofits, researchers, and yes, even pharmaceutical companies.

Let's be honest, Big Pharma has an awful lot of money, but they also have a bad habit of sitting on research unless they can figure out how to make a big profit. The problem with that? It slows down innovation and can put life-saving treatments out of reach for millions of people who need them.

Enter collaborative models like the Medicines Patent Pool (MPP), which encourage partnerships to make drugs more accessible. MPP helps create agreements between manufacturers, governments, and nonprofits to increase the availability of affordable medicines—particularly in lower-income countries. Think of it as a medical team-up where the goal is global access rather than individual profit.

And while we're at it, let's imagine a world where public health research isn't about companies patenting life-saving drugs to lock them up for decades, but about an open-source world where knowledge flows freely, and life-saving medicines are made accessible to all. It sounds like something out of a futuristic sci-fi movie, but guess what? It could happen in our lifetime.

Now, imagine if the World Health Organization (WHO) or even universities began publishing data about drug development in real-time. Researchers worldwide could jump in, tweak formulations, share new findings, and collaborate on treatments at a much faster pace. The possibilities for accelerating progress would be limitless. This isn't just a pipe dream—it's the type of collaboration that could bring us a cure for malaria or a universal flu vaccine.

Collaborative drug development isn't just about speed; it's about making sure life-saving treatments are available to everyone, everywhere. When research is open and shared, it reduces the barriers that are often created by patents, exclusivity deals, and the control of essential medicines by a handful of players. The real beauty of open-source development is that it flips the entire system on its head, putting patients first—not profits.

Why Should We Care? A Little Competition Never Hurt Anyone (Except Maybe Prices)

So, why is this partnership thing so important? Well, because when public and private sectors team up on drug research, it creates a level of competition and innovation that benefits everyone. It's not just about letting Big Pharma do its thing behind closed doors; it's about creating a market where public and private entities work together to push the boundaries of medical science.

Who doesn't like a little friendly rivalry? Think of it as the academic equivalent of a science Olympics, where the best and brightest compete not for gold medals but for life-changing breakthroughs. More participants in the game mean more ideas, more innovations, and lower prices when drugs are developed. Companies can't just sit back and relax if everyone else is moving forward at full speed. A little public-private competition can kick start innovation and bring prices down, helping to make these innovations accessible for all.

One great example of this is the way some countries are using public-private partnerships to tackle neglected diseases, like tuberculosis or malaria. Governments fund basic research, nonprofits get involved to test potential treatments, and private companies step in to produce the drugs. Everyone benefits when these partnerships work in unison, and patients get better treatments at lower prices.

What Can We Do? How Can We Be Part of the Solution?

The solution isn't just about sitting back and hoping for the best. It's about advocating for stronger public-health and research partnerships. That means pushing for:

Increased government funding for public health research, especially for diseases that don't always get the attention they deserve.

Encouraging more open-source initiatives and global collaborations to ensure the benefits of research are shared equitably.

Supporting nonprofit organizations that foster this kind of collaboration and helping to hold big pharma accountable for their pricing practices, while recognizing the need for innovation that benefits all.

You can get involved by supporting policies that encourage transparency in drug development, advocating for more public health funding, or simply educating yourself about where drugs come from and how they're developed. Share that knowledge with others—because informed consumers and activists are the ones who can demand more ethical practices and better collaborations between the public and private sectors.

Stronger partnerships between public health and research can transform the future of healthcare—not just in terms of innovation but also in making life-saving treatments more affordable and accessible. The more we encourage collaboration, transparency, and a people-first approach to drug development, the closer we'll get to a world where medicine is made for the masses, not just for the elites.

In the end, the pharmaceutical industry can't—and shouldn't—hold the monopoly on life-saving innovations. By promoting partnerships that place the focus on global collaboration, public health, and accessibility, we can build a future where innovation isn't just something to profit off of, but something that everyone benefits from. So, let's roll up our sleeves, get the government on board, and encourage those partnerships that can reshape the pharmaceutical landscape—for the good of all.

Hold Pharmaceutical Executives Accountable:

No More Golden Parachutes, Please!

Ah, pharmaceutical executives—those high-flying, private-jet-owning, multi-million-dollar-salary types. They're the ones who make headlines not just for groundbreaking medical discoveries, but often for their jaw-dropping bonuses and salary packages that make the rest of us feel like we're in a completely different financial universe. While most of us are sweating the high cost of insulin or trying to figure out how to afford the latest cancer treatment, some of these executives are living the dream—a dream built on the backs of people who just want access to affordable medication.

If we really want to fix the pharmaceutical industry, we need to start with the big cheeses—the ones at the top. These executives call the shots, and it's their decision-making that often puts profits ahead of people. It's time to hold them accountable—no more looking the other way while they cash in on outrageous salaries and bonuses, all while raising the prices of life-saving drugs. Let's break down how we can rein in the extravagant corporate excesses and make sure these companies are working for the public good rather than just fattening their pockets.

Executive Compensation Reform: How Much Is Too Much?

If you've ever felt a little dizzy reading about the pay packages of pharmaceutical CEOs, you're not alone. We're talking about multi-million-dollar salaries, stock options, performance bonuses, and even golden parachutes (just in case they ever leave the company—don't worry, they'll be fine). In 2021, the CEO of a major pharmaceutical company made over $20 million in total compensation—while the price of insulin continued to skyrocket. Hmm, you don't have to be a math genius to see how these two things might not be totally fair.

Now, before we get all hot under the collar, let's acknowledge that executive pay isn't inherently evil. The logic is that CEOs, especially of large corporations, need to be compensated well for their vision, leadership, and ability to guide a massive company. But there's a fine line between rewarding someone for effective leadership and giving them excessive pay that's wildly out of sync with the company's core mission—especially when that company is in the business of providing life-saving medications to people who can barely afford them.

Here's the deal, executive pay should be aligned with the company's performance and public impact, not just the stock price or quarterly profits. If a pharmaceutical company is raking in record profits by hiking up prices on critical drugs, yet the CEO still gets a fat bonus, something's off. It's like rewarding the chef who makes your meal three times more expensive while serving you a smaller portion than you ordered. Executive compensation reform should be about accountability and ensuring that these leaders aren't just focused on short-term gains, but on creating long-term, sustainable solutions that benefit everyone—not just themselves.

Pay for Progress, Not Profits

Let's consider a different approach to paying pharmaceutical executives. Rather than rewarding them based on immediate profits, why not tie their compensation to positive social outcomes? For example:

Lowering the price of essential medications for consumers.

Increasing access to life-saving drugs in underserved communities.

Investing in public health initiatives that improve overall health outcomes, especially in marginalized populations.

By linking their bonuses to how well their company improves public health and lowers prices, we can create a better incentive system. Instead of paying CEOs for inflating prices and maximizing profits, we could reward them for making medications more accessible and affordable. Imagine a world where saving lives and helping people is what drives the success of pharmaceutical companies—now that's a vision we could all get behind.

Ethical Standards for Corporate Governance: Making It About the People

Pharmaceutical executives are in a unique position to influence public health on a global scale. Their decisions can determine who gets access to life-saving treatments and who doesn't. But the sad reality is that many executives seem more concerned with their bottom lines than with improving public health.

Incorporating stronger ethical standards in corporate governance would ensure that the values of transparency, accountability, and public good guide the decision-making at the top levels of pharmaceutical companies. A few key ideas for improving corporate governance could include:

Transparency in pricing: Companies would need to disclose not only the costs of research and development but also the true cost of drugs, including manufacturing and distribution. No more "black box" pricing schemes.

Audits on pricing practices: A third-party audit could be instituted to check if drug prices are fair and aligned with actual costs, ensuring that they are not inflated for profit maximization.

Clear ethical guidelines for executive decision-making, making it clear that decisions should prioritize human health over profit motives. This could include commitments to sustainable pricing, ethical marketing practices, and a focus on long-term health outcomes.

If the people in charge of these companies couldn't hide behind opaque practices and were required to be more transparent and accountable, it would shift the industry toward practices that are focused on public health and well-being—not just profit margins.

The Golden Parachute Dilemma: Time for a Change

Ah, the golden parachute—the golden handshake or the exit package that ensures an executive lands on their feet with a soft cushion when they inevitably leave the company, whether voluntarily or not. While these parachutes might seem like an employee benefit for top brass, they often seem downright insulting when they come at the expense of customers who are struggling to afford basic medications.

It's time to make some changes here. If a CEO leads a company that unethically raises drug prices, puts profits over people's lives, or engages in shady business practices, why should they be entitled to millions in severance pay when they're ousted? Let's be real—Golden parachutes should be reserved for those who truly deserve them, not for those who profit off of people's health struggles.

One way to tackle this is by capping executive compensation based on ethical benchmarks that reflect a company's contribution to society. This would ensure that if an executive is pocketing large sums of money, it's because their company is doing good, not because they've driven up prices of essential medications or engaged in price-fixing schemes. Financial rewards should be tied to social good—not just market manipulation.

Holding Executives Accountable: The Public and Politicians Have a Role

While reforming executive pay is one part of the equation, holding pharmaceutical executives accountable requires a broader societal shift. Politicians, regulators, and the public all have a role to play in ensuring that these companies act in the best interests of society. Let's be honest: when a company's actions are hurting public health, it's the job of government to step in and enforce accountability. If pharmaceutical executives continue to price-gouge, refuse to make their drugs accessible, or put profits ahead of public well-being, regulators must hold them accountable—through fines, price controls, or even breaking up monopolies that limit competition.

And let's not forget about consumers. We have the power to hold these companies to account by demanding ethical practices and supporting companies that prioritize health over profit. Voting with our wallets, whether through boycotts or by supporting more ethical brands, can send a loud message to pharmaceutical executives that their practices matter.

Making Ethics the Bottom Line

Pharmaceutical executives have a responsibility to their customers—not just to their shareholders. Holding them accountable for unethical behavior, excessive compensation, and harmful pricing practices can help transform an industry that's built on public health and trust. By instituting compensation reform and ethical guidelines that prioritize people's lives over profits, we can reshape the pharmaceutical landscape into one that serves the public good.

After all, if a company is making billions in profit, it's not unreasonable to ask for reasonable pricing and ethical governance. And if these executives are getting paid millions to improve public health, shouldn't they actually be doing that? Let's hold them accountable for changing lives—not just their bank accounts. The real reward, after all, is in making sure that everyone has access to the medications they need at prices they can afford.

Advocate for Global Cooperation on Drug Pricing:

A Global Problem, A Global Solution

If you've ever found yourself scratching your head in disbelief at the sky-high prices of prescription drugs in the United States, or maybe shaking your fist in frustration at a pharmaceutical monopoly, you're not alone. The price of essential medicines can vary dramatically from country to country—sometimes to the point where it seems like we're living in parallel universes when it comes to access to healthcare.

In wealthier nations like the U.S., pharmaceutical companies can set sky-high prices for life-saving drugs, while in developing countries, the same drugs might be available for a fraction of the cost, often thanks to international aid or generic alternatives. This price disparity is a glaring example of global inequity in the pharmaceutical market, and it's a problem that demands a global solution.

Can we get the world to come together to fix this? It may seem ambitious, but it's not as far-fetched as it sounds. With global cooperation on drug pricing, we could ensure that essential medicines are priced fairly and equitably—so that people in both rich and poor countries have access to life-saving treatments without being financially devastated in the process.

International Price Agreements: Leveling the Playing Field

One of the major challenges in global pharmaceutical pricing is the discrepancy between what different countries pay for the same drugs. In the United States, for instance, consumers often face astronomical prices for medications that are sold at a fraction of the cost in other parts of the world, such as Canada or India. This isn't because the drugs are inherently more expensive to produce in the U.S.; it's due to a lack of price regulation and market competition.

So, what if countries came together and agreed on standardized pricing for certain essential medications? This would be game-changing.

Countries could come to an agreement that, for example, insulin, a life-saving medication for people with diabetes, should not cost more in the U.S. than it does in Mexico or Germany. This kind of international price agreement could level the playing field, ensuring that prices reflect the true cost of production—not just the profits of pharmaceutical giants.

You may be thinking, "But won't the pharmaceutical companies just fight this tooth and nail?" Well, yes, they probably will. But if governments and international organizations like the World Health Organization (WHO) coordinate their efforts, it's possible to build a framework that makes these agreements enforceable, with penalties for non-compliance.

Imagine a global drug pricing treaty, where countries collaborate to create fair pricing standards for drugs. The idea is to ensure that wealthy countries don't keep hiking up prices, while developing nations aren't left with the scraps or forced to rely on aid. Everyone, no matter where they live, could get affordable access to the medications they need. It's about global solidarity, and in a world where we are more connected than ever before, this idea is not as far-fetched as it may seem.

Patents and Access to Medicine: Intellectual Property Isn't Always the Best Idea

Let's talk about patents. Ah, patents—those little legal certificates that pharmaceutical companies use to protect their intellectual property (IP). On paper, patents are great—they reward innovation and allow companies to recoup the costs of research and development. But in practice, patents can delay access to affordable medicines, particularly in poorer countries. Big Pharma often uses patents to maintain monopolies on drugs, charging high prices by preventing generics from entering the market.

Take HIV/AIDS medications, for instance. For years, the high cost of HIV medications kept millions of people from getting the treatment they needed to survive. In some countries, the price of a year's supply of antiretroviral drugs was several thousand dollars. Meanwhile, in countries like India, generic versions were available for a fraction of the cost. But because of patent laws and the influence of large pharmaceutical corporations, these cheaper alternatives were not available in many parts of the world.

Now, imagine if the patent system were overhauled globally. Instead of allowing patents to protect monopolies, we could create a system that balances the need for innovation with the need for universal access to essential medicines. Patent pools, like the Medicines Patent Pool (MPP), have shown that this is possible. The MPP is a collaboration where pharmaceutical companies voluntarily license their patents to allow for the production of affordable generics, especially for diseases like HIV/AIDS and hepatitis C. It's a model that could be expanded globally to allow for broader access to essential drugs without sacrificing the incentive to innovate.

A Global Pharmaceutical Pricing Framework: The Case for an International Treaty

We're talking about something big here—a global pharmaceutical pricing framework. This would involve countries coming together to create a set of rules and standards for how pharmaceutical companies price their drugs. Rather than letting each country negotiate on its own or be subject to the whims of pharmaceutical giants, an international framework could create equity in the system, ensuring that people in every country have access to affordable medications.

How would this work in practice? Well, let's break it down:

Global Price Benchmarking: Countries could agree to benchmark prices for certain essential drugs against the lowest price available in other countries. For instance, if a drug is sold in the U.S. for $1,000 but is sold in Canada for $200, the U.S. could be required to set its price closer to the Canadian price.

Price Transparency and Public Disclosures: Pharmaceutical companies could be required to disclose not just the cost of manufacturing, but also the prices they charge in various markets. This would ensure that pricing is fair and transparent, and governments could use this information to regulate prices accordingly.

Subsidies for Low-Income Countries: Wealthy nations could pool resources to provide subsidies for drugs in low-income countries. This would help ensure that life-saving medications are available to people who need them most, regardless of where they live.

International Regulatory Oversight: An independent global body could be created to oversee this framework and ensure compliance. The World Trade Organization (WTO), the United Nations (UN), or even a specialized health authority could take on this role, setting and enforcing pricing standards and ensuring that countries stick to the agreement.

While creating a global treaty for pharmaceutical pricing is no small feat, the benefits would be enormous. Not only would it ensure that people across the world have access to the medications they need, but it would also create a more fair and transparent global market.

Why Does This Matter?

We live in a world where globalization means that issues in one country can quickly affect others. The pharmaceutical industry is one such issue—it doesn't matter where you are on the planet; people everywhere need access to the same medicines. However, right now, access to medications is largely dependent on where you live and how much you can afford. This is not just a health crisis—it's a moral crisis.

By pushing for international cooperation on drug pricing, we can tackle one of the biggest disparities in global healthcare today. It's not just about making drugs cheaper; it's about making them accessible to everyone, no matter their income, no matter their country. This is a cause that benefits everyone—rich or poor, developed or developing—and it's a step toward making the world a fairer place for everyone.

The global drug pricing crisis isn't something that can be solved by any single country or corporation. It's going to take global cooperation to address the systemic flaws in the pharmaceutical industry and ensure that everyone, everywhere, has access to life-saving medicines at a fair price. The solutions are out there—international agreements, patent reforms, and global frameworks—and we have the power to make them a reality.

So, let's make it happen. It's time for a global shift in how we think about pharmaceuticals. No more letting big corporations profit at the expense of people's lives. Instead, let's build a system that puts public health first, and makes sure everyone gets the medicine they need, at a price they can afford. Affordable healthcare is a global right—and the time to make that right a reality is now.

Promote Ethical Investing:

Putting Your Money Where Your Morals Are

If you've ever thought about putting your money in a retirement account or some shiny new investment opportunity, you've probably been bombarded with options. But did you know that how and where you invest could have a profound impact on industries you might care deeply about, like the pharmaceutical sector?

The concept of ethical investing isn't just about picking stocks that make you feel warm and fuzzy inside—it's about aligning your financial decisions with your personal values. It's a powerful way to encourage positive change, and guess what? The pharmaceutical industry is no exception.

Imagine for a moment, you have the chance to directly influence how pharmaceutical companies behave—without ever having to go to a protest, write a letter to your congressperson, or even stand on a soapbox shouting "We demand lower drug prices!" (though, if you do that, power to you). Instead, you can do it with a few clicks, a little research, and a bit of strategic thinking. That's the magic of ethical investing.

What Is Ethical Investing, Anyway?

In its simplest form, ethical investing (also called socially responsible investing or SRI) means putting your money into companies that align with your values and avoiding those that contribute to things you find morally questionable. For example, some investors choose to avoid industries like tobacco or firearms, while others might focus on supporting clean energy, fair labor practices or pharmaceutical companies that prioritize patients over profits.

With ethical investing, you're making a direct statement that you care about how companies operate. And with the pharmaceutical industry, this statement matters more than ever. After all, these are the companies that create life-saving medicines—and, unfortunately, sometimes price them so high that many people can't afford them. That's where your dollars come in. Your investment choices can help push the needle toward a more equitable, transparent, and patient-centered industry.

Divestment: A Powerful Tool for Change

One way ethical investing works is through divestment—essentially, selling off shares in companies that are doing more harm than good. Imagine you're holding stock in a pharmaceutical company that, let's say, has been caught price-gouging on a life-saving drug. Every time the price of that drug goes up, the company's stock goes up, and you're unknowingly profiting from people's suffering. Not exactly a good look, right?

By divesting from these companies, you're not just avoiding putting your money in a place that feels icky—you're sending a message. You're saying, "I don't support this behavior, and I'm going to vote with my wallet."

You might be wondering, "But do I really have that much power?" Well, turns out, you do! In fact, divestment has been used in numerous social movements throughout history, from the anti-apartheid movement to the climate change movement. When enough people start pulling their money out of unethical companies, the stock price goes down, and the pressure starts to build for these companies to change. It's a great way to hold big pharma accountable—without a single protest sign.

And it's not just for individuals. Institutional investors (like universities, pension funds, and even governments) have the power to influence entire industries by choosing to divest from pharmaceutical companies that exploit pricing or engage in unethical marketing practices.

Supporting Ethical Pharmaceuticals: The Good Guys of the Industry

But wait, you don't just have to sit back and passively avoid the bad guys. You can actively invest in pharmaceutical companies that are doing the right thing—those that put patients over profits, that engage in fair pricing, and that prioritize transparency in both their research and business practices.

These companies are out there! They're the ones who make life-saving treatments available at a fair price, the ones that support affordable access to medications in developing countries, and the ones that disclose their pricing structures instead of hiding them behind closed doors. By investing in these companies, you're not only putting your money to work for you—you're putting it to work for social good.

For example, companies that develop generics (which are cheaper versions of branded drugs) are often innovators in the true sense of the word. Not only do they improve access to affordable medications, but they also create healthy competition in the market, which can drive down prices for everyone. These companies may not make as much profit as their brand-name competitors, but their mission-driven approach makes them worthy of your investment.

Another example is companies that are open-source in their approach to research and development. These companies are working toward collaborative solutions to the world's biggest health problems, rather than hoarding patents for financial gain. When you invest in such companies, you're supporting a model of drug development that values public health over private profits.

Ethical Investing: Not Just a Trend, but a Movement

In recent years, ethical investing has exploded in popularity. More and more people are waking up to the idea that investing isn't just about getting rich

—it's about getting rich in a way that doesn't contribute to the world's problems. And when it comes to pharmaceuticals, this is an especially important shift.

Here are some reasons why ethical investing in the pharmaceutical industry could be your next big move:

The Moral Imperative: There's a lot of talk about how big pharma exploits patients and markets life-saving drugs at prices that are, frankly, outrageous. By investing in ethical pharmaceutical companies, you can put your money where your heart is, ensuring that the companies you support are contributing to the greater good. If you're tired of hearing about price-gouging and over-prescription, ethical investing is your chance to be part of the solution.

The Power of Consumer Choices: As an investor, you're essentially a consumer of the stock market. Just as you might opt for products that are sustainably made or ethically sourced, you can choose companies whose practices align with your values. The power of choice isn't limited to what you buy at the store—it extends to your investments, too.

It's Good for Business (Really!): Here's the kicker: ethical investing isn't just a feel-good, fluffy thing to do—it makes sense financially. Studies show that companies with strong ethical standards and social responsibility outperform their peers in the long run. Investors who prioritize sustainability and social good often see returns that are just as strong (if not better!) than those who focus solely on the bottom line. So, you can feel good and make money. Who says you can't have it all?

Global Health and Impact: The pharmaceutical industry touches millions of lives around the world. The impact of your investment choices could be far-reaching, helping to make life-saving medications more affordable and accessible in both developed and developing nations. Your money could literally be contributing to a healthier, more equitable world.

How to Get Started with Ethical Investing

Do Your Research: Start by identifying companies that align with your values. Do they have transparent pricing practices? Do they prioritize access to affordable healthcare? Are they involved in open-source research or generics development? Resources like the Ethical Investment Association or SRI Funds can help guide you toward companies that prioritize health over profits.

Look for Ethical Funds: If you don't want to pick individual stocks, you can invest in mutual funds or exchange-traded funds (ETFs) that focus on ethical businesses, including pharmaceuticals. Many funds focus on companies that meet environmental, social, and governance (ESG) criteria.

Stay Engaged: Investing ethically isn't just about buying stocks—it's about staying involved in how the companies you invest in operate. Engage with the companies through shareholder meetings or by supporting shareholder advocacy groups that push for changes in the industry.

Consult a Financial Advisor: If you're new to ethical investing, it might be worth chatting with a financial advisor who specializes in socially responsible investments. They can help you navigate the complex world of ethical investing and ensure that your portfolio reflects your values.

Putting Your Money Where Your Values Are

At the end of the day, ethical investing is about empowering yourself to make a difference in the world—while also ensuring you're making sound financial decisions. By investing in companies that prioritize transparency, fair pricing, and public health, you're helping to reshape the pharmaceutical landscape in a way that benefits everyone, not just shareholders.

So next time you're thinking about where to park your hard-earned cash, ask yourself: Is this investment helping to make the world better? Because with ethical investing, you have the power to choose—not just where your money goes, but what kind of world it helps create.

The pharmaceutical industry plays a crucial role in providing life-saving treatments and innovations, but when profit-seeking drives the pricing of essential medications to unsustainable levels, it is a moral and economic failure. Tackling this issue requires the concerted effort of governments, businesses, consumers, and civil society. Whether it's through stronger regulations, price transparency, the promotion of generics, or ethical business practices, we can create a system where public health, not private profits, is the priority. The challenge is complex, but the opportunity to reshape the pharmaceutical landscape in a way that benefits everyone — not just those at the top — is within our reach.

Theres No Place Like Home

The Housing Crisis – Where's Home?

Imagine for a second that you've just moved into a new city for a fresh start. You've found a job, gotten your bearings, and are excited about what the future holds. But there's one small problem: housing. After spending a few days scouring online listings, your optimism begins to fade. The only affordable places you can find are either tiny studios in questionable neighborhoods or apartments with walls that seem thinner than a piece of tissue paper. If you're lucky, you might find something that's "affordable" by the standards of this very city—though it's still well beyond what your paycheck would allow.

Now, picture someone else in the same scenario: maybe they're an elderly woman living on a fixed income, or a young single parent trying to make ends meet. Housing is not just a nuisance for them—it's a matter of survival, and finding a roof that doesn't cost a fortune becomes their full-time job. Unfortunately, this is the reality for millions of people in cities across the globe.

In many urban centers, housing costs are skyrocketing while wages remain stagnant, leaving a growing number of individuals and families unable to access affordable housing. As a result, homelessness and housing instability are becoming more prevalent, affecting not only those directly impacted but entire communities.

Why does this matter? Because housing is more than just a roof over your head; it's the foundation for stability, health, and social mobility. Without a stable place to live, people struggle to maintain jobs, care for their families, or even access basic services like healthcare or education. The cycle of poverty becomes more entrenched, and communities become divided between those who can afford to live comfortably and those who are left scrambling for a place to call home.

But here's the good news, change is possible, and it starts with collective action. If we want to create a more just, equitable society, we need to tackle the root causes of homelessness and housing instability—and that begins with affordable housing.

Why Affordable Housing and Homelessness Matter

The Housing Affordability Crisis: A Perfect Storm

The cost of housing has been rising steadily for decades, but recent years have seen an alarming acceleration in both prices and rents. In many cities, average rents have increased by 20% or more in just the last few years, while wages have barely budged. According to recent studies, affordable housing is defined as housing that costs no more than 30% of a household's income. Yet, in major cities like New York, San Francisco, or London, people are routinely paying over 50% of their income on rent. In other words, people are being forced to spend more than half their paycheck just to live somewhere they can barely afford.

The numbers are equally concerning when it comes to purchasing homes. Housing prices, especially in urban areas, have surged dramatically. The cost of buying a home in places like Silicon Valley or Manhattan is out of reach for all but the wealthiest individuals. As a result, many people who are unable to buy a home are locked out of the market altogether, while others are left with no choice but to rent—if they can find something within their price range.

This affordability gap isn't a coincidence—it's a symptom of a larger systemic issue. A lack of affordable housing stock, coupled with an influx of wealthier individuals and gentrification, is exacerbating the situation. For example, developers often opt to build luxury condos in areas that are being rapidly gentrified, rather than affordable housing. The result is a shrinking pool of affordable options and a growing population of people pushed further to the margins.

This isn't just about the individuals who are struggling to pay rent or find a home. It's about the entire community. When large groups of people are priced out of the housing market, it leads to an increase in homelessness and displacement, which puts pressure on social services, healthcare systems, and local economies. Cities begin to look like a patchwork of luxury apartments surrounded by tent cities, with no sense of connection or community between the two.

The Ripple Effect:

How Lack of Housing Affects Other Aspects of Life

Affordable housing, or the lack thereof, is not just a housing issue. It's an issue that touches virtually every part of life—from health to education, social mobility, and even the overall well-being of communities. In fact, housing instability doesn't just have a few ripple effects—it sends out shockwaves that affect every other aspect of life in profound ways. Imagine dropping a stone into a pond and watching the ripples spread out. The stone is homelessness and housing insecurity; the ripples are everything else.

Health: Not Just a Roof, But a Foundation for Well-Being

Let's start with the obvious, health. When people don't have a stable place to live, their health often suffers in ways that go beyond the physical toll of being homeless. A roof might keep the rain off your head, but it doesn't do much to protect your mental and emotional well-being. Stable housing is foundational to physical health, too.

Here's how housing insecurity impacts health in many interconnected ways:

1. Mental Health Challenges

Living without a stable home is a mental and emotional strain. Think about it: how can anyone thrive when they're constantly worried about where they'll sleep tonight or if they'll have a roof over their head next month? Housing instability can lead to anxiety, depression, and feelings of hopelessness. These emotions are often amplified by the societal stigma that comes with homelessness. Feeling isolated, ashamed, or unsupported can have long-term impacts on mental health.

On a biological level, stress itself can cause a cascade of negative health effects: increased cortisol (the stress hormone), sleep deprivation, and weakened immune systems. Over time, chronic stress can exacerbate existing mental health conditions or create new ones, leading to a cycle that's difficult to break.

2. Chronic Physical Illnesses

Without a stable home, individuals are more likely to face serious chronic health conditions that go untreated. Without access to a kitchen or regular meals, nutrition becomes a critical issue. Instead of a balanced diet, many people experiencing housing instability rely on fast food, food banks, or even skip meals altogether. Malnutrition weakens the body's immune system, leaving individuals more susceptible to infections and illnesses like respiratory infections, diabetes, and cardiovascular diseases.

Additionally, the lack of consistent access to healthcare is a huge concern. Homeless individuals often don't have regular access to doctors, let alone the medications or therapies they need. A minor health issue that could be easily treated with proper care becomes a serious condition when left unchecked, leading to hospital visits that could have been avoided. Emergency rooms, not primary care doctors, become the de facto healthcare system for many people without stable housing.

3. Exposure to the Elements

Let's not forget the weather—which in many parts of the world can be an unforgiving adversary. Homeless individuals are exposed to extreme conditions: the cold of winter, the blistering heat of summer, rain, and sometimes even dangerous storms. This can result in hypothermia, heat stroke, and other weather-related conditions that drastically affect health. Simply being exposed to harsh elements can cause long-term damage, from respiratory issues to frostbite. And since many of these individuals do not have access to hygiene facilities, they are also at higher risk for infection and skin conditions.

4. The Vicious Cycle of Poor Health and Homelessness

When you're struggling with your health, it's hard to work. When you can't work, it's hard to afford housing. And when you don't have housing, your health continues to decline. It's a vicious cycle, one that's incredibly difficult to break. Without stable housing, it's nearly impossible to focus on self-care—whether that means going to the doctor, eating well, exercising, or simply sleeping soundly. All of these factors contribute to the long-term struggles people face when trying to regain stability.

Education: The House That Learning Built (Or Didn't)
Next, we move to education—which is essentially the gateway to a brighter future. But what happens when the gateway is locked, not because the kid doesn't have potential, but because they don't have a place to live?

1. School Absenteeism

Children who lack stable housing are more likely to miss school. Imagine trying to study for a test or finish homework when you're unsure where you'll sleep that night. When your family is forced to move frequently due to housing instability, kids end up missing valuable school days. Chronic absenteeism means missing out on learning opportunities, which can lead to falling behind academically. In fact, a recent study found that students in unstable housing situations were twice as likely to miss school compared to their peers.

2. Mental and Emotional Strain on Children

The emotional strain of not having a permanent home also impacts a child's ability to focus in class. The psychological burden of housing insecurity can lead to difficulty with attention, concentration, and memory. For children, these challenges make it even harder to keep up with lessons or develop the foundational skills they need for future success. Additionally, when kids are concerned about their living situation, their mental health suffers, which can result in increased anxiety, depression, and behavioral issues.

For children who grow up in an environment where housing instability is common, it can also affect their sense of identity and self-worth. Being constantly uprooted can create feelings of uncertainty, fear, and a lack of control over their own lives, all of which can undermine their confidence and self-esteem.

3. Lower Graduation Rates

The culmination of all of these struggles—absenteeism, emotional distress, and lack of focus—often leads to lower graduation rates. In many cases, kids living in unstable housing situations may drop out of school to help support their families or because they've fallen too far behind to catch up. Without an education, these young people are locked out of better opportunities and are more likely to experience poverty and homelessness as adults.

Social Mobility: The Unclimbable Ladder

Housing insecurity also undermines social mobility—the ability to improve one's socio-economic position through education, work, and other opportunities. Without stable housing, it's nearly impossible to move up the economic ladder.

1. Employment Challenges

Stable housing is critical to maintaining steady employment. Employers are more likely to hire someone who has a stable address and can show up to work regularly, without the risk of needing to take time off due to an unstable housing situation. For someone without a permanent address, even the basics of applying for a job—filling out forms, going to interviews, or showing up consistently—can become daunting obstacles.

Additionally, those struggling to afford housing may need to work multiple low-wage jobs, which can be physically exhausting and leave little time for career advancement, further education, or networking. And without a stable address or phone number, it's hard to connect with potential employers or access job opportunities in the first place.

2. Stuck in a Cycle of Poverty

The lack of affordable housing means that people are often stuck in neighborhoods with few resources. These communities might have high unemployment rates, underfunded schools, and limited access to services like childcare or healthcare. When individuals are confined to these areas, they can find it incredibly difficult to escape poverty. Without housing that allows for mobility, families are trapped in a cycle of poverty that spans generations.

3. Limited Access to Social Services

Without a permanent address, people are often denied access to vital social services. Things like government assistance programs, health insurance, and food stamps require an address. When someone is experiencing homelessness or housing instability, these programs may be harder to access, which exacerbates the financial and emotional burdens they face. It's hard to pull yourself out of poverty if the very systems that are supposed to help you are difficult to access.

Community Well-Being: A Fragmented Society

The impact of housing instability is not just individual—it affects entire communities. As people are displaced from their homes, neighborhoods become fragmented, and the social fabric that holds communities together starts to erode.

1. Displacement and Gentrification

When people are displaced from their homes due to rising housing costs, gentrification, or lack of affordable housing, the neighborhood suffers. Long-standing community connections are disrupted, and people are often forced to relocate to areas far from their support networks. This creates a divide between wealthier residents and those struggling with housing instability. What was once a diverse and vibrant community becomes a patchwork of enclaves, where access to resources, opportunities, and social services is unequal.

2. Social Isolation and Stigma

Homelessness, in particular, leads to a deep sense of social isolation. When individuals lose their homes, they are often cut off from their community and from society at large. The stigma of being homeless can lead to feelings of shame and alienation, making it difficult to reintegrate into social networks or access support systems. Without social connections, people are less likely to regain their stability, and communities lose the diversity and richness that come with a mixture of people from different backgrounds.

How to Improve: Concrete Steps Toward a Solution

Let's be real, solving homelessness and the housing affordability crisis is not going to be a quick fix. If only there were a magic wand to wave and solve the problem overnight! But here's the good news: there are practical, achievable solutions. While the challenge is vast, a combination of policy changes, community engagement, and targeted investments can make a huge difference. The key is making housing a priority—not just as a problem to fix, but as an opportunity to transform communities, support families, and build a fairer, more equitable society. Let's explore how we can all be part of the solution.

1. Supporting Affordable Housing Initiatives: Building More Homes for More People

Let's start with the obvious, we need more affordable housing. There's no sugarcoating it: there simply aren't enough affordable homes for the people who need them. So, how do we increase supply? Here are some concrete steps that can create more affordable options for people who need them the most.

A. Government Funding: Invest in Building Housing for All

Governments at the local, state, and federal levels have a critical role to play. For starters, we need public funding to build more affordable housing units. While the private market can only do so much—especially when profits are the top priority—public funds can help bridge the gap. Governments can allocate money for new housing projects, particularly those focused on low-income families and individuals.

This could include a mix of subsidized housing programs where rents are set at a rate that's affordable for people earning below the median income, or direct investment in public housing projects, similar to what many countries have done (and not just the U.S.). In places like Singapore and Vienna, governments have demonstrated that providing affordable housing doesn't just make economic sense—it creates stronger, healthier, and more vibrant communities.

It's not a dream. It's a proven model, and it can work in more places.

B. Incentivizing Private Developers: The 'If You Build It, They Will Come' Principle

Here's where things get a little tricky, developers often shy away from affordable housing because it doesn't yield high profits.

Understandably, it's hard to get a real estate developer excited about a project that won't make them a boatload of cash. But what if governments could offer tax incentives or zoning variances to encourage developers to build affordable housing?

One way to do this is through mixed-income housing. This involves integrating affordable units into larger developments that also include luxury apartments or condos. The idea is to create a balanced neighborhood where people of different income levels live side by side, which reduces social segregation. Developers might be more willing to include affordable units if they're able to make some money on higher-priced units.

Imagine this, a luxury condo building, but with affordable units on every floor—the best of both worlds. The penthouse owner can live next door to someone paying a fraction of the price for a smaller apartment, and it's all thanks to well-structured policy incentives. It's a win-win.

C. Rent Subsidies and Vouchers: Bridging the Gap

The cost of rent keeps going up, but wages? Not so much. The disparity between income and rent has left many families on the brink of homelessness. Housing vouchers and rent subsidies can help close this gap. Programs like the Section 8 Housing Choice Voucher Program are already in place in many areas and allow low-income individuals and families to pay a portion of their rent, while the government helps cover the rest.

This system can be expanded and streamlined to help even more people—especially as rent prices continue to rise. Vouchers allow people to rent homes in the private market without being crushed by skyrocketing rents. As a result, these programs don't just keep families housed—they give people choice and dignity, enabling them to live in decent homes without the constant threat of eviction.

2. Rent Control and Stabilization: Making Sure No One Gets Left Behind

Rent control policies often have a bad rap, but here's the thing: they're not just a landlord nightmare—they're a tenant lifesaver. Sure, some argue that rent control discourages investment in the housing market, but many experts believe it's essential for keeping vulnerable tenants from being priced out of their homes.

A. Preventing Displacement

In rapidly gentrifying neighborhoods, rent hikes are a major cause of displacement. As neighborhoods become more desirable, landlords hike up rents, often pushing out long-time residents who can no longer afford to live there. Rent control can prevent this by capping rent increases at reasonable levels. Imagine a grandma who has lived in her apartment for 30 years—without rent control, she could be priced out of her home by an unreasonably high rent hike. But with rent control, she can keep her apartment, live in peace, and continue to be part of the community she helped build.

B. Protecting the Most Vulnerable: Seniors, Disabled, and Low-Income Renters

Some of the most vulnerable groups—seniors, people with disabilities, and low-income tenants—are often the ones who suffer most from rising rents. Rent control offers these individuals a safety net to help them stay in their homes, even if they are on fixed incomes or struggling financially. Without rent control, they could be forced to choose between paying rent or affording food and medicine. Rent stabilization can ease this pressure and make life more manageable.

C. Keeping Neighborhoods Stable

Rent control is not just about protecting tenants; it's about stabilizing neighborhoods as a whole. Without rent control, neighborhoods can experience rapid turnover, with long-time residents replaced by higher-income newcomers. This leads to social fragmentation—neighbors don't know each other, community ties weaken, and the neighborhood's unique identity can be lost. Rent control, however, helps preserve the character of a neighborhood, allowing long-term residents to stay and maintain the fabric of their communities.

3. Zoning Reforms: Rewriting the Rules to Build More Homes

Zoning laws are one of the most restrictive barriers to affordable housing development. Traditional zoning codes often prioritize single-family homes and luxury condos, while making it illegal to build much-needed multi-family housing, particularly in desirable areas. These zoning restrictions increase housing scarcity, driving prices up and leaving many people with fewer affordable options.

A. Relaxing Zoning Laws: Let's Build, Baby!

It's time to rewrite the rules. By relaxing zoning regulations, cities can open up more land for affordable housing development. For example, allowing multi-family buildings (like apartment complexes or townhomes) in areas that are currently zoned for single-family homes can dramatically increase housing supply. If cities create more space for developers to build affordable units, they can lower prices across the board.

B. Encouraging Density: More Homes on Less Land

Cities don't have an infinite supply of land, especially in highly sought-after areas. But they do have the opportunity to build vertically. Higher-density developments (like apartment buildings or condo complexes) allow more homes to be built in smaller spaces. This helps create more housing in urban areas, reducing the pressure on suburban sprawl and allowing people to live closer to public transportation, jobs, and services.

C. Incentivizing Affordable Housing Development: Sweetening the Pot

To encourage developers to prioritize affordable housing, cities can offer incentives such as tax breaks, reduced fees, and expedited permitting processes for affordable housing projects. The idea is to make it easier (and more profitable) for developers to include affordable units in their projects. This could be in the form of density bonuses, which allow developers to build more units in exchange for setting aside some of those units as affordable housing.

4. Increasing Public Awareness and Community Engagement: Changing the Narrative

Homelessness and housing affordability are issues that can sometimes seem distant or abstract to those who aren't personally affected. That's why public education and community involvement are so critical to creating change.

A. Public Education Campaigns: Shifting Perceptions

Too often, the issue of homelessness is misunderstood. People think it's simply a matter of personal failure or poor decision-making, rather than a systemic problem tied to poverty, rising rents, and lack of affordable housing. Public education campaigns can help reframe the narrative, showing people that homelessness is an issue that affects all of us—and that solutions like affordable housing, rent control, and increased government investment can help everyone.

B. Community-Led Solutions: Empowering Local Voices

The best solutions come from those who are directly affected by the housing crisis. Community-led housing initiatives—like community land trusts, cooperative housing, and affordable housing advocacy groups—allow residents to have a say in the decision-making process. When communities are involved in designing and building housing solutions, the outcomes are more likely to meet their needs and be sustainable.

It's like the old adage: "If you want something done right, do it yourself." Empowering local communities to be part of the solution leads to more effective, inclusive housing projects.

Breaking the Cycle

The lack of affordable housing doesn't just affect the individuals who are struggling—it ripples out and affects entire families, neighborhoods, and societies. From health issues to education challenges, social mobility, and the well-being of communities, housing insecurity creates a cycle that's difficult to break.

But here's the silver lining, tackling the housing crisis, creating more affordable housing, and improving access to stable homes can have a transformative effect on health, education, and social mobility. When people have access to affordable housing, they can begin to break the cycles of poverty, improve their quality of life, and build the foundation for a better future for themselves and their families.

A home is not just a place to live—it's the key to unlocking a better life. And when we invest in affordable housing, we're not just putting up walls and roofs—we're building stronger communities and creating a brighter future for everyone.

So let's make sure that when we think about housing, we don't just think about a place to sleep—we think about the opportunities it can create for health, education, work, and a better tomorrow.

Public Transportation

Underfunding Public Transportation and High Auto Insurance Rates Are Literally Driving Us Further Into The Wealth Gap

Let's face it, in today's world, getting from point A to point B is not as simple as hopping on a bus or a bike. It's more like navigating a labyrinth of expensive choices: do you shell out a chunk of your paycheck for car insurance, or do you roll the dice and pray your 20-year-old car doesn't break down on the way to work? Or—if you're lucky enough to live in a city with public transportation—do you pray your bus is actually on time for once?

This dilemma is not just an inconvenience—it's a serious driver of inequality in America. When we talk about the wealth gap, we often focus on issues like wages, education, or healthcare. But transportation—specifically the lack of affordable, reliable options—is a huge factor that often goes overlooked. So, let's take a ride through this issue, with a few detours to make it fun (and let's be real, you deserve a little comic relief).

Car Ownership: The "American Dream" That Costs a Lot More Than You Think

So, you live in the suburbs or a rural area, and you need a car. Why? Because if you want to get anywhere—like, say, work or a doctor's appointment—public transit is about as reliable as that one cousin who "always says they'll show up but never does." So, you go out and buy a car. Easy, right? Well, no.

First, there's the sticker price. Cha-ching. Then there's the maintenance —those tires aren't going to rotate themselves. And don't forget gas, tolls, and the parking tickets that will inevitably follow if you ever forget to read the "No Parking" sign (we've all been there). But perhaps the biggest kicker is auto insurance. Depending on where you live, your driving history, and your car's color (yes, apparently that's a thing), you could be paying anywhere from $1,500 to $2,000 a year for insurance. For many low-income workers, that's a substantial chunk of their paycheck.

Auto insurance premiums discriminate, especially against people of color and low-income communities. If you live in a zip code that's considered "high-risk" (often a euphemism for low-income or predominantly Black or Latino neighborhoods), your premiums are sky-high, regardless of your actual driving record. Talk about a financial kick in the teeth.

The Public Transportation Problem: It's More Like "Public Non-Transportation"

Public transportation is supposed to be the great equalizer. It's supposed to be a cheap, reliable way to get to work or go grocery shopping without selling your kidney to afford gas. But if you've ever been late for a meeting because your bus arrived 30 minutes late, or stood in the rain waiting for a train that never showed up, you know that's not always the case. And don't even get us started on cities where buses are about as frequent as a solar eclipse.

And in rural areas? Forget it. Public transit is almost a mythical concept, like unicorns or a quiet toddler in a restaurant. If you live outside a major city, you're basically looking at a choice between buying a car or having a complete social and economic isolation experience. Need to get to that better-paying job 10 miles away? Well, better start saving for a car. And good luck getting anywhere if your only option is walking or hitching a ride with a neighbor who doesn't have gas money either.

When public transportation isn't available, people are left to rely on expensive car ownership, perpetuating the cycle of financial strain. That's bad enough. But what really makes the wealth gap worse is that transportation is essential to economic mobility. Without reliable ways to get to work, school, or doctor's appointments, low-income people can't access the opportunities they need to get ahead. It's the kind of thing that's hard to measure but still drives the divide between rich and poor.

The Wealth Gap: A Mile (or 20) Wide

The bottom line is this: when transportation options are limited and expensive, people's ability to work, save, and invest is severely restricted. And when you don't have access to good-paying jobs or the resources to keep those jobs (thanks to the car payment or insurance bill), it's hard to get ahead.

Now throw in the fact that communities of color are more likely to live in areas with poor public transit and higher car insurance rates, and it's clear that these transportation issues aren't just inconvenient—they're discriminatory. The playing field isn't level. And when transportation costs take up a huge chunk of your income, you don't have much left to put into savings, retirement, or other wealth-building activities. So let's talk about how we can fix this situation.

1. More Funding for Public Transit: Let's Fix That Bus Schedule

Let's start with the obvious solution, more funding for public transportation. Cities and states need to massively invest in upgrading public transit networks, especially in underserved areas. Buses and trains should run more frequently and be more reliable (maybe even show up on time once in a while). The best way to do this is through long-term investment in infrastructure, as well as partnerships with tech companies to create more efficient, on-demand services (think: a Lyft for the bus). Imagine a future where you can use an app to book your seat on a bus that picks you up right outside your door instead of waiting at a sketchy bus stop.

2. Affordable Auto Insurance: No More Pay-to-Play

Next, let's talk about those auto insurance premiums. It's high time we fix the discrimination built into the system. We need to outlaw practices that use zip codes and race to set rates. Insurance should be about driving behavior and actual risk—not where you live. Additionally, more state-level regulations should be put in place to ensure that auto insurance is affordable for everyone, particularly for low-income families.

3. Self-Driving Cars: The Future Is (Almost) Now

Now, hold on to your steering wheel because here's where things get futuristic. Self-driving cars could be a game-changer, especially for those who can't afford to buy and maintain their own vehicles. Imagine a network of autonomous cars that you can hail through an app, just like Uber. These cars would be cheaper than traditional rideshare because they wouldn't have a driver to pay. They'd also help reduce traffic congestion, which means getting places faster. While we're not quite there yet with full autonomy (thanks, tech companies, for still ironing out the kinks), this could radically change how we think about transportation.

4. Intercity Electric Community Cars: Sharing Is Caring

Why should I own a car when I can rent one for a few hours? Enter the world of electric community cars. Imagine city-run electric cars that residents can rent by the hour. These cars would be low-cost, environmentally friendly, and available for everyone who needs them. Think of it like a public library, but for cars. People could use them for commuting, grocery runs, or even weekend trips, all without the hefty cost of ownership. And guess what? They don't need to pollute the air while doing it.

5. Bikes and Scooters: Two Wheels, One Solution

For short trips, we don't need cars at all. Bike-sharing programs and electric scooters are already making waves in cities around the world, and they're a fast, green, and affordable way to get around. Why not expand this model? Imagine a future where you can hop on a scooter for $1 to get to work or school, instead of waiting for a bus that's perpetually late. Plus, they're great for the environment (and for avoiding traffic). And hey, if you're lucky, you might even get a few extra calories burned in the process.

6. Regional High-Speed Rails: The Train to a More Connected Future

What if you could wake up in Chicago, have breakfast, and then hop on a train that whisks you to St. Louis in just a couple of hours. Or, you grab a cup of coffee in Los Angeles and, before you know it, you're meeting clients in San Francisco, skipping the hours of gridlock and the stress of airport security. This isn't some sci-fi daydream—it's the future we could build with regional high-speed rail systems.

In countries like Japan and France, high-speed trains are already a staple of everyday life, moving people between cities at lightning speeds (think 300+ km/h or 186 mph). But in the United States? We're still stuck in the 20th century with planes and cars as our primary modes of intercity travel. High-speed rail—especially between major urban centers—is an opportunity we've largely missed, and it's time to change that.

Why High-Speed Rail is a Game Changer

The U.S. is massively underdeveloped when it comes to regional high-speed rail, especially in comparison to other developed nations. But why is this so important? Here's the case for high-speed rail:

Faster Than Driving, Cheaper Than Flying: High-speed rail is a viable, cost-effective alternative to both driving and flying, especially when you consider the stress and hidden costs of air travel (airport parking fees, baggage fees, and those $18 sandwiches). You can catch a train, work or relax while traveling, and show up at your destination feeling less like a jetlagged zombie and more like someone who just made a smart decision.

No More Traffic Nightmares: In cities like Los Angeles, where traffic can make you feel like you're trapped in a slow-motion car chase, a high-speed rail system would be a game changer. Imagine traveling between L.A. and San Francisco in about 2 hours, instead of enduring a 7-hour drive or suffering through the chaos of airports. High-speed rail would relieve congestion on highways, ease the pressure on airlines, and take millions of cars off the road, reducing carbon emissions and cutting down on the urban sprawl caused by excessive reliance on cars.

Economic Boost for Smaller Cities: High-speed rail isn't just for the big cities—small and mid-sized towns can benefit as well. By connecting regional hubs with major urban centers, smaller cities like Kansas City, Birmingham, and Cincinnati could see a surge in tourism, business investment, and job opportunities. This could make these cities even more attractive places to live and work, helping to balance out the current urban-rural divide.

Sustainable Transportation: If we're serious about tackling climate change, transitioning from car and air travel to electric-powered trains is a major step forward. High-speed rail produces significantly fewer greenhouse gas emissions than cars or airplanes, making it a far greener option. Plus, many countries have already demonstrated that it's entirely possible to run high-speed trains on renewable energy, making them a win for both the environment and your carbon footprint.

The Need for Investment: It's Time to Catch Up

High-speed rail isn't just an idea—it's a pressing need. But, to make it a reality in the U.S., we need massive investment in infrastructure. Right now, the federal government spends billions on highways and airports, but we're lagging behind when it comes to rail. The 2021 infrastructure bill did allocate some funds for rail development, but it's only a small portion of what's needed.

The good news is that there's growing momentum for change. Several states, like California and Texas, have already started planning and building high-speed rail systems. California's Central Valley high-speed rail is a key example of how regional systems can help connect more densely populated areas and encourage sustainable transportation options. And in Texas, the proposed Dallas-to-Houston high-speed rail line could take just 90 minutes, compared to the 4-hour drive.

We also have to look beyond just building the rails themselves. Creating a seamless travel experience—with affordable, reliable schedules, easy transfers between cities, and connectivity to local public transportation networks—is key. High-speed rail needs to be a practical, hassle-free alternative to flying or driving, not just another niche service that only appeals to a small segment of the population.

The Future of Regional Travel: Let's Get Moving

When you think about it, high-speed rail is the kind of infrastructure that could totally reshape the way we live and work. Instead of treating cities as isolated bubbles, we could create a web of connected communities where people are no longer limited by their geography. Jobs, businesses, and opportunities could be more accessible, and regional inequalities could be bridged. High-speed rail could make it possible for people to live in affordable areas and still have access to the opportunities of larger urban centers.

In a country where time is money, high-speed rail offers a more efficient, sustainable, and equitable way to travel. Plus, it's way less stressful than flying or getting stuck in traffic. Imagine sitting back, watching the landscape zoom past, and knowing you're not just making your commute—you're helping to reduce the wealth gap and improve the environment, too.

So, what are we waiting for? It's time to stop talking about high-speed rail and start building it. Let's stop being the country that lags behind and start becoming the country that leads. And if we can do that while making commuting a whole lot less miserable? Well, that's just the high-speed cherry on top.

Let's Close the Gap and Drive Toward a Better Future

Transportation isn't just about moving from point A to point B—it's about creating opportunity. When we make transportation more affordable and accessible, we give people the freedom to reach better jobs, education, and healthcare, which in turn helps narrow the wealth gap.

By investing in public transit, regulating insurance rates, and embracing new technologies like self-driving cars and electric bikes, we can transform the way we move and live. So let's stop treating transportation like a luxury and start seeing it as a basic right that should be available to all—no matter how much money you make or where you live.

And remember, a world with less traffic, lower insurance rates, and faster public transit isn't just a nice dream. It's a road we can actually drive down.

Corporate Greed In Essential Services

The Ethics of Profiting Off of Necessities

The privatization of essential services—water, energy, education, and healthcare—has become one of the most debated ethical issues of the modern era. Essentially, we're talking about turning things that should be accessible to everyone into commodities for profit. In a world where every household needs access to clean water or electricity to survive, is it ethical to let private corporations control these basic necessities? Should the pursuit of profit govern our ability to live with dignity and security?

The Rise of Privatization:

What Does It Mean for Public Goods?

In simple terms, privatization refers to the process where governments sell public assets (like water systems, schools, or energy grids) to private companies, or allow private companies to take over the delivery of these services. The idea is that businesses, driven by competition, can provide these services more efficiently and cost-effectively than government-run programs

In theory, this sounds plausible. Efficiency and competition—who doesn't love that? Except... as we've seen in practice, things tend to go sideways when profit becomes the driving force behind the delivery of something as fundamental as clean water or energy.

Water Privatization: Liquid Gold?

Water, we need it to drink, cook, clean, bathe, and, you know, survive. It's arguably the most essential resource on Earth—without it, life doesn't exist. And yet, in a shocking twist of irony, this life-sustaining resource is increasingly being privatized, turning it into a commodity that is controlled by corporations. As if it weren't enough that we already pay for our bottled water, it turns out, water itself has become a goldmine for some of the world's largest companies.

Let's take a deeper dive into the issue of water privatization—and how it turns something as basic as drinking water into a luxury.

1. The Nestlé Water Wars: Bottled for Profit

Let's start with Nestlé, the global food and beverage giant that has been at the center of controversy over its groundwater extraction practices. In places like California and Michigan, Nestlé has been accused of extracting large quantities of groundwater—sometimes during drought conditions—bottling it up, and selling it for a profit. In fact, Nestlé has been referred to as the "Water Pirate" for its efforts to take water from public sources, often without sufficient oversight or respect for local water needs.

Nestlé operates numerous bottled water brands, like Poland Spring and Pure Life, which are sold across the globe. Yet, many communities near Nestlé's extraction points, particularly in areas suffering from water scarcity, have found themselves without access to sufficient clean water. The problem isn't just that Nestlé is bottling water from local sources—it's that the profits from these sales often don't go back into the community, but into the pockets of shareholders and executives.

In 2017, Nestlé agreed to sell its North American bottled water business for nearly $4.3 billion to private equity firms, but the damage had already been done. The company faced ongoing protests from local communities who argued that their access to water was being exploited for profit, leaving them without enough water during droughts or times of scarcity. Nestlé's operations in places like Michigan and California, where water resources are already stretched thin, have drawn sharp criticism for exacerbating water shortages.

Meanwhile, Nestlé's bottled water prices often make you wonder whether you're paying for water or buying liquid gold. A bottle of Poland Spring can cost anywhere from $1.50 to $3, even though the company is essentially taking water from local aquifers—water that, in many cases, belongs to the public.

2. Flint, Michigan: The Privatization Failures on Full Display

Then there's Flint, Michigan, a city that is still grappling with water contamination issues years after its infamous water crisis. For those who don't remember, in 2014, the city switched its water source from Detroit's water system to the Flint River as a cost-saving measure. The result? Lead contamination that poisoned thousands of residents. Despite years of public outcry and government promises to fix the problem, Flint's water is still not entirely safe to drink, and residents are still facing serious health problems.

The Flint crisis was not only about mismanagement and government failures but also about the privatization of water. The private companies involved, like Veolia, were tasked with managing the water system and were found to have failed to ensure the water's safety, leading to one of the most devastating public health crises in recent U.S. history.

At the same time, while Flint residents have had to battle for clean water for years, corporations that privatize water services are not accountable for making sure the water is safe or affordable. In fact, when water services are privatized, costs tend to rise, and the quality of service tends to decline. Privatization, in theory, is meant to improve efficiency—but when water is controlled by a company whose primary goal is profit, residents get stuck paying more for worse service.

Flint's water crisis exemplifies how privatization of an essential resource like water creates an environment where basic human rights are subordinated to corporate interests. People in Flint can't afford to pay for bottled water—yet they're still paying for the poisoned water that comes out of their taps. The disconnect between profit-driven companies and basic human needs couldn't be clearer.

3. Rivers Dammed, Communities Droughted: Corporate Control of Fresh Water

The privatization of water extends beyond just bottled water and municipal systems. The issue of damning rivers for hydroelectric power has profound implications on water access, particularly for indigenous populations and rural communities. Dams built to generate power for private corporations and urban areas often have a devastating impact on surrounding ecosystems and the people who rely on those rivers for their livelihood.

In places like the Amazon Rainforest, the Colorado River, and even here in the U.S. along the Mississippi, river damming has led to water shortages in downstream communities. The diversion of rivers for hydroelectric plants, industrial use, or agricultural purposes has created droughts, leaving some communities with little to no access to water for drinking, farming, or everyday needs.

One of the most devastating effects of this is felt by indigenous communities, many of whom have had to fight for decades just to retain control over their traditional water sources. Indigenous peoples in places like the Ganges River, the Murray-Darling Basin in Australia, and in the Southwest U.S. are often left with little access to clean water, despite being some of the most water-dependent populations in the world.

For example, Native American reservations, particularly those in the Southwest U.S., experience severe water shortages as their water sources are often either privatized or overused by agricultural and industrial operations. In Arizona, Native American tribes like the Navajo Nation have to drive hours every day to get access to clean drinking water, often from distant wells or government water stations. In stark contrast, urban areas and corporate farms have direct access to water sources, yet the government has done little to address the needs of indigenous communities.

4. The Human Cost: Access to Water as a Luxury, Not a Right

As access to water becomes more and more corporatized, the impact on vulnerable communities is undeniable. Water, once considered a basic human right, is rapidly becoming a luxury for those who can afford it. This creates a two-tier system where the wealthy and corporations can pay for water, while the poor—especially those in underserved or rural areas—are left to scramble for clean water.

This means that, for many, clean water isn't a given anymore. It's a commodity that is controlled by a few corporations—and that doesn't bode well for public health or economic equality.

In the case of Flint, and places like Detroit, where water services have been privatized or underfunded, water costs have skyrocketed. As a result, many people are now paying higher rates for water that is unsafe to drink—yet they have no choice but to continue paying, because they cannot live without water. Meanwhile, Nestlé continues to extract water from places like Michigan, California, and Oregon, paying almost nothing for the water they bottle and sell for a profit. In some cases, Nestlé and other bottlers don't even have to pay taxes on the water they use, leaving local communities stuck with the bill—while corporate profits soar.

5. Water as the New Gold: The Moral and Ethical Costs

So, what's the endgame? A world where water, the lifeblood of humanity, is increasingly controlled by corporations, and access to it depends not on the basic need for survival but on the ability to pay. When corporate interests take over, clean water becomes a luxury—like a high-end designer handbag, only it's a lot more crucial to your day-to-day existence.

The ultimate irony? In some places, you could end up paying more for water than you would for beer. This isn't just inconvenient; it's a moral disaster. People shouldn't have to worry about whether they can afford water—yet that's the reality in many places, especially where water rights are held by private corporations.

The Thirst for Justice

The privatization of water isn't just a business decision—it's a human rights issue. When access to clean, affordable water is restricted by private corporations, it deepens inequality and undermines public health. While companies like Nestlé bottle water and sell it for a profit, people in places like Flint and the Navajo Nation continue to fight for the basic right to clean water.

We need a world where water—that most basic of human needs—remains in the hands of the people, not the corporations. Because when water is treated like liquid gold, it's the people who are left thirsty.

Energy: Powering Profits, Not People

Let's get down to the dirty truth about energy: it's a basic necessity—one that powers your home, your workplace, your appliances, and yes, your TikTok obsession (we know you're scrolling). And yet, for millions of Americans, energy costs are skyrocketing, while the infrastructure that delivers this power remains outdated and crumbling. Why? Because energy companies are primarily driven by one thing: profit. And to keep their profits high, they keep raising rates—quarter after quarter—while offering nothing in return to consumers except higher bills.

It's not just that energy rates are climbing; it's that prices have been rising drastically with little to no improvement in service or infrastructure. Let's break this down and look at how energy companies continue to rake in profits, pay massive bonuses to their CEOs, and actively block greener, more sustainable energy practices—all while leaving consumers stuck paying the price.

1. Rising Energy Prices: When Your Bill is Bigger Than Your Rent

You've probably noticed it in your own monthly utility bill—rising energy rates. According to the U.S. Energy Information Administration (EIA), between 2000 and 2020, electricity prices for consumers increased by about 45%, and natural gas prices rose even higher in some regions. While you're getting your electric bill every month, your local energy company is getting fat off of it.

Now these price hikes often come quarter after quarter. Every few months, your energy provider hikes the rates under the guise of "necessary cost adjustments" or "increased fuel costs." And yet, despite this constant price inflation, the service that consumers receive seems to stay stagnant, at best, or get worse, at worst. Power outages? No problem, your bill is still going up. Cracked infrastructure? Hey, you still have to pay for it.

So where does all the extra money go? Well, let's follow the money:

Corporate Profits and CEO Salaries

The CEOs of many energy companies are among the highest-paid executives in the country. A prime example is Darren W. Woods, CEO of ExxonMobil, who made nearly $23 million in 2022, despite the company making record profits (which, for the record, was around $55 billion in 2022). But it's not just oil and gas companies—the same trend is happening with electric utilities.

For instance, Pacific Gas and Electric (PG&E), a major utility in California, has been criticized for its role in devastating wildfires, but that hasn't stopped its executives from pocketing large salaries and bonuses. In fact, PG&E's CEO, Patricia Poppe, earned $10 million in total compensation in 2022, despite the company's financial troubles and history of catastrophic mismanagement. PG&E has even had to file for bankruptcy twice in recent years, yet its executives continue to earn hefty bonuses while ordinary people face blackouts, fires, and unsustainable utility rates.

So, the story is clear, energy companies keep raising rates to increase their bottom lines, while their executives rake in enormous salaries and bonuses. But for you, the consumer, the only thing you get in return is an increased energy bill and unreliable service. That's a pretty raw deal, don't you think?

The Infrastructure Ruse:

No Updates, Just Price Hikes

Now, let's talk about the infrastructure, because this is where the scam gets truly offensive. Energy companies regularly hike their prices by claiming they need the additional funds to "modernize infrastructure"—to build new power plants, improve transmission lines, and update aging equipment. But here's the thing: the infrastructure is still falling apart, and there's little sign that consumers are seeing any tangible improvements.

Take Texas, for example, which was hit hard by the winter storm in February 2021. Millions of Texans were left without power for days, and many people lost access to heat and water, leading to deaths and widespread suffering. While the energy companies were busy raising rates before the storm (and continuing to raise them after), they had failed to invest in winterizing infrastructure or improving grid reliability. Texas has some of the highest electricity rates in the nation, and yet their grid was woefully underprepared for a winter freeze. So, where did the money go? Certainly not into maintenance or upgrades.

This isn't a one-off. Across the U.S., energy providers have faced allegations of neglecting to invest in infrastructure and instead prioritizing shareholder returns and executive bonuses. Take Consolidated Edison (Con Edison) in New York City, where customers face consistently high utility rates, while the company has faced lawsuits for poor service and aging infrastructure. Despite these issues, Con Edison continued to report large profits—profits that certainly didn't seem to be going into repairing the outdated and vulnerable system.

In essence, energy companies are making huge profits by charging customers more, while offering no significant improvements in service. They raise prices, tell us it's for "upgrading," and then proceed to ignore necessary updates because, well, those upgrades don't line the pockets of shareholders. Why fix what's not broken—financially speaking?

Lobbying Against Cleaner Energy:

Corporate Greed and the Environment

Now let's talk about the elephant in the room, greener energy alternatives. You've probably heard the buzz about renewable energy sources—solar, wind, geothermal—technologies that could help reduce our reliance on fossil fuels and lower carbon emissions. The only problem? Energy companies don't want to lose their profits, which is exactly what would happen if we switched to cleaner energy sources that don't rely on oil, coal, or gas.

This is where corporate lobbying comes into play. Energy companies spend millions of dollars annually to lobby against regulations that would limit carbon emissions or encourage a shift to renewable energy. Why? Because renewable energy means fewer profits for the traditional power players. If the world moved to 100% renewable energy, companies like ExxonMobil, PG&E, and Duke Energy would see their revenue streams shrink dramatically.

For example, Duke Energy (which operates in the Southeast and Midwest) has lobbied against renewable energy policies in multiple states, arguing that transitioning to clean energy would "raise prices for consumers". Meanwhile, Duke Energy continues to invest heavily in natural gas and coal plants, despite the growing evidence that these energy sources are harmful to both the environment and public health.

This kind of corporate behavior isn't unique. In fact, energy companies have been among the largest contributors to anti-environmental legislation, working to block or delay climate action that would threaten their profit model. This isn't just a business strategy—it's an ethical travesty. These companies are standing in the way of a sustainable future, all because they're addicted to the profits generated by dirty energy.

The Energy Industry's Disaster Response:

Negligence, Corporate Greed, and Broken Promises

When a natural disaster strikes—whether it's a hurricane, wildfire, flood, or severe winter storm—there's a natural expectation that utilities will act swiftly to restore essential services like electricity, heat, and water. These are the lifelines that millions rely on for their safety and well-being. But far too often, energy companies fail to respond with the urgency or accountability needed, leaving communities without power for days, weeks, or even longer. What's more, the response to these crises raises troubling ethical questions about how companies are using government funds, how they prioritize profits over public good, and the way they exploit disaster relief efforts for self-promotion.

It's not just inconvenient or frustrating—it's downright negligent and insulting. And here's why.

1. The Long Delays in Power Restoration: A Matter of Life and Death

When natural disasters hit, especially major events like Hurricane Katrina, Superstorm Sandy, or Hurricane Maria, power restoration can take days, weeks, or even months. After these storms, people are left without electricity for extended periods—no lights, no heat, no ability to cook or refrigerate food. Worse, without power, hospitals, emergency services, and communication systems can be severely impacted, putting lives at risk.

Take Puerto Rico, for example, after Hurricane Maria in 2017. The island was without power for nearly 11 months, despite the billions of dollars in federal relief funds allocated to the utility companies. While Luma Energy (which took over operations in 2021) and Puerto Rico Electric Power Authority (PREPA) received enormous federal grants for reconstruction, the restoration efforts were sluggish and ineffective, and the power grid remained fragile. In contrast, Texas after Winter Storm Uri in 2021, another state plagued with a lagging response, faced weeks of blackouts, despite receiving federal funding and assurances from companies like ERCOT (Electric Reliability Council of Texas) that the grid would be fixed.

It's one thing to face challenges during a disaster, but what's even more egregious is the lack of accountability and delay in action—especially when energy companies have been given ample resources to prevent exactly this kind of disaster.

2. Government Grants: Money for Infrastructure—But No Improvements

Energy companies receive huge sums of money from federal and state governments to improve infrastructure and provide disaster response. After disasters, they are awarded grants and emergency relief funds to rebuild and upgrade their infrastructure to ensure that these problems don't happen again.

These funds are public money, meant to serve public good. Yet, far too often, these funds are used for anything but improving infrastructure. Instead, they are funneled into corporate profits, executive bonuses, and shareholder dividends.

For example, after Hurricane Katrina, the utility giant Entergy New Orleans received over $400 million in federal grants to help restore power, but many residents were still waiting for power to be restored for weeks. Entergy made headlines for its exorbitant executive pay packages (even amid the disaster), while it delayed making necessary upgrades to the grid. Even in the case of PG&E in California, the company has been awarded billions of dollars in state and federal funds following natural disasters like wildfires, only for the infrastructure to remain woefully inadequate, and for the company to continue increasing rates. In 2020, PG&E received over $1.1 billion in disaster relief from the state of California to help recover from wildfires, yet their infrastructure remained vulnerable and outdated, resulting in more fires and blackouts.

Where does this money go? Not into the grid. Instead, it often goes into the pockets of executives, who get huge raises and performance bonuses—even as the public continues to suffer from inadequate services.

3. Charitable Donations: Advertising, Not Altruism

Another aspect of this corporate negligence is how energy companies use disaster relief efforts for self-promotion. During major natural disasters, these companies often flood the media with advertisements highlighting their "charitable donations" and their commitment to disaster relief. They proudly announce that they are donating millions to help rebuild affected communities and support those in need. But here's the catch: these donations, while often touted as part of their corporate responsibility, rarely match the scale of the actual federal funds they've received for recovery.

Take Consolidated Edison (Con Edison), for instance. After Superstorm Sandy, Con Edison launched a highly publicized media campaign to show their "generosity," donating $1 million to relief efforts. Meanwhile, Con Edison reported profits of nearly $2.5 billion that year, and its executives took home substantial bonuses. Not to mention that the company had received federal disaster relief funds for infrastructure repairs. In this case, the money spent on the charitable donation looks like chump change compared to the actual funds that were available to them.

In fact, it's almost as if these companies are spending more money on advertising their charitable donations and patting themselves on the back than they are actually donating to the people who need it. Charity, in this sense, is more of a marketing tool than a genuine act of goodwill.

4. The Rate Hike Scam: Payback for a Crisis

After energy companies take billions in disaster relief funds, pat themselves on the back for their charitable efforts, and take their sweet time restoring power, here's the kicker: they turn around and raise your rates. These rate hikes often come within months of a natural disaster, long after the emergency funds are in place. They'll justify it by saying that they need the money for infrastructure repairs (which, remember, they received relief money for in the first place), or to "cover the cost of rising operational expenses." But the truth is, many of these rate hikes are simply a way to boost their profits—especially after they've already been given federal relief money.

After Hurricane Sandy, for example, Con Edison raised its electricity rates by 8.5%—just a few months after receiving $1.2 billion in federal aid to repair the grid. Despite the increase in rates, the utility did not make any significant changes to prevent future outages or improve infrastructure. The money was, once again, used to pad the balance sheets and line the pockets of executives.

In fact, PG&E has raised rates multiple times over the years, despite receiving millions of dollars in government aid and failing to significantly update its infrastructure.

It's simple, when these companies receive federal funds for disaster recovery, they often do little to nothing to actually improve the infrastructure. Instead, they use it as a justification to increase consumer rates, turning the cost of the disaster into a windfall for themselves. And, once the rates go up, there's very little accountability or regulation to ensure that the money is actually being used for the purpose it was intended: to improve services and prevent future disasters.

5. Lack of Accountability: Who's Holding These Companies to Task?

The real problem is that there is no one regulating these practices effectively. Energy companies are essential services, but they are not held accountable for their failures, their greed, or their negligence. Government oversight is often weak or nonexistent. Even when federal or state funds are distributed for disaster recovery, there is often no accountability about how those funds are spent or whether they result in tangible improvements.

In many cases, these companies are allowed to lobby for policies that benefit their profits while dodging regulations that would protect consumers. Their lobbying power is immense, and they often use it to ensure that rate hikes are approved, that disaster relief funds are disbursed with minimal oversight, and that clean energy reforms—which could actually benefit consumers—are blocked because they would reduce long-term profits.

While we the consumers foot the bill through higher energy rates, energy companies continue to maximize their profits and avoid meaningful investment in improving the infrastructure that people rely on. And as for the federal relief money? It often gets siphoned off for executive bonuses or funneled back into advertising campaigns.

In the end, the failure of energy companies to respond quickly and adequately during natural disasters isn't just an inconvenience—it's a gross act of negligence and corporate greed. These companies receive billions in government aid and flood the media with feel-good ads about their "generosity," yet their disastrous responses and continued rate hikes reveal a much uglier truth: their commitment is to their profits, not the communities they serve.

Until we hold these companies accountable—demanding transparency, stricter regulation, and meaningful investment in infrastructure—we'll continue to see this same cycle of corporate exploitation, government waste, and consumer suffering. The next time your lights go out during a disaster, remember: you're not just waiting for the power to come back on—you're waiting for a company that took your money and failed to use it for the public good.

The Cost to Consumers:
The Bigger Picture

What does this all mean for you, the consumer? Skyrocketing energy prices without significant service improvements. Outdated infrastructure that leaves you without power during storms or extreme weather. And an industry actively working to block greener energy practices that would help reduce your bills in the long term.

And who pays the price for all of this? You do. While CEOs and shareholders of these energy companies continue to pocket massive salaries and bonuses, ordinary people are left with the ever-increasing cost of their electricity, gas, and heating bills.

This corporate greed in essential services is a key factor in the growing wealth gap. While the rich get richer—thanks in part to their investments in these companies—regular folks are stuck paying higher prices for essential services. It's a classic case of the rich getting richer, while the poor get stuck with the bill.

The Ethical Dilemma:
Should Necessities Be Governed by Profit?

Now, let's get to the heart of the ethical issue: Should essential services like water, energy, and education be driven by profit?

The answer, for many, is no. At its core, the idea of privatizing essential services raises the question: should the basic necessities of life—things that everyone needs to survive and thrive—be controlled by corporations whose primary goal is to make money? Essential services are not optional; they are the building blocks of a functional society.

When we allow corporations to control these services, we risk creating a two-tier system—one where the rich can afford to live comfortably, with access to the best services, while the poor are left to struggle. It perpetuates inequality and reinforces the wealth gap.

The Wealth Gap:

How Corporate Greed Exacerbates Inequality

The wealth gap—the chasm between the richest and poorest Americans—is widening at an alarming rate. According to a 2020 study by the Federal Reserve, the top 1% of U.S. households hold about 40% of the country's wealth, while the bottom 90% control only about 27%.

Privatizing essential services is one of the key drivers of this disparity. Here's how it works: the wealthiest individuals and corporations control the means of production for essential services. They charge higher prices and cut services to maximize profits. Meanwhile, the working class and the poor, who are dependent on these services, bear the brunt of the costs.

If you're wealthy, you can afford to live in a neighborhood with privately-run schools, uninterrupted electricity, and clean, bottled water.

If you're poor, you're stuck with underfunded public schools, sky-high utility bills, and unreliable water sources.

In other words, privatizing essential services creates a system where the wealthy get better services, and the poor get stuck with the bare minimum.

The Call for Change: What Can Be Done?

So, what's the solution? How do we solve the ethical dilemma posed by privatized essential services and bridge the wealth gap?

Stronger regulations and transparency: We need governments to regulate energy companies more effectively. This means cracking down on price hikes, forcing companies to invest in infrastructure upgrades, and implementing clean energy mandates to push for greener, sustainable practices. If privatization is going to occur, there must be strong regulatory frameworks to ensure that companies don't exploit the public for profit. This could involve price caps, service guarantees, and strict accountability measures.

Advocate for public ownership: Public ownership of services like water and energy can ensure that these services are managed with the public good in mind, not profit motives. Publicly run services are generally more accountable to the people they serve.

Ultimately, the ethical problem with privatizing essential services is simple, it creates a world where people's basic human needs are subjected to the whims of the marketplace. Profit-driven models work for consumer goods (you know, things like gourmet popcorn or designer sneakers), but not for necessities like water and energy.

By allowing corporations to profit off essential services, we are not just increasing the wealth gap—we are making human dignity and equality harder to attain. Public goods should serve the public good—and not be a vehicle for wealth accumulation.

The rise in energy prices, lack of infrastructure improvements, and resistance to greener energy practices aren't just unfortunate outcomes of corporate greed—they are symptoms of a broken system where the needs of people are secondary to the desire for profit. Until we put people before profits, until we stop letting CEOs and lobbyists call the shots, we're stuck paying the price—literally and figuratively.

So, the next time you hear about a "water company" or a "utilities corporation" ask yourself: Is this a service, or is this just another opportunity for someone to cash in on the things we need to survive?

It's time to put the "public" back in "public services"—before the "gap" gets any bigger.

Hurricane-Prone Areas And The Insurance Scam

Paying for Protection that Doesn't Protect

Living in a hurricane-prone area should come with a simple reassurance: you'll have access to affordable insurance that will actually help if your home is damaged in a storm. Unfortunately, for many living in the hurricane belt, this simple expectation has become a pipe dream. Instead, they are forced into a situation where they pay sky-high premiums for coverage that doesn't actually cover much—and then, when disaster strikes, they find themselves without the help they desperately need. The whole situation stinks of corporate greed, market monopolies, and a system that favors profits over people's well-being.

1. The Flood Insurance Shuffle: Forced to Pay, Left High and Dry
Imagine this, you live in a beautiful, coastal town where hurricanes are a regular guest on the weather radar. The home you've worked hard for is nestled just a few miles from the water, and you've poured time and money into making it your own. Then a storm approaches, and suddenly you are faced with a grim reality: insurance companies don't want to touch your property unless you pay for flood insurance. Even though you've been paying homeowner's insurance for years, flood insurance is a whole separate beast—and an additional financial burden you can't avoid.

This is a common scenario for homeowners in places like Florida, Texas, Louisiana, and other hurricane-prone states. The issue is simple: flood insurance is either unavailable, unaffordable, or doesn't actually cover much of the damage when it's most needed. The government's National Flood Insurance Program (NFIP) is often the only option for homeowners in high-risk areas, but even that program leaves gaping holes in coverage, and the premiums can skyrocket.

So, say you pay $1,200 a year for your homeowner's insurance—and then, to comply with federal requirements or to protect your mortgage, you also have to buy flood insurance. Depending on the flood risk, that can run anywhere from $500 to $2,000 annually. That's a hefty amount, right? You're already putting thousands of dollars a year into insurance. You'd think that would cover you in case of a flood. Wrong.

2. "Sorry, Your Basement Doesn't Count": The Limits of Flood Coverage

Now, here's the real kicker. After you've been dutifully paying for flood insurance, you think you're protected when disaster strikes. But when the storm comes and floods your property, you find that your flood insurance won't cover basement damage. Wait, what? The basement—where you've turned that extra space into a cozy living area—was, according to the insurance company, not meant for living. So, despite the fact that you've turned your basement into a perfectly functional part of your home, the insurance company deems it an "unfinished space" or "storage area". And, of course, they won't pay for any of the water damage.

This is an especially cruel blow to lower-income homeowners who often have to make the most of their space. For many families, the basement is not just a utility space, but a vital part of the home—used for bedrooms, offices, or even extra rental income. It's a clever way to get around paying out claims. Insurance companies may argue that the basement is technically not for living (because, heaven forbid, it was finished into a legitimate living space), so they don't have to provide compensation when it floods.

The frustration here is palpable. If you live in a hurricane zone and you're forced to purchase flood insurance, and then that insurance won't cover flood damage to the most vulnerable parts of your home, you're being left out in the rain—literally and figuratively.

3. The Monopoly of One: The Insurance Giant in Your Neighborhood

Now, let's talk about the lack of competition in the insurance industry, particularly in high-risk areas. Imagine having one insurance company in your entire region that you're forced to buy from. That's what homeowners in certain states face. For flood insurance in some coastal areas, there might be only one provider—and it's typically the government-run National Flood Insurance Program (NFIP) or a single private company that's been granted exclusive rights. That's not just a monopoly—it's corporate dictatorship.

This lack of competition means these companies don't have to worry about offering competitive rates or even honoring their claims fairly. They know they have you cornered. In fact, if your area is deemed a high flood risk, there's a strong chance you'll pay a premium for flood insurance whether you want to or not, and you may not have any real bargaining power.

What's worse? Many of these companies also rely on fine print and technicalities to avoid covering you when it matters most. Want to know what they call it when you try to file a claim for flood damage to your basement? "Uninhabitable space." This might be the most insulting part of the entire system—they pocket your premiums for years, only to leave you high and dry when you need them most.

4. Hurricane Insurance and the Growing Wealth Gap: The Cost of Living in High-Risk Areas

So what does all this have to do with the wealth gap? Well, it's simple, insurance costs are skyrocketing, and those in lower-income communities—especially people of color—are disproportionately affected. When you live in a high-risk area, you're forced to pay for insurance coverage that may or may not cover your needs when disaster strikes. And, as the costs of living in hurricane-prone areas continue to rise, it becomes even harder for the working-class and low-income families to afford the protection they're required to purchase.

To make matters worse, wealthy individuals and corporations can often afford to take the risk and self-insure, while middle-class and low-income families are left scrambling to pay for overpriced policies that provide limited coverage. This exacerbates the wealth gap, as those who are already struggling to make ends meet find themselves spending a larger percentage of their income on insurance premiums—only to have that money go straight into the pockets of big insurance companies that don't actually have to live up to their promises.

As insurance premiums rise and coverage becomes more difficult to obtain, the economic divide widens. Wealthier homeowners are more likely to have the resources to weather the storm (literally and figuratively), while lower-income families are at the mercy of a system that forces them to pay for protection they will likely never receive.

5. Where's the Accountability? Who's Watching the Insurance Industry?

The truth is, insurance companies have a lot of power, and the lack of regulation in the industry allows them to exploit people who are already at a disadvantage. In some hurricane-prone states, the lack of competition and the monopoly control exercised by a few big players means that residents are stuck paying for subpar insurance that's designed more to line the pockets of executives than to actually protect homeowners when disaster strikes.

So, where's the oversight? Where's the accountability? Regulatory bodies have failed to keep up with the growing demand for coverage in these high-risk areas, and state and federal governments often fail to ensure that companies are acting in good faith. As a result, we're left with a system that doesn't just fail to protect us—it punishes us for living in risky areas, while corporations profit from our misery.

6. The Investor Takeover: Wealthy Opportunists Buying Up the Broken Pieces

As if the whole system weren't frustrating enough for lower-income homeowners, there's another disturbing dynamic at play: wealthy investors swooping in to buy damaged properties after a disaster strikes—often in lower-income areas—because the original homeowners can't afford to rebuild. It's like a shark circling its prey while the vulnerable struggle to keep their heads above water.

Here's how it typically plays out: After a hurricane or other natural disaster, the homes of those already living on the financial edge suffer devastating damage. For many of these homeowners, the insurance payouts are a fraction of what it would actually cost to repair or rebuild their homes. Remember those limited flood insurance policies we talked about earlier? They don't cover much, and when it's all said and done, the homeowners are left with only enough money to pay for some quick patch jobs—if they even get that.

But what happens to those properties once the damage is done and the owners can't afford to fix them? Well, wealthy investors—who likely own multiple properties or have deep pockets—step in, buy up those homes for pennies on the dollar, and flip them for huge profits. These investors can afford to absorb the cost of repairs because they have the resources to rebuild and restore the property.

Meanwhile, the previous owners, often lower-income families, are stuck either foreclosing or selling for a fraction of the home's value. In many cases, these homeowners cannot afford the high deductibles or the cost to rebuild, and so they sell their property to these opportunistic investors, who now own a home that's been devalued by the storm, but they're in a position to turn it into a high-priced asset once the repairs are complete.

A Tale of Two Realities:

The Rich Reap the Rewards, the Poor Get Left Behind

This scenario is all too common in the aftermath of major disasters. A recent example comes from New Orleans after Hurricane Katrina—one of the most infamous examples of how disasters disproportionately affect low-income communities. After the storm, wealthy real estate investors were able to buy up damaged properties in neighborhoods that were historically home to Black and low-income families. These areas were hard-hit by flooding, and many residents were forced to leave, either due to the devastation or because they couldn't afford repairs.

The problem was twofold, the flood insurance payouts were often not enough to cover the costs of rebuilding (remember that frustrating basement clause?), and the government's response to rebuilding was slow and inequitable. This left opportunistic investors to sweep in, buying properties in bulk for a fraction of their market value, and then gentrifying the neighborhoods. In many cases, these homes were then sold at inflated prices, and the original residents—many of whom had lived in the community for generations—found themselves locked out of the housing market altogether.

This is happening right now in other places like Puerto Rico, Florida, and Texas, where wealthy investors and real estate firms are buying damaged properties for cheap and renovating them for resale at a huge profit—leaving displaced families with nothing but the remains of a destroyed home and no way to rebuild. It's a clear example of how the wealthy continue to capitalize on disaster—literally buying up opportunities in communities that are most vulnerable to these disasters in the first place.

Insurance Companies and the Wealth Gap

So, what does this have to do with the wealth gap? Everything.

The ability of wealthy investors to buy distressed properties at bargain prices and flip them for a profit is a direct result of a system where low-income homeowners are forced to pay into a system that doesn't actually help them when disaster strikes. These homeowners are left with insufficient insurance payouts (if they get anything at all), and as a result, they're unable to rebuild or repair their homes. When these vulnerable communities can't afford to fix their properties, investors with money take advantage of the opportunity to purchase these homes for cheap, turning a disaster into a windfall.

This creates a feedback loop that widen the wealth gap. On one side, you have low-income families who have been struggling to build wealth in the form of homeownership, but who are now facing financial ruin because their homes are uninsured or underinsured. On the other side, you have wealthy investors who can afford to weather the storm—literally—and make a profit off the misfortune of others.

The result? Displacement, gentrification, and an even larger wealth divide. The cycle of poverty and inequality becomes more entrenched, while corporations and investors continue to benefit from the very disaster that devastates the communities that can't afford to rebuild.

A System That Prioritizes Profits Over People

At the end of the day, the situation surrounding home insurance and natural disasters reveals a lot about the deep inequalities built into the system.

Homeowners are forced to pay high premiums for flood insurance, but when it's time to make a claim, they don't receive enough compensation to cover their damages. At the same time, wealthy investors are buying up properties in neighborhoods that have been devastated by disasters, turning a profit off the misfortune of families who couldn't afford to rebuild in the first place.

This is a textbook example of how corporate interests and wealthy investors are able to capitalize on disasters, while the poor and vulnerable are left behind, trapped in a system that takes from them but gives them nothing in return. It's an issue that is fueled by greed, and it only continues to widen the wealth gap, pushing people out of their homes and neighborhoods—while making it easier for the rich to take advantage of the broken system.

Until we reform the insurance industry, increase competition, and hold insurers accountable, we will continue to see the same cycle play out: communities devastated by natural disasters, wealthy investors swooping in for bargains, and ordinary people left to pick up the pieces of a system that was never designed to protect them.

What Can We Do? Leading the Charge for Positive Change

While the situation surrounding insurance companies, natural disasters, and the growing wealth gap can feel overwhelming, change is possible—especially if we come together and start demanding reform. The system is stacked against us, but collective action, policy change, and public awareness can make a huge difference. Here's how we can begin to turn the tide:

1. Advocate for Insurance Reform: Transparency, Accountability, and Fairness

One of the most important steps toward positive change is pushing for stronger regulations on the insurance industry. Right now, insurance companies are able to operate with a shocking lack of accountability and transparency, particularly in high-risk areas. To fix this, we need better oversight at both the state and federal levels.

Demand comprehensive insurance coverage: We should push for flood insurance policies that actually cover all property damage, including basements and unfinished spaces. If people are required to purchase insurance, the least the system can do is make sure that insurance actually protects them.

Fight for stronger consumer protections: We need stricter laws that prevent insurance companies from denying claims based on loopholes and technicalities. If you've been paying into the system for years, you should not have to jump through hoops or find ways to get the coverage you were promised in the first place.

Push for price transparency: Insurance premiums should be transparent and comparable across providers. Monopolistic pricing in certain regions, especially for flood insurance, must be addressed, and we need options—not just one overpriced choice. More competition will drive down prices and improve service.

End the practice of "redlining": In some areas, insurers refuse to provide flood coverage to people in historically marginalized communities because they are deemed "high-risk." We need to demand that insurers stop discriminating based on geography, race, or income. Insurance should be available to everyone, regardless of where they live or their economic status.

2. Push for Government Support: Strengthening Public Resources

In the aftermath of a natural disaster, we often see the government step in with federal aid, but that assistance is often inadequate, and it's not always evenly distributed. We need better disaster relief programs, including more effective rebuilding efforts and financial assistance for people who are hit hardest by hurricanes, floods, and other catastrophic events.

Strengthen the National Flood Insurance Program (NFIP): The federal flood insurance program is the only option for many homeowners, but it is severely limited in its capacity to help. We need to reform and expand the NFIP to ensure that it provides sufficient payouts for flood damages, including rebuilding costs, not just quick fixes.

More direct aid for low-income homeowners: The government should focus on helping people rebuild by offering grants or low-interest loans that actually cover full repair costs. Homeowners shouldn't be stuck in a system where they are forced to accept an insurance payout that doesn't cover the full cost of rebuilding. Special focus should be placed on low-income communities that are often left behind after a disaster.

Develop affordable housing solutions: Many people in disaster-prone areas are unable to rebuild simply because housing prices have skyrocketed due to gentrification. Local governments need to prioritize affordable housing solutions and ensure that communities aren't displaced in the wake of disasters.

3. Fight for Stronger Environmental Regulations: Protecting Our Communities

The greed of the fossil fuel and utility industries often plays a huge role in environmental damage that exacerbates the frequency and intensity of natural disasters. By supporting green initiatives, clean energy policies, and climate change mitigation strategies, we can begin to reduce the long-term effects of global warming on our communities.

Advocate for stricter environmental regulations: We need stronger regulations on polluting industries, particularly fossil fuels, and we must hold them accountable for their role in exacerbating climate change. Disasters like hurricanes are made worse by the failure to protect the environment, and big polluters must be forced to pay for the damage they cause.

Push for clean energy alternatives: Investment in clean energy such as solar and wind should be a top priority. In many parts of the world, communities are being devastated by climate change, but they also lack access to renewable energy sources that can reduce their dependence on fossil fuels. Advocating for green energy is not just about the environment—it's about providing a more equitable, sustainable future for all.

Support local climate resilience projects: Flood control measures, coastal restoration, and green infrastructure like rain gardens and levees can help protect vulnerable communities from the worst effects of climate change. Supporting these projects will reduce the need for future insurance payouts and ensure that less money is lost to environmental disasters.

4. Combat the Real Estate Investor Problem: Protecting Homeownership

To address the hoarding of properties by wealthy investors in disaster-stricken neighborhoods, we must create policies that protect homeownership for lower-income families and prevent displacement.

Increase property tax incentives for low-income homeowners: Property taxes in high-risk areas can skyrocket after a disaster. We need to freeze property taxes for homeowners in vulnerable communities so that they aren't forced to sell due to rising costs.

Create affordable homeownership programs: Policies should be put in place to ensure that low-income individuals and families can still buy homes and remain in the communities they've built. This includes down payment assistance, rent-to-own programs, and tax breaks for first-time homebuyers.

Ban corporate ownership of distressed homes: We need stricter laws that limit corporate ownership of homes in neighborhoods devastated by disaster. These laws would prevent large companies and wealthy investors from buying up properties in areas where homeowners are already struggling to rebuild.

5. Raise Public Awareness and Organize for Change

Sometimes, the most powerful tool for change is public awareness and collective action. The more people are aware of these issues, the more likely they are to demand change. If we work together, we can apply pressure on lawmakers, corporations, and policy-makers to change the system.

Support advocacy groups: There are many organizations already working to fight for insurance reform, climate action, and housing justice. By supporting these groups, whether through donations, volunteering, or simply amplifying their message, we can help keep these issues on the national agenda.

Sign petitions and participate in protests: When citizens stand together to demand change, lawmakers take notice. Whether it's signing a petition for affordable insurance policies, protesting corporate greed, or lobbying for government action, public pressure can make a huge difference.

Vote with your dollars and your ballot: At the local, state, and national levels, elected officials make decisions that impact the policies we live with. By voting for representatives who support insurance reform, climate action, and affordable housing, we ensure that the people making decisions are working in the best interest of all communities.

While the problems surrounding insurance companies, disasters, and the wealth gap may seem insurmountable, there's a clear path forward if we choose to walk it together. By advocating for insurance reform, supporting environmental policies, fighting for homeownership protections, and raising awareness about the issues facing vulnerable communities, we can begin to shift the balance of power back in favor of those who need it most.

It's time to hold the insurance industry accountable, demand better disaster relief, and push for policies that prioritize people over profits. It's time for change—and it starts with us. Let's make sure the wealthy no longer get to profit from other people's misfortune, and that the vulnerable are given the support they need to rebuild.

How The 1% Manipulate The Narrative

If you've ever felt like you're stuck in a loop of sensational headlines, polarizing political debates, and outrage culture—but that none of it ever really leads to meaningful change—well, there's a reason for that. The truth is, much of what we see on the news, and the issues we debate endlessly in politics, are distractions designed to keep us fighting amongst ourselves while the real decisions that shape our world are made behind closed doors.

At the heart of this system is a relationship between mainstream media and the wealthy elite—specifically the 1%—who are invested in keeping things the way they are. When you look closer, you'll see that corporate media is often a mouthpiece for the interests of the wealthy, prioritizing narratives that don't challenge the status quo and that deflect attention from issues that might threaten the billionaire class' profits. Meanwhile, the political theater that plays out in Washington and state capitals is a smoke-and-mirrors game designed to keep the public divided and distracted from real, systemic reforms that would actually make life better for the majority of people.

Corporate Media:

The Puppet Master Behind the Curtain

Let's start with mainstream media, because it's the vehicle through which most of us get our news—and it's no accident that the narratives we consume are often skewed in ways that protect the interests of the wealthy elite.

Corporate ownership of media outlets: The reality is that most of the news we consume comes from a handful of corporations—like Comcast, Disney, ViacomCBS, and News Corporation—which, in turn, are controlled by billionaire families or corporate conglomerates. These entities have enormous influence over what gets reported, how it gets reported, and which stories get swept under the rug. When advertising dollars are involved, the incentive is not to challenge the economic system that allows these corporations to profit. Instead, the media focuses on sensationalist stories—like celebrity scandals or clickbait headlines—that grab attention without questioning the structural issues that hold power in place.

The role of advertisers: Many mainstream news outlets are heavily reliant on advertising revenue from major corporations—including those that profit off of the very issues that are being discussed. When a media outlet depends on advertising dollars from big pharma, oil companies, and Wall Street firms, it's in their interest to downplay or ignore stories that might hurt these industries. For example, have you ever noticed that news outlets rarely run in-depth pieces on things like corporate tax avoidance, climate change, or labor rights abuses? Instead, we get endless coverage of political scandals or the latest media circus —which leads us to the next part of the equation: politics as spectacle.

Politics as Distraction: Keeping Us at Odds Over Petty Divisions

Have you ever thought about how polarizing political rhetoric seems to ramp up at key moments—especially when it distracts us from discussing real issues that could challenge the economic power of the wealthy? Whether it's the left vs. right debate, the culture war, or the endless scandals and finger-pointing between politicians, it often feels like we're watching a reality show rather than engaging in meaningful conversations about how to fix the problems facing everyday people.

Political theater over policy

Let's face it, a lot of the political debates we see aren't really about solving problems. They're about keeping people angry, scared, and divided. The issues that dominate our political conversations—abortion, gun control, immigration, and even the occasional moral outrage—often overshadow real, structural reforms that would actually improve the lives of millions. For example, universal healthcare, a living wage, affordable housing, and corporate tax reform are issues that could actually reduce inequality and benefit the majority of society—yet we rarely see them dominate the headlines. Instead, we get a steady stream of performative politics that appeals to people's emotions and identities rather than addressing the economic systems that perpetuate inequality.

There's a reason why politicians and media outlets seem to focus so much on cultural issues that divide us, whether it's debates over identity politics, social values, or race relations. These issues are important, of course, but when they're manipulated to create divisions, they distract us from real systemic problems. If people are constantly fighting over issues like CRT, voter ID laws, or cancel culture, they're less likely to focus on the fact that the 1% are hoarding wealth, dodging taxes, and buying up politicians.

The media and politicians also use scapegoating to shift blame away from the actual culprits—the corporations and billionaire elites—and onto things that can't really be solved through legislation. It's easier to blame immigrants, welfare recipients, or foreign interference than it is to blame the billion-dollar companies that are skimming off the top while evading taxes and replacing real workers with automation or low-wage labor. By making us focus on the "bad guys" in our own neighborhoods or across the globe, the media and politicians can avoid addressing the deeper issues of wealth concentration and corporate greed that keep society unequal.

The Real Issues We're Not Talking About

If you strip away the divisive headlines and the political soap opera, you start to see what's really happening. Corporations are profiting off our misfortune, and billionaires are avoiding paying their fair share of taxes. These structural issues should be the focus of our attention—not the daily drama that's designed to keep us distracted. Here's what we should be talking about:

Tax reform: The richest individuals and companies have the ability to avoid paying taxes through loopholes, offshore accounts, and corporate subsidies. If the 1% paid their fair share, it would fund social programs like universal healthcare, education, and infrastructure improvements that would benefit the public.

Corporate monopolies: Big corporations are buying up smaller competitors, driving up prices, and controlling markets in ways that hurt consumers and workers. Antitrust laws should be strengthened to prevent monopolistic practices and ensure that markets remain competitive.

Climate change and environmental destruction: The fossil fuel industry and other polluting companies are largely responsible for the climate crisis we're facing. Rather than seeing these industries as untouchable giants, we need to hold them accountable for the damage they cause to our planet—and for the disproportionate burden climate change places on low-income communities.

Universal basic income (UBI): Instead of debating about whether people "deserve" healthcare or a living wage, we should be discussing a universal basic income that guarantees everyone a basic level of financial security.

The Bottom Line:

It's All About Profits, and the Wealthy Are Winning

At the end of the day, the system we live in benefits the wealthy at the expense of the rest of us. Mainstream media, controlled by corporate interests, spends its time sensationalizing issues that keep us divided and distracted. Politics is often reduced to a game of divide-and-conquer, where the real issues —like tax reform, corporate power, and wealth redistribution—are either ignored or downplayed because addressing them would threaten the profits of the 1%.

We need to stop getting distracted by the latest political circus and start focusing on the real issues that affect our collective future. Only then will we be able to create a society that works for everyone, not just the ultra-rich.

The Road Ahead

Together, We Can Make a Difference

As we stand at the intersection of countless challenges and opportunities, it's clear that the path to a brighter future doesn't lie in one grand gesture or singular policy change. It's woven together by a collective effort, driven by the shared belief that we are capable of not just surviving—but thriving. From the very beginning of this book, we've explored how quality of life, citizen happiness, and societal advancement are all tightly connected. These aren't just abstract concepts or lofty ideals; they are the foundation of a society that works for everyone, not just the lucky few. And while the wealth gap may feel like a chasm at times, it's important to remember: every journey begins with a single step. That step is us—together—moving forward.

Now, let's be honest. We know this won't be easy. It's going to take hard work, a little creativity, and, quite frankly, some elbow grease. But isn't that what makes it worthwhile? Whether we're advocating for policy change to close the wealth gap, supporting education and training to unlock opportunity, or promoting local businesses to build stronger communities, each action, no matter how small, adds up. Think of it like a potluck dinner. Everyone brings something to the table, and together, we end up with a feast. Sure, some of us might bring a bag of chips, but hey, chips are still part of the spread!

We've also taken a deep dive into the very things that make or break a community: access to healthcare, fair employment, financial literacy, and the often-overlooked issue of mental health. After all, what's a society without its people feeling healthy, financially secure, and emotionally supported? The challenges in these areas are complex, but not insurmountable. If we can rally around a common goal—fairer, more affordable healthcare for all—then surely we can tackle the rest. And, let's not forget: while healthcare and pharmaceuticals are often seen as the serious, business-end of societal issues, we can't allow Big Pharma to run the show with their golden parachutes and price gouging. It's time for a new script—one where the people, not the profits, come first.

In all of this, we also highlighted the importance of civic engagement—because, let's face it, if you don't vote, you can't complain. And frankly, we're all tired of listening to complaints about things we can fix if we just roll up our sleeves and engage with the process. Voting isn't just a right—it's a responsibility. From voting on local issues to advocating for global cooperation on drug pricing, we've got a lot of work to do—and no one can afford to sit on the sidelines. The power is in our hands, and we have the tools to make change happen.

Now none of this happens in a vacuum. We've got to work together. Whether it's building coalitions to fight for equitable workplaces or supporting ethical investing to ensure our dollars align with our morals, the future will be shaped by the partnerships we form today. It's not about being perfect, but about being better together. So, let's get to work. It's a lot like building a house—it's not just about picking the right materials, but about working with the right people.

And yes, we've spent some time talking about education reform—because, let's be real, no one wants to live in a world where a good education is a privilege and not a right. The truth is, the future of any society hinges on how we equip the next generation. So, let's make sure that education is not just the key to a better life, but the door to a more equitable future for all. A good education isn't just about learning how to solve a math problem or memorize a history lesson—it's about preparing people for the challenges ahead, giving them the tools to thrive, and teaching them to work together.

So, as we close this book, let's take a moment to reflect on one undeniable truth: change doesn't happen overnight, and it doesn't happen by waiting for someone else to do it. It starts with us—each of us—doing our part. Whether it's engaging in a conversation, writing to your local representative, supporting a local business, or just sharing a good idea, we all have something to contribute.

Yes, the road ahead will be tough, but isn't it worth it? After all, it's a road we're all on together. And if we play our cards right—if we embrace the challenges, support each other, and stay committed to our shared vision of a fairer, more prosperous world—then who knows? We might just get there faster than we think.

When we invest in each other, we all rise. The journey toward a better world begins now—and there's no better time to start than today. So let's spark some conversations, and get to work. The future is waiting—and we're ready for it.

www.ingramcontent.com/pod-product-compliance
Lightning Source LLC
Chambersburg PA
CBHW071018240526
45469CB00006BD/1979